# One Black Man's Story and the Woman Who Loved Him

**Dwayne Erroll Hall I**
**One Black Man's Story and the Woman Who Loved Him**

All rights reserved
Copyright © 2025 by **Dwayne Erroll Hall I**



Published by Spines
ISBN: 979-8-89691-804-2

# One Black Man's Story and the Woman Who Loved Him

Dwayne Erroll Hall I

# One Black Man's Story

A deeply moving memoir unfolds, tracing the resilience of a family across decades, love's guiding light through trials of health, incarceration, and societal change. Embracing kinship and the pursuit of dreams.

The narrative resonates with the harmonies of life, echoing the enduring power of devotion, the relentless pursuit of redemption, and the unbreakable spirit of togetherness.

Navigating the complexities of love, ambition, and identity, this tapestry of experiences reminds us of our unbound capacity to love.

# One Black Man's Story

## &
## The Woman Who Loved Him
### Our Fifty Year Journey
### By
## Dwayne Erroll Hall

**Formatting and Photo Restoration
By
James Edward Lewis**

**A Time Designs Media Publication**

"I dedicate this book to my children, grandchildren
and future generations.
May it provide you with insight and guidance.
With age, comes wisdom. With wisdom, peace of mind.
Proceed with kindness."
- Dwayne Erroll Hall

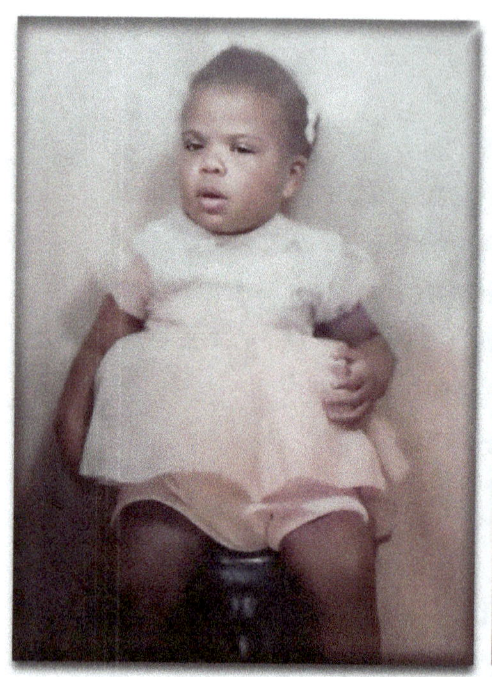

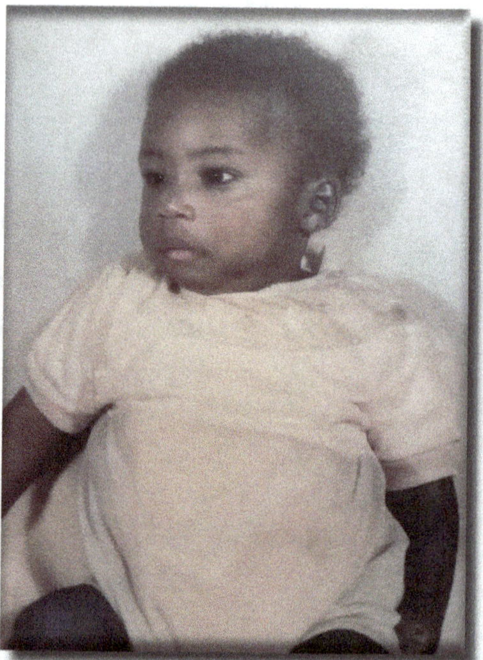

# Our Fifty Year Journey

# Forward

I would like to thank my parents for finding each other this lifetime. To witness the reflection of true love, dedication, perseverance, friendship, compassion, trust, honoring vows, honoring each other as humans, loyalty, recklessness, joy, fun, kinder spirits, passion, devotion, beauty, and gratitude for fifty years was a work of art only your two spirits could have achieved. During the journey that you two embarked on, you influenced the trajectory of lives and souls.

Your love story will always remain the standard of finding the one person on this earth who completes you. I'm proud that my father never lost who he was due to circumstance. My mother was and is his air, and without her, he breathes differently, but he breathes.

As you laugh, cry, and enjoy this expression of love and devotion that my father had for my mother, try to find and implement the *Jewels* that my Daddy drops throughout the book. If you knew him, you would have heard these jewels directly from him. These jewels have changed the thousands of lives he and my mother have touched; may yours be one. To the Man I call a Legend I salute you, I honor you, and I'm proud to call you my Daddy!

Love, *Lil Ma*, aka Laticia Hall.

## Here By Myself

Everybody's got a story to tell, if you just take the time to listen. I'm writing this book because our lives together meant everything to me. I hope our story inspires others to follow their hearts, to be true to who they are, and to be willing to let each other grow.

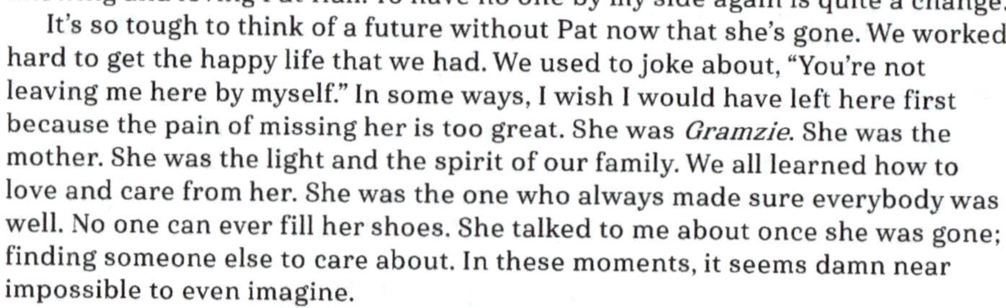

As I sit here on my front porch wondering, "What does the future have in store?" It reminds me of another time in my life when I was young and alone. My motivation to keep going is at its lowest point ever; then and now. The only difference is that now I know I was blessed to have had the privilege of knowing and loving Pat Hall. To have no one by my side again is quite a change.

It's so tough to think of a future without Pat now that she's gone. We worked hard to get the happy life that we had. We used to joke about, "You're not leaving me here by myself." In some ways, I wish I would have left here first because the pain of missing her is too great. She was *Gramzie*. She was the mother. She was the light and the spirit of our family. We all learned how to love and care from her. She was the one who always made sure everybody was well. No one can ever fill her shoes. She talked to me about once she was gone; finding someone else to care about. In these moments, it seems damn near impossible to even imagine.

## Our Story As I Remember It

Our story begins on January 1st, 1972. I was a young man sitting on the curbside, wondering what life was going to be like and asking God if he could give me a sign. That was the afternoon I met Patricia Alexander.

I was 18 years old, and my sister Francine asked me to give her a ride to the store. The next thing I knew, she was asking Pat to slide in and sit next to me. I had never seen her in our neighborhood before. From the moment our blue jeans touched, I felt a spiritual connection.

Stevie Wonder's, *Superstition* was pumping from the radio. The air was cool and fresh. My heart was inspired. I felt a calm come over me in her presence. Six months after we met, we were married. July 15th, 1972, and we've stayed side by side ever since. Fifty years strong!

The car I first took her to the store in was my parents. I wrecked mine coming home from the Christmas party at work after taking mushrooms and drinking! I ran over a rock, or, I should say, a boulder. I messed up my beautiful 1965 T-Bird with the convertible top and swivel seats.

I knew after New Year's night that something had to change in my life. I loved that car so much. I had saved my money since I was 14 to be able to buy it. Even though my car was wrecked, we spent a couple weeks sitting in it, talking and listening to every 8-track tape we've ever collected. I mean, we listened to everything from Chicago, Santana, Cat Stevens, Jimmy Hendrix, and Led Zeppelin. In East Palo Alto, where we lived, the teenagers didn't really listen to that type of music. It was important for us to have those things in common.

## A Lot in Common

It begins with the two of our births; me, born to Barbara Williams and Willie Hall, and Pat, born to Dorothy White and Odell Crosby. Both of our single mothers were too young to take care of us on their own, and both of our fathers were not ready to be fathers.

The time we spent in our grandparents' homes from birth to five years old was a wonderful time in both our lives. Being the firstborn and having the love and attention not only of our mothers but also of our grandparents was very special. The birth of our siblings would change our lives forever. No more being the special one. We were both being raised mostly by our grandparents. Things would change when our mothers met their new husbands, Frank and Ernest.

## Stepchildren

We both became known as stepchildren, and we talked about those changes early on in our relationship. Being the oldest in our families meant watching all of our brothers and sisters; making us a second parent. Having that in common, we had the same patience and understanding when it came to handling our younger siblings. After my mother had me, she had four more kids. Ritchie, Francine, Tony, and Cheryl are all from her marriage with Frank. Since the time my first sibling, Ritchie, was born, I've always had someone to care about and make sure that they were good!

## New Daddy

One day, my mother comes home, takes us all to my cousin's house, and drops us off for four months. Then she returned and took us all to East Palo Alto. My mother was now with a new man, and I was introduced to my new stepfather, Patrick Patterson, or 'Pat' for short. We were never told why my mother was no longer with Frank, the father of my stepbrothers and sisters. It blew our minds that she did not have this conversation with all her kids!

It was like, "Here's your new dad!"

My brother wants to know what happened to his father Frank. My mother never had this conversation with us about how some marriages don't work out. Not having that conversation gave my brothers and sisters a tough time in their lives. When you don't know the truth you try to fill in the holes, and make something up. Stupid shit like, "I should have been a better kid, and maybe he would have stayed with us."

In thinking back, I guess my mother handled it the best way she could. She grew up not knowing who her father was, and never found out her whole life. None of her kids could ever say that they didn't know who there father was.

It felt devastating to us, and we were kind of forced to act like everything was all right. Nobody liked him except our baby sister, Cheryl. The rest of us were *acting the fool* whenever we could. Eventually, we couldn't keep the anger up and accepted the life that he was now providing us.

He used me like a dog. He'd shoot a bird, then make me go and get it. One time, the bird wasn't dead yet. The male pheasant was on his back and had his talons out, pushing his wings off of the ground, trying to get me with his talons. That was the last time I went hunting. He still forced me to clean up the birds that he shot. I would have to soak them in hot water, pull the feathers off, and then cut them to take the guts out. No more hunting!

My stepfather kept the pressure on me about refusing to go and called me many names. I had another abusive man in my life and I prayed that I would grow up quickly so I could whoop his ass on any given Sunday.

There were certain things about East Palo Alto that I really loved. I had hung out by the railroad tracks and caught tadpoles in little ponds in San Francisco and had a lot of fun there.

In East Palo Alto, there was a marsh half a block away from my house. I was finally able to have all the Huckleberry Finn adventures on a raft, pretending to be a pirate. I would also catch the train and ride it for several miles. It was a great time. I could be all alone out there, having adventure after adventure. There were fruit trees on everybody's lawn, and white people and black people played together. I know now that I needed this period in my life to adjust.

Within five years, all of the white people moved out of the neighborhood. I noticed it as a kid and didn't really pay much attention to it. Shortly after, Latinos started moving in. The city had really changed in those five years.

One thing I remember about those early years was that our house got burglarized. I had never seen this type of burglary before. We got home from the dentist, and our front door was cracked.

We rushed in, and everything from every room is sitting in the living room. The jewelry has already been stolen, and the rifles that my stepfather used to hunt with are also gone. I was happy to see that they stole my stepdad's rifle because I hated hunting. To kill something is not for me. These people had planned to come back with the semi truck and move the whole house out! It was devastating. If we hadn't come back, all our stuff would have disappeared. The thing that devastated me the most was that they stole my radio. They stole my music. 'How could they?'

## I'm Almost Grown

Once, when I was a teenager, we did have a fight. In the couple years I've been with my 'New Daddy,' I've taken karate classes and grown a few inches taller. When I first got my car, he tried to restrict my driving. One day he decided that I couldn't go somewhere because I didn't cut the grass. He tried to snatch the keys out of my hands. He grabbed for my furry ball that the key was on; that's all that he got—the furry ball. I still had the key. He lunged at me, and I blocked his hands. We both threw a couple punches until I grabbed him, took him down to the ground, and put my knee in his nuts, just like my teacher had instructed me to do. I told him that I was going to kill him at that point. My mother snatched me by the back of my shirt and pulled me off of him.

That kind of sums up the relationship I had with him until I left the house. In my later years, I can even give him a little credit for creating a part of me that has to get the job done, no matter how badly I don't want to do it.

He was a military man in the Navy. He would wake us up at 6:00 a.m. every morning to take care of our pigeons, pheasants, quail, and rabbits. Feed them and clean up their shit. We had to do it before school every day.

When me and my brother Richie would have our temper tantrums, we would holler at him, "We're not your slaves!" Storm off and barricade ourselves in our room. We would put the dresser up against the door, and when we did that, it would make him go crazy. We were in pain: "Didn't nobody care?" "Who are you, dude?"

## A Rocky Start

My wife endured five miscarriages with me and one before me that we only spoke of once. The emotional pain was challenging for her. For years, Pat blocked out the traumatic memory of her first stillborn child. I admired her for coming to terms with her loss, and I appreciated her coming to me to help her find peace within. We decided not to have any children at this time. We went through all kinds of mental bashing from other people.

It made us cry and depend on each other even more. I was trying to get over all of the talk that everybody had said about our relationship not making it. Our romance was only going to last six months because we were too young. We heard all that bullshit and still believed in ourselves.

## Looking for a Miracle

After four miscarriages, we were wondering, "What have we done to God to have been denied the opportunity to have kids?" Then we were blessed with a doctor who had perfected a new technique and told us that Pat was a perfect candidate. If we allowed him to use this new method, we could get a baby. With optimism in our hearts, we took a chance.

The decision for us to try to have children again was really hard on both of us. When I say she fought for this family, I mean that. She risked her life. With all of my heart, I know I couldn't have done it. Pat basically gave up her professional life for nine months so that we could have our baby. Bed rest was the biggest requirement. We followed the doctor's orders, and after so many disappointments, Laticia was finally born! You think men are strong? Pat was stronger. I know I couldn't have done it. A majority of women couldn't have done it. God wasn't punishing us; God did believe in us. He answered our prayers when Laticia came!

With the birth of Laticia, all of our doubts about not being parents and the fear of whether or not Pat and I were going to make it went away. We took the responsibility of being parents very seriously.

Now that Pat isn't here, things are pretty strange. I have two adult children. She is no longer here to give me those clues about when I'm supposed to do my 'daddy thing'. Whether they just need some of my wisdom or just another way to look at a situation, I am proud to have raised them to take care of themselves. They both have successful lives of their own. They now look after me, which is pretty amazing.

## Two Miracles

Now it's time to be great parents. We did the same procedure to have our son, Dwayne E. Hall II. Pat named our son and I named our daughter Laticia Faye Hall. The only problem I had was that Pat wanted to name him Dwayne Jr. Most of the 'Juniors' I knew were unhappy with the Jr. thing. It seems like they can never reach their father's status. That's why he's the II and De's son is the III.

*Dwayne II & Dwayne*

Being a junior just never seemed right to me but Pat insisted on naming him after me. We agreed that he would be Dwayne II. I am very grateful for him to be named after me. His wife, Maggie, started a tradition by naming my first grandson Dwayne E. Hall III, and she decided to give all five of my grandbabies my initials, D.E.H.

## She Saw the Music in Me

Pat insisted I keep pursuing music. She bought me a set of congas, found out about jam sessions, and introduced me to people that she thought could help my career. She always wanted me to have a career in music.

*Pat's Grandfather
'Big Daddy'*

It wasn't until 45 years later that I found out why she enjoyed music so much. Her grandfather was a professional guitarist. He would love to play for her as a baby and a toddler. She always had live music in her home and in her soul.

One of our first serious conversations was about two days into our relationship. She said to me, "I'm all about my family. I visit my grandfather every week. I visit my grandmother every week, and I take my siblings to play every week. If you have a problem with that, we're not going to be able to work it out."

I didn't know it then, but I was looking for a woman who was passionately devoted to her family. I had never seen anyone that young and committed to their family like Pat was. It just made me love her more.

When we met, we both had jobs. She worked at a grocery store, Bodega Corner Market, and I worked at Raychem, where they made hand grenades and other deadly destructive weapons for the Army. I had just graduated, and she was still in high school. I would pick her up from there.

## Life and Death

Death is something we all have to deal with. The more people you love, the more you deal with death. My dealings with people leaving started at a young age, around 7 or 8 years old. We were at the Russian River in California, playing in the water holding hands, when a riptide took my friend in. We didn't find him until two days later. For some reason, the adults in my life felt it was necessary for me to see him in the casket.

It messed me up for the rest of my life. What I did understand was that the plans we had made would never be fulfilled. After that, I lost my aunt, uncle, and cousin before I was 10. From 10 to 15, I lost three more cousins and my godfather. From a very young age, I understood how precious life is. Through all the things that Pat and I went through, we always knew that tomorrow wasn't promised.

Arguing and holding grudges wasn't working because, at any time, you could be gone. In the beginning of our marriage, we made some rules that we stayed true to for 50 years.

## The Rules

Rule 1: No calling each other names
Rule 2: No telling each other to get out
Rule 3: No physical or verbal abuse
Rule 4: Not to be like our parents
We watched our parents fight, and we wanted no part of that.

## The Promise

The first five years of our marriage were a lot of pain; the majority of the miscarriages happened during that time. Pat came to me and told me she wanted to split up! I was devastated. Through my tears, I asked her why. She told me, "You want to have kids, and I can't do that for you."
I told her at that moment that if we never have kids, I still want to spend the rest of my life with her. I can say that since that moment, in fifty years, we have never said we wanted to break up with each other. We have had some tough times and gone through tons of disagreements. We always stayed with what we started with: love. We knew we were going to be challenged in this relationship, and what's so amazing to me now, looking back, is that she never gave up on us.

## Where's God?

People didn't think that I believed in anything. Pat knew that I chose God as my father since mine didn't want to be one. I didn't think about it before. I guess that's what we did. We walked on "Faith Lane", my wife's favorite saying. We were sixteen and eighteen years old. What do we know about love and making a relationship work? Both of us were not virgins. We both had previous sexual experiences. To be in a real relationship? We had no clue. We were teenagers in an adult world.

I'm going to honor her final request to continue on. To be a grandfather and a father to our kids until my time runs out. I feel like I'm in the desert searching for water, and I just can't find it. I am thirsty for her kisses and her touch. I miss her so much.

## Finish What We Started

Writing this book has helped me deal with her absence. Also, this will give my grandkids, now too young to understand, the opportunity to learn that there was a lot more to Pat than just Gramzie and how much she loved them.

My kids can reflect on what she endured for them to have breath. A chance to see all of who we were for fifty years, the good and the bad.

## Little Haters

During the early years we weren't perfect. Sometimes we were not happy about other people having babies. We really were hard on people who we felt didn't take care of their kids. It made us feel mad and sad at the same time.

We recognized that seeing life through this lens wasn't going to solve anything. It would only continue to destroy us inside. Patricia was my balance and my opportunity to see life from a different perspective. She told me every day in those last months how happy I made her, and knowing that gives me peace. I'd like to know: What do I do now?

## Someone Else's Shoes

Finally, we were blessed with a daughter. In that moment, a fear came over me that made me ask the question, "How in the hell do I raise a daughter?" To ask myself that question made me aware that her birth changed me forever.

I was finally able to try to look at life through a young woman's eyes. Yeah, it's hard out there for a black man, and it's hard for a black woman too. Especially for those who are pretty, smart, and strong.

I knew Laticia would be just like her mother. That's when I started asking my wife more questions about how she felt about this world. She said that being a woman came with a lot of stuff. 'How pretty am I? Will someone love me? Am I good enough to be a mother?' Things I never knew before. Now I have to raise a daughter. How do I give her the confidence to walk through this world?

We all know that this world can be a scary place.

## I Can Learn

I was finally beginning to gain some confidence in myself. In those years, Pat gave me the confidence to love myself. We were young when we met. I couldn't even read properly when I first met Pat. I couldn't spell the name of the street that we moved on. Me and Pat started studying, pulling words off of the Phil Donahue show, looking them up in the dictionary, and finding out what they meant. We taught ourselves.

For the first time in my life, I realized the power of wanting to achieve something. I bought my first car at fifteen and a half; I achieved that. I had a job at sixteen; I achieved that, but this learning after being away from school was different.

We taught ourselves every day until we got to the point where teaching ourselves how to read and write was one of our first joint achievements. We felt more comfortable in this world. Watch out world! Here we come!

## Secret

Pat says the harmony was shattered in her family when she found out that her dad wasn't her biological father. She said, "Something broke in her." Things got really bad; respect was lost, and she ended up being a ward of the county at around 14. She lived with her foster parents and then with her aunt May. I met her while she was still living with her aunt. They say that Pat was a, "Wild child." I guess for all people, there's another person who can cool them out and make them see their full potential. Appreciate the moments they have with each other. Feel like they're being heard, and see you as you truly are.

Luckily, Pat and I were that for each other. People said how much happier she seemed since our relationship began. They said how much she had changed. Pat was a different person now, self-assured, focused, and devoted to her family.

## Little Black Boy

I was born in Santa Barbara, California, on November 11, 1953. The people in my life were my grandfather, my grandmother, and my mama. And a Latino babysitter who was teaching me Spanish at that young age. I got all the attention; this was the one time in my life that I was spoiled.

When I turned 5, I moved from Santa Barbara to San Francisco, and I was introduced to 8 to 10 different cousins of various ages. I learned that I had to take care of myself.

Every summer, I stayed with my cousins who lived in the Fillmore District of San Francisco, Hunter's Point, and the Mission District. My aunt was, in other words, very lenient.

## Learning to Hustle

At 9 and 10 years old, I was making sure I took care of myself. My first job was at a used car lot, wiping down the cars from the morning dew in the Bay Area. And then I would go across the street and work at the Bodega on the corner, which gave me breakfast every morning. Eating at my aunt's house was a struggle. They used to put out one box of cereal and a can of Pet Milk (evaporated milk in a can), and everybody was supposed to eat off of that, like cats? Well, not me. After fighting a few times to get my share, I was done, and I wondered why my cousin Johnny never put up a fight. He would watch the mayhem and then disappear.

My big cousins would always win. I'm crying my eyeballs out, and he comes to me and says "Let me show you, man, you don't have to cry."

He showed me how to collect soda bottles and turn them into the store to make a little money to buy sunflower seeds that I would put in my pocket and that would last me all day.

My older cousins took advantage of us youngsters, so I found a way to eat!

Me and my older cousin Johnny used to get on the bus and go to Playland Beach to shine shoes. At that time, the sailors were stationed in San Francisco. Dressed sharply with money to spend. Their black, shiny shoes always needed a shine. On the way back home, when the sun started going down, we would buy roasted chicken and wouldn't have to fight with the rest of them to eat. That started me out on being self-reliant, not afraid to work, and making sure I was taken care of.

## Young Entrepreneurs

I guess this was the beginning of my hustling life, educated by my cousin Johnny and the *Pimps* and *Ho's* on the street, giving a young man *game* that would follow me and actively be a part of my whole life. I don't look at the hustle mentality as a bad thing; I look at it as something that gave me the energy to achieve. In our community, hustling is a good thing and a bad thing; it all depends on how you apply it to your life.

Are you the type of hustler that helps people achieve things along with yourself, or are you the type of hustler that takes advantage of people to gain what you want? Which makes you more of a conman than a hustler.

## The Art of Negotiation

Hustling from a young age taught me the art of negotiation. Negotiation is a really big part of life, which I don't know if everybody understands. At a young age, I did.

One story I remember is that when I was with my mom, I would always venture out to the railroad tracks to catch tadpoles and frogs and throw rocks at rats.

Me and a couple friends stumbled across the Planters peanut factory and the Bazooka gum factory. We young kids jumped the fence, rummaged through all the boxes, and found wonderful peanuts. The guy who worked there was so upset that he chased us. He didn't catch any of us, though he scared the shit out of us.

The following week, I went by myself and asked the Planter's guy if I could get the rejects. If the label didn't fit on the pack of peanuts, they would reject them. They were perfectly good; just the packaging wasn't right. I made a deal with him to just straighten up a little bit and pick up all the discarded papers, and I could have all the peanuts I could carry. Well, since that worked out for me, I went to the Bazooka bubble gum place, and I got the same answer! Yes! Negotiation.

I used to go once a week and then sell them to all the kids at school. It was one of my first major hustles! I loved making money and I loved making deals, although it would lead me into trouble later on in life.

## Wild Child

Age 12 through 17 was a rough time for Pat. Her world had been knocked off its  axis, and she was spinning out of control. She could no longer live at her parents house. Pat started doing things that would ease her pain, or at least that's what she thought. She started doing drugs; she used to say acid was her favorite before I met her. She said it was the one thing that stopped her from thinking about all the bad stuff in her life. She took it one time while we were dating, and she had a really bad trip. I helped her through that, and she never did it again.

Back in the 70s and 80s, during our teen years, drugs were a big part of our lives. I had been selling weed for a couple of years.

When I first met her, of course I had some, and she asked me for a joint. I guided her to my bedroom and shut the door. It was a little awkward for a second because both of us could feel the sparks that we had for each other.

I reached up into the raptors and pulled out a pound, and she busted up laughing. Not sure why, I asked her, "Why are you laughing?"

She said to me, "I would have never thought it; you don't seem like the type. You seem really square."

## Business Partner

After that, she started bringing customers to me, or maybe I should say she gathered her own group of customers. That's how our partnership began.

She never looked at herself as a great businesswoman, but she was. Before I met her, I was *slinging that stuff* and making pretty good money, probably about $600 a month.

Part of that money went to buy my beautiful 65 T-Bird with a removable top, swivel seats, a tilting steering wheel, and silver chrome baby moon tires. My car was as low as a pack of Kool's with an 8-track tape player and red crushed velvet seats.

I had learned the hustle game pretty well from the streets of San Francisco. When I got to East Palo Alto, I thought I was the 'shit'. I bought this car at 15 and a half, and I was bragging my ass off. Not in words, just in the way that I was moving. Fresh clothes and, even back then, tennis shoes could make a statement. I always had a pair that nobody else did.

## Lessons in the Game

One day at school, while hanging out with a couple girls, a bully decided enough was enough with this dude, and he came over. We exchanged words, and he slapped me so hard that I ended up under my car!

The car had put me in the spotlight of jealousy. My first lesson was that bragging and *stunting on people* was dangerous. I met up with the guy that slapped me up under the car later in life, and the outcome was a little different; this time weapons were involved, but I'm still here.

## Buffalo Soldier

School was not that enjoyable for me. But there were a couple things that I took from high school. The love of cooking and horseback riding. My Photoshop teacher invited me for the weekend to ride horses. I fell in love with it. He was a real black cowboy. I would go down every other week and help out on his ranch. Outside of Gilroy, next to a national park, you could ride for miles.

I rustle cattle and eat beans and tortillas by the camp fire under the moonlight. It was a wonderful hobby. I took Pat a couple of times with me. She enjoyed the horseback riding. But she didn't want any parts of the work on the ranch. When I rode, it made me feel like I went back in time.

I was a real 'Buffalo Soldier' in those moments. I continued to ride for a few years after we were married but stopped when Laticia was born.

## Whipping Her Ass

In the first year of our love story, I lost my mind for a second and tried to slap Pat. She packed her clothes and left me. It was only for two days. I lost my mind. She told me that she grew up with her dad whipping her ass, and she sure wasn't going to live the rest of her life with me whipping her ass.

Damn, I messed up. I begged her to come back. That's when we created the four rules that were mentioned earlier in our story.

Like I said, we followed those for 50 years, and I never put my hands on her again. I was young and dumb and had never seen a respectful marriage. I had two stepfathers, so I didn't grow up seeing a successful relationship.

## Runaway Child

When Pat found out she had a biological father, all she wanted to do was find out more about that side of her family. From what I understand, she was a pretty sheltered kid up until age 12, and her parents pretty much controlled whatever environment Pat was in.

Pat said that when her breasts started growing, her parents put more restrictions on her. When a father sees his daughter develop like that, it's a *whole new ballgame*. From 'Daddy's Little Girl' to someone that men are now staring at.

The fear of what could happen to somebody in their youth—the fear that someone could talk them into doing, "The Deed" before it was time—is just all kinds of crazy stuff. Pat's stepfather didn't handle it very well, and in his mind, he knew how cruel some men can be.

Pat started running away from home at 12, and that's why she lived with foster parents and then her aunt May. She tried several times to go back home, but it just didn't work for her anymore. Pat always wanted to be her own person. As they say, "Dance to the beat of your own drum."

## You Got A Daddy?

Pat and her mother bumped heads for a while over her visiting her biological father's side of the family. When junior high and high school came, she got a taste of a little bit of freedom. They arranged for her to go and visit that side of the family, and during those visits, a lot of crazy stuff went on. One thing for sure happened: she was raped and became pregnant behind it. She had a stillborn, and it really messed her up before I even met her. She felt like her parents abandoned her during her darkest time, and that abandonment would play out in many ways over the 50 years we were together.

Sitting here in this sadness, it reminds me that when I met Pat, she was the one who took away my sadness. I haven't felt this way since I was a kid, and my dad said he was coming to get me. I used to sit out and wait for him to come, but he would never show up. And now I'll never see her again. This amount of sadness I haven't had to deal with in a long time.

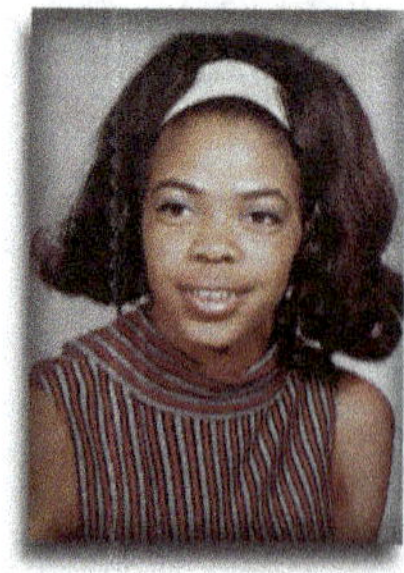

## The Little Dark Kid

I mentioned my grandfather earlier, my mom's stepdad. He was a white man; we think he may have been Creole, but we don't know for sure. He was the only father I knew, and he gave me all that I try to give to my kids. All of the knowledge, reassurance, and love. I grew up with a white grandfather and a white stepfather. My stepfather was Hungarian-American. He didn't always treat me the best; he abused me. Not sexually, but physically.

**Frank Fetkyol**
**Dwayne's**
**Step Father**

He would make me kneel on my knees for hours or spin around in circles until I threw up. I was carrying all that baggage when I met Pat. Now we had each other and no one would ever do anything like that to us again. I did everything I could to please my stepfather, but he never really accepted me as his son. I was just the kid that was there before he came into our lives.

## Are You Worthy?

Even though Pat was really happy about our relationship she still needed her parents approval. She was mad at them for the years that she had to spend away from her brother and her sisters. She loved them to death. She wanted me to meet her parents and of course they broke her heart.

**Pat's Parents**
**Ernest & Dorothy**

The first time I met them, they gave me a verbal lashing. Asking me if I was on heroin and a variety of other stupid questions. They even asked us if we already had sex, which let me know right then that they didn't think I was worthy of their daughter.

I had a lot to prove. They made us really doubt our future together. When we left and hugged each other, we said, "We don't give a damn," and set out to make anyone who doubted us into a liar.

## Man Money

Our families were not strangers. They played cards and partied together. Her Aunt Dusty, Aunt May, and my mother used to organize these parties. You know, barbecues, dominoes, and card parties. Her aunt, Dusty, who lived across the street from me and my family; was like my second mother. She let me smoke cigarettes in her backyard before my mother let me smoke at the house. She always used to tell me, "You make man money, so you should be able to do man things."

Pat and I used to sit in her driveway and listen to music in my broken-down car. Auntie May and Dusty were very happy about our relationship because they saw how happy Pat was over the couple months that we had been together. We loved them, and they had our backs.

My mother yelled, "No fucking way, not over my dead body." All kinds of crazy shit, but in the six months I had known Pat, I had really grown up a lot. I was able to tell my mother that she couldn't tell me what to do with my future.

It soured our relationship for a while, but when she saw how stubborn we were, it came down to us telling them that we would elope. Then they backed off a little. Pat's mom and my mom did the wedding. The ceremony was nothing that we wanted; we went along with it because we knew our freedom wasn't too far away.

## Two Different Worlds

When I was a kid, it was like I lived in two different worlds. With my mom, everything was 'Father Knows Best.' When I went to my cousin's house, it was 'Street Life.' I was baptized Episcopalian, kind of like Catholic. I went to church on Sundays and Bible study on Thursdays at the church.

I never understood the words in the songs, which were prayers. They were in a different language. Greek or Portuguese, which I still don't know to this day. When we moved to East Palo Alto, I was introduced to the Baptist Church. I think I was about 11 or 12.

We walked into the church, and I got my mind blown. People were dancing, catching the 'Holy Ghost', fainting, and 'talking in tongues.' They also had a live band. What a huge difference between the two sides of my family! One is calm and very structured; the other is loud and energetic. Two sides of the same religious coin. Both preach love and happiness. It really blew my mind.

That experience inspired me years later to read the Bible and the Quran. I later learned about Buddhism and Hinduism, which led me to create what I call my personal religion. I believe in reincarnation because I don't think that you can become one with God in one lifetime.

I believe you have to experience everything that the earth has to offer. Being rich, being poor, being black, being white, being crippled, being handsome or ugly, pretty, smart or not so smart. I think every time you learn something, you change yourself. If you take the information and use it in the right way. We all have choices.

## My Real Family

Shorty & May

I got a chance to meet the people that Pat called family: Shorty and May, Sandra and James, and her uncles and aunts. The night that we left her parent's house, I knew that she was a *Ride or Die*, as they say, *10 Toes Down*. "That woman got your back," is what we used to call it.

James & Sandra

She really had my back that night. It was strange to have someone defend me with all of her heart. It impressed the hell out of me. To stand up to your parents, wow!

Now looking back, she was used to that fight, trying to get her parents respect. They lost Pat's respect for them that night. They had created a wall that they had to get over. When something bad happens, you can let it define you, let it destroy you, or let it strengthen you.

Pat discussed with me a lot about why she felt her mother didn't give her the love that she needed. She had a lot of different theories, and that's something that I guess I'll never know the truth about.

I'm glad that in the last months, or maybe I should say the last couple years, her mother started to express how much she loved Pat after 60 years of her not knowing it. I'm quite sure she has the answer now that she can see the whole picture.

Having Pat in my life made me look at things through her eyes—from a different angle. Move just a little bit, and you might see it in a different way. Pat taught me about family. Not just your immediate family, but the family that you create with those you truly love. Pat loved to love and be loved. Her greatest strength was her loving heart.

## Child Raising Thing

I remember when we had our daughter. I was sitting there with her in my arms when I asked Pat, "What are we going to do now?" She said to me, "Everything that our parents didn't do." We were going to flip the script with our kids, and from that moment on, we took it seriously. She said, "They'll have rules, but good ones, and we'll use our intuition. Now you can't do everything perfectly, but we were going to try our best."

We were both grateful to know that our kids appreciated the way that we raised them. To have them let us know was one of the biggest highs we've ever had.

Me and Pat made some big mistakes, and the kids let us know about those too. But they were allowed to talk to us. To question things, to ask why we were doing certain things in a certain way, and to respect them for trying to do their best.

Growing up was the opposite for me and Pat. Looking back, we were kind of lost about the whole child-raising thing. We questioned ourselves about everything, and Laticia was intelligent and very aware of her own personal identity. She really challenged us, and when the same stuff started coming out of our mouths as our parents, we took a pause on that. We kind of knew that when something was wrong, we would change our approach.

## The Dynamic Duo

After we taught ourselves how to read and write, we went to the bookstore. We bought a couple of self-help books on how to communicate with people better and how to make your situation better. We put those techniques to work.

Too many young black people are just married, with their whole future ahead of them and not many opportunities. We learned how to use that knowledge to our advantage. We worked through a lot of situations in our favor, and we realized that we were a team to be reckoned with.

Putting our minds together in those early years, we realized we were a dynamic duo. I'm an introvert, and she's an extrovert (yin and yang).

We could do anything but have kids. We would have those highs of success and making it in this world. Until we thought about the miscarriages. Back and forth: sadness, happiness, sadness, happiness. We were emotional wrecks by the time the doctor knocked on our door.

Dr. Richard Chamberlain was an obstetrician who was researching methods for childbirth. He had discovered a technique for which Pat was an ideal candidate. When I say he came knocking, he literally knocked on the front door one night while we were eating dinner. He came in and assured us that we would have a good chance of having a child if we consented to the procedure.

Back before Laticia came, we were living life to its fullest, snatching all the fruit that we could. We both worked jobs; I went to jam sessions on the weekends, and the weed business was booming.

We sold to all of the employees at the places that we worked. We liked selling through other people. You know the kind that likes to brag? We always played it low-key, based on the lessons that I had learned back in the streets. Before I met Pat, I had stuck my foot in the deep end of the weed business.

I was the *mule*, bringing back 40 pounds every two weeks.

## Want To Be A Player

In high school, I planned on being a chef. I took the culinary arts class for 2 hours every day. That was the only class I never cut. School was really hard for me for some reason. I only liked the culinary arts, the wood shop, the video class, and photo shop. Yeah, I got kind of popular when I took photo shop class because all I did was go around and take pictures of the girls. They were all up on me, and I had a car. I was lucky girls weren't a problem (ha ha ha).

I did a lot of cooking contests, traveled to a lot of other schools, and met a lot of different people back then. I should say white people. They had the connections (the drugs), and my having a white grandfather and a white stepfather is what made it a little easier for me to connect with them.

I think fear comes from not knowing about something. My grandfather taught me to 'fear no man' and 'command respect.' I wasn't intimidated by white men; I looked at them as my equals.

If you smoked weed, you called yourself a *head*. That's how you would identify those who participated in that activity. I made a lot of connections. I would travel from East Palo Alto to Santa Cruz to pick up the 20 packages, weighing 2.2 kilos in each package, and bring them back to the guys who paid me to do it.

## It's Not Free

When I met Pat and she found out about that situation, she made me promise to not do that anymore. I told her," I get four and a half pounds for free." She said, "It's not for free. If you get caught, I won't see you again."

We were half-owners in a hydroponic setup. This was in the 1970s; it was unheard of back then. We spliced plants and made our own strains. The favorite brands were Acapulco Gold, Panama Red, Thai Stick, and Mexican Brown Weed with a whole lot of seeds.

At some point, I started doing more and more music. Then music became my life. In our everyday lives, Pat was always my manager. I would listen to her opinion because I understood it was for the best of both of our futures.

## My White Grandfather

I'm so glad that my grandfather was in my life. Growing up without my father, he taught me a lot of the values that I still follow and teach my kids. I asked him, "Are you going to teach me how to be a man because I don't have a father?"

He said to me, "I can't teach you to be a black man; there are too many ways to be a black man in this world. I can help teach you to be a good man that your family will love and honor."

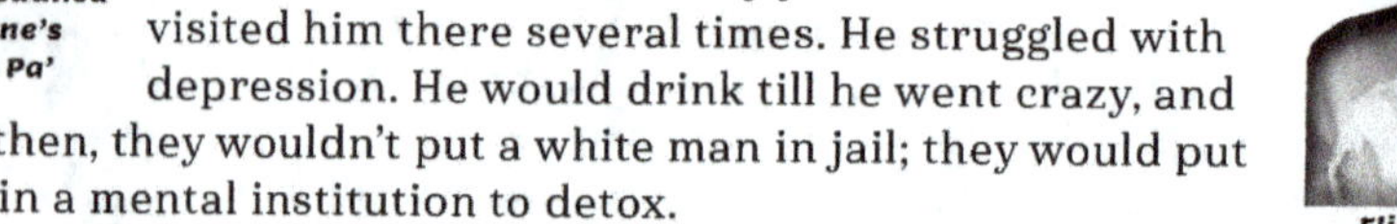

My grandfather was a beast, and he took no shit from no man; you know, he was a *real man*. He married my grandmother, a black woman. Back in those days, he could have been killed or lynched for having loved her, and he had been threatened on many occasions. He had a chip on his shoulder for any man who looked at his wife cross-eyed.

I believe he was a railroad conductor. He had a bad drinking problem that landed him in a mental institution a few times in my youth. I went and visited him there several times. He struggled with depression. He would drink till he went crazy, and back then, they wouldn't put a white man in jail; they would put them in a mental institution to detox.

*Chuck Beaulieu Dwayne's Gran Pa'*

*Elinor Beaulieu Dwayne's Gran Ma'*

When he came back home, he'd be fine for another few months. When he was home, he gave me all the loving care I needed. I wouldn't be me if it weren't for all the love, the lessons, the joy, all the fishing trips, and the trips to the desert.

He was the first man I met when I was a baby—the first man to ever hold me. I'm glad I was mature enough to thank him for being in my life. Did I see a white man? No, he was my grandfather. Even though he passed away in my twenties, he loved me and he loved Pat. He said marrying her was the best thing I'd ever done. He knew that she had my back, and he told me not to fuck it up. Well, Pops, I didn't fuck it up.

## Making Music

Now was the time for me to, "Open my mind and my ass would follow." I learned everything that I could about the music business. I have been a performer and did shows in my *Doo Wop* group, The Mystics, but this was different. My music is starting to heat up a little. The jam sessions that Pat would find for me started to pay off. After one of the jam sessions, a guy named Rason walks up to me and says, "If you ever want to start a band, let me know. Here's my number." After that, I got a lead on a songwriting job. I was good at writing lyrics and *hooks*. It didn't make money, but the time I spent on the songwriting team sharpened my skills. We were writing songs for Smokey Robinson. He had several writing teams in different cities and collected their music annually.

*The Mystics*

**Pat**          **Smokey Robinson**          **Dwayne**

After a whole lot of writing and a whole lot of waiting, he accepted one of
our songs. Then it all went bad. The song we wrote was chosen for a movie
soundtrack, but the movie never came out. During the time I was creating
music, Pat and I discussed the whole band thing. We decided I might as well go
and see what was going on with Rason. "Nothing ventured, nothing gained," was
just one of the things *Gran Pops* told me.

## Investing in the Future

I was lucky. Rason was a bass player and had some pieces of equipment. All
of a sudden, it became an investment. I had to buy more equipment.

There was a list of things: a mixing board, microphones, speakers, monitors,
chords, stands, and equalizers—all kinds of stuff that I didn't know we needed.
It takes a lot to make a band, and someone has to run this stuff while you try to
perform!

Pat and I sat down and discussed what we were getting into. She said to me,
"Let's do it!" On her advice, I started my music career. We came up with a plan
to get our half of the money to buy the equipment, and Rason came up with his
half.

This is about two and a half years into our marriage, and I still have all of
my connections from my teen years. We put together a couple of nice deals and
came up with the money. Practice began, but we still needed a drummer, a good
rhythm guitarist, a lead guitarist, and keyboards.

Of course, I was modeling my band, *Midas Touch* after one of my favorite
groups: *Earth, Wind, and Fire*. Which meant I needed three horn players:
a saxophone, a trombone, and a trumpet. We started putting ads in BAM
Magazine (Bay Area Music) for different members of the group. A lot of people
came and went. Since Rason was the bass player and he was the one that
offered me this opportunity to start a band, it was kind of 50/50. As time went
on, I started to realize that band members were coming because they believed
that my voice could get them where they wanted to go. Several months in, we
realized that we could cut the members of the band by getting specialized
people like a horn player who could play several horns or a keyboard player
who could play horn parts and string parts. There were guitar players who
could play rhythm and lead guitar.

So we cut back on band members, and everyone got a little bit more
money. We practiced for almost a year to have 40 songs to be able to play in a
nightclub. I learned a lot in that year when I was in a singing group, but I had
three other guys with me. Now I'm the *front man* and all of this is new to me.

Midas Touch

Midas Touch

Midas Touch
. . . cordially invites you
to
A PRE-ROAD PARTY
Friday — October 28
at the MC Breed Roadhouse
2147 Pulgas in East Palo Alto
10 pm until 3 am
$1 at the door

**Midas Touch**
Circa 1975

# I Can Do It!

At first, I used to sing while looking at the floor. There were anxieties that I had to overcome, but I was always one to try to make myself better. I pushed on, and I got a little better. When the time came for our first performance as Midas Touch, we invited people to come over and listen to us in the practice room. Now we were going to play for a real audience!

Once I got in front of that audience, I turned into a different person, one that I didn't even know. At that moment, I knew 100% that music was what I needed to do for the rest of my life! The band and I had looked up the top 10 songs of the month or year and chosen keys where I could sing them. I didn't have as many choices back then. I had to figure out different techniques. I sang some female songs with my voice.

The thing for the audience was that they had just heard it on the radio, and in that way, we always made that connection with the people. We were current. They used to say Midas Touch played all the new songs. In this world, you have to create an edge over the other bands.

## The Show Must Go On

One of our first performances was at Stanford University's bookstore in Palo Alto. We played for 45 minutes for free during lunch just to get the stage experience and let people know, "We are here!"

After that, we played at a couple *dive bars* to, "Tighten the wig." It took a whole hour to set up all our equipment. We were hungry for knowledge. Every night, problems occurred. We learned how to fix things in the moment. "The Show Must Go On," no matter what happens.

During this time, Pat had a miscarriage, and that knocked us off our feet once again. We pushed on, and the band started getting the opportunity to play at weddings, birthday parties, and graduations. We even played at Pat's sister Carolyn's and Chris's wedding. We performed their favorite song by The Commodores, *Stuck On You*. That's what we were good at: taking requests and satisfying our clients' wishes. Our moneymaker was the parties that the college kids would throw. College kids like to have a lot of fun at their frat parties.

We started to really catch on in the Bay Area. We played at several different colleges. San Jose State, Foothill College, and De Anza College, just to name a few. Colleges were good money; they always paid you. For some of the jobs we did, we would get paid in drinks! We started playing in different cities. Opened up for Tony, Toni, Toni in Oakland, and also played in San Francisco.

We were really getting hot. We were booked a year out for New Year's Eve parties, Halloween parties, weddings, and corporate events. Things were going pretty well. We had a couple of touring booking agents looking at us and giving us offers, but we weren't ready yet!

When the band was ready to gig, Pat was pregnant again. She had started with the new procedure that the doctor had recommended. We could finally have a child! During this time, it was a real challenge trying to make sure my wife was good while generating enough money to pay for a practice place and enough money to keep my band members happy. I was under a lot of pressure. Pat convinced me that I have been making good choices and got the band this far with my ideas, but I could not see that because I was in the middle of it. I started to understand that I was the key. The band members started only listening to me. I didn't have the confidence to really be the band leader.

"Midas Touch" sang at a recent performance on the Campus green. They are (left to right): percussionist, Larry Beck; bassist, Rason Sampson; saxophonist, Ray Cordova; congas-lead vocal, Dwayne Hall; lead guitar, James Lewis.
(Photo by Doug Smothwaite)

## Man Up

I had a lot of areas to grow through; my wife counseled me, and I started to take responsibility as the band leader.

At this point, my wife said it was time to have a conversation with Rason, the bass player, and tell him that I was the leader of the band. The band members wanted it that way, and they wouldn't have it any other way. They were going to walk, so I had to stand in that light now. I'm the band leader now, and I have to lead this band in the right direction. My wife is pregnant at home. I said to myself at that time, "You wanted to be grown up; this is what comes with it."

## 'Razor' James

At one of our performances, a young man came up to me during our break and told me, "I can blow your guitarist off the face of the earth; are you looking for anybody?" I gave him my number. The guitarist who was in the band was on his way out. James came to the audition, and he was really good.

We asked him to join the band that night, and the rest is history. He had just returned from the University of California, San Diego, to study music as his major and was currently enrolled at San Jose State.

He knew what he needed to do. Be a professional musician! The chance to go on tour with a *Soul Dance* band was exciting. The biggest challenge was to learn 40 tunes in less than a month prior to leaving the San Francisco Bay Area and traveling throughout the Northwest and Canada. After hundreds of performances, we still work together to this day. Collaborating on this book.

With the introduction of James, the band started sounding better. He had the knack of putting the musical side together. He was really pushy about it. Whether it sounded good or bad, he had an ear for it. He was soft-spoken, but not when it came to music.

His words would cut like a knife, and I ended up giving him his stage name, 'Razor James.' He brought a youth full fire to the energy of the band. Later on he had to make tons of decisions in the studio. You know, what sounds to use, what takes to keep, stuff like that. All I had to do was focus on my rhythm on the congas and sing!

With him joining the band, James took a certain amount of pressure off of me. After the talk I had with the bass player, Rason, he started to *cop an attitude* and not work as hard as he used to.

## Go For It

At this point, I was a band leader, a husband, a son, a brother, and an uncle. I worked in a warehouse for 8 hours a day. Something had to change. As I said, we were getting pretty big in the Bay Area. The offers started coming in from the booking agents once again. 'Was this the opportunity? Could I quit working an 8-to-5 and finally have music take care of my family?'

Pat and I had decisions to make. The booking agents were offering multiple city tours five nights a week, which made pretty good money back then. I just left Hewlett Packard after working there for a couple years and was driving a truck for Memorex. I had a steady paycheck. Playing in the band was a good check, maybe once a month. Could I make this all work?

I'm afraid to quit my job because of the security of the steady checks, and she's telling me, "These opportunities won't always be here, and you won't always be young; you have to go for it." 'Go For It' is one of the first songs I wrote inspired by that conversation.

"Will we be all right?" I didn't know the answer to that, but I had to believe her. If she was willing to take the risk, I had to be willing too. I had to believe in myself and all of the hard work it took to create the band.

Pat is on bed rest, but luckily, with good neighbors, family, and friends, she always had someone with her. Her pregnancy is going well, and we're starting to get *juiced!* Are we going to be parents this time? Wow! We continue to play gigs, and Pat continues to get bigger. Every day that goes by, I get more and more anxious.

## Teamwork

I did not know music theory, chords and stuff but I knew how 'vibes' felt to me. James knew music theory so Rason's position diminished.

James and I started writing songs together. The first time I was able to write music he said to me, "You hear it in your head, right?" I said, "Yeah." He said, "Just sing it to me." I'd sing it to him and our first song was created. He had given me the ability to get ideas out of my head. I didn't write music but the way that he worked with me gave me confidence.

Creating music had finally come to life. I was always good at coming up with hooks. We made sure there were plenty of them. He got me to look at the bigger picture: "What do we really want to achieve with the band? I never felt that I needed to get rich off of this music thing. I would just love to be known as a great singer. Whatever money was made was just icing on the cake. The spirit of music lives through me; I have no choice but to let it out." For the first time my mind turned to writing and recording and I started on the journey to put together a home studio to get my ideas out.

I was going to make an album. As mentioned Earth, Wind, & Fire was my favorite band. Me and Pat had seen them every time they came to town—at least 15 times or more.

Pat and I loved going to concerts. It was one of our favorite things to do in the first five years of marriage. We would be at concerts like, Level 42 and Phil Collins and be the only black people in the theater. I sat through many Luther Vandross and Teddy Pendergrass concerts because Pat loved their music so much.

We always made it to the 'Day On the Green' concerts at the Oakland Coliseum. The home of the Oakland A's baseball team. You bring a blanket, and everybody lays out on the grass and listens to all the funk bands. War, Parliament, Cameo, Gap Band, Average White Band, Tower of Power, and Santana. We tried to go even after Laticia was born.

## Crowd Danger

We took Laticia one time, and it sounded like shots were fired, and the whole crowd began running. It was a stampede, and I had to knock people to the side. I only weigh about a buck fifty. My baby was in danger. I'm pushing people aside while Pat gets Laticia up off the ground because the crowd is coming. We made it out of there safely; we left some diapers, blankets, and some other little things, but our baby was safe. We never went to any more concerts

there, but Laticia's young life was filled with music and concerts. Every one of my grandkids loves music. It's in their blood. Now the little ones are growing up with their papa's music videos. I could never imagine that back then.

## The No No's

We started writing and got a nice collection of original songs. As Midas Touch we were known as a cover band that played Top 40. But we would try some of our hotter original dance songs at some of our gigs. It was kind of a 'no-no' to play original music in a nightclub setting. We only picked the most dance-able of our originals to play. The bartenders, waitresses, and owners never knew it was our own stuff and loved it!

It gave me and James a lot of encouragement. We were rebels and kept on writing. Pushing boundaries to the edge, playing whatever we felt the club would groove to. They really loved dancing to our original songs, and we knew we were headed in the right direction.

## Cop Troubles

I'm still dealing weed. It had always been my hustle to make sure we had what we needed. I had been lucky over the years. The police stopped me regularly, but I was never caught with any weed on me. The time I did get caught, the cop took a smell of it, put it in his pocket, and told me to go on about my business.

I have been getting stopped by the police throughout my driving history. It really got intense in the fifth month that I was with Pat. The cops had seen me in my fancy T-Bird, and now I had this beautiful Bonneville with oval tires and chrome everywhere and this beautiful woman sitting next to me.

How do you get jealousy from the cops? They just knew I was selling drugs. They would ask me where I got the money from, and I would show them my pay stub. That didn't slow them down. They started stopping me every time they saw me.

I've been thrown on the ground with shotguns pulled out many times. I even had a warning shot fired when I was in my teens at the school playing soccer. They put me in the cop car, took me to where a burglary had taken place and asked the people if I was the one. They said "No." They just let me out of the car and I had to get home by myself. As Rodney Dangerfield would say, "No respect." This one cop felt like it was his duty to take me off the streets. He stopped me and gave me a ticket on my way to work.

I used to work graveyard shift at RayChem and in the morning when I'm leaving work he says to me that he only has two more times to give me a ticket and then he would have my license suspended. I'm dealing with the cops and I'm also dealing with the draft. I didn't know if I was going to Vietnam or not.

The paranoia started to creep in and this *street life was gettin' real*. That cop is one of the reasons why I asked Pat to marry me because I was getting out of this town and I couldn't leave without her.

## Big Boy Moves

I felt I had to get out of this town. I rented a room from one of my high school friends in Menlo Park. That way, I wasn't in East Palo Alto all that much. My mother didn't like that I stopped paying her rent. In the six months that I knew Pat, the amount of growth that I went through was hard to believe. The changes that were happening to me included having love in my life. It truly made me feel like somebody was on my side.

For the first time, I wasn't tripping over why my dad didn't love me. I had somebody doing her best to love me. Amazingly, that confusing feeling went away. "Why wasn't I good enough?" Well, I was good enough. She made me believe that in a short amount of time. Looking back, it was a hell of a growth spurt.

Back then, you didn't *shack up*, and I wasn't going to leave her. We couldn't get married because she was only 16. We planned together; as soon as she turned 17, we were going to get married on her birthday, July 11th. We were going to elope. It was four days after her birthday on July 15, 1972, that we were married.

The one thing we had on our side was that Pat's social worker, who now had custody of her, was surprisingly impressed by Pat's attitude over the six months she had been with me. Pat had really given them hell over the last couple years with her attitude.

She was willing to sign for Pat to get married as soon as she turned 17, and I'm praying that I don't get drafted before then. Pat's parents didn't want us to get married, but they surely didn't want us to elope. Her parents didn't have any say in our getting married. The social worker had the power. Both our parents threw the wedding in order to feel like they were still in control of Pat's life.

## Ready Or Not!

It's that time. Contractions have started. It was a bit early because she's only about 8 months pregnant. A little too early. We're scared and excited at the same time. We had made it past the dangerous months. We had prayed to get to this point. We were hoping everything would go okay, and we were praying with all our might, 'God, you can't let us down; please don't; it would destroy us.' We've had so many failures. I'm totally blown away. I'm a nervous wreck.

Pat is in pain, and I can't do anything. This is how nature works. Oh man, finally she pushes that last time, and we find out that we have a little girl! I cut the cord and named her Laticia shortly after she was born.

Pat's blood pressure, or something of that nature, went sky high, and it caused a certain amount of worry and concern among the staff, so they rushed her out to intensive care. 'We've got the baby here! Now something's going to happen to you?' Oh no, I couldn't even comprehend raising the baby by myself. My heart dropped, and for the next 40 minutes, I was trapped in limbo.

Am I happy, or am I sad? Finally, the nurses let me know that everything was alright. Thank God. You can't wait until life isn't hard anymore before you decide to be happy. Worrying is a wish for something bad you don't want to happen.

## Our First Miracle

Thank you, God. We finally have our baby girl. The life that we envisioned starts now! I had been juggling a lot of things. Band, relatives, and warehouse work. I just took a deep breath and put fear to one side. Here we go.

We were the happiest we had ever been in our whole lives. The light in Pat shined brightly. Being a mother was everything to her, and she wore it well. She took it quite seriously. She had her mini-me. Laticia was a beautiful baby, and to us, she acted like she really was supposed to be with us. She was exceptionally beautiful. The pride that we felt every time someone told us those things about her. That look we would give each other like we already knew each other was proud as hell and a little conceited. We know she is beautiful, and we created her.

## Time To Get Fitted

Okay, it's time for me to sign with the booking promoter and we're going to start playing five nights a week. Laticia is here and the band is sounding tighter. Through the booking agent, The Anderson Agency, we are performing at Holiday Inns and Ramada Inns in the Bay Area. Now that we're playing in these places, we have to get a wardrobe.

I take the band to San Francisco to see the Chinese lady who has been making my clothes since I was a kid. I knew that she was good enough to make clothes for the band. We sketched out three costumes, and they were tailor-fit. The band was sounding great and looking even better. We were getting paid, and we knew we were a professional band. We're doing okay. Laticia is about 6 months old now, and I'm playing five nights a week. I'm living a musician's life. I play every night, and I'm loving it, and I'm loving having a family. It took me to another level of becoming a man. I really had responsibilities now, and I took them very seriously. My confidence as a performer is rising, and James and I are cranking out the original songs.

## Our Wedding

Well, I guess I kind of got ahead of myself and skipped over the pain that we hid. You might ask what happened at our wedding. The pictures may look beautiful, but Pat and I were fed up.

We had, for the last month, been in constant arguments with our parents about the wedding. We didn't have anything planned for our wedding. If we had anything to do with the wedding, we would not have played *We've Only Just Begun*

by The Carpenters as our song if not for her parents. We were getting ready to be together forever; we just wanted to get it over with. It was also the beginning of us dealing with difficult people together.

## That Thing Called Death

Death is unavoidable. It happens to the people we love. The first time I heard the phrase, "Death comes in threes." My uncle George got electrocuted while messing with an air conditioner. On our wedding day, this was also the day that I stopped listening to my mom and truly started thinking for myself and what was best for Pat.

We weren't having a wedding reception, as far as I can remember. I just remember being pressured into getting in the car and going to Oakland. To grieve instead of celebrate. We were unable to begin our honeymoon in our brand new apartment. They did not have to ruin our day with sadness; that's the way we both felt. Death comes in threes was the phrase.

Shortly after my uncle passed away, Pat's uncle James passed away. A vibrant young man, was killed in an automobile accident. In those 6 months, he had been like a big brother, giving me advice on relationships so I could treat his niece right.

Pat really loved her uncle James. She looked at him as a big brother and took it really hard. I don't know the whole story, but I know that she helped him

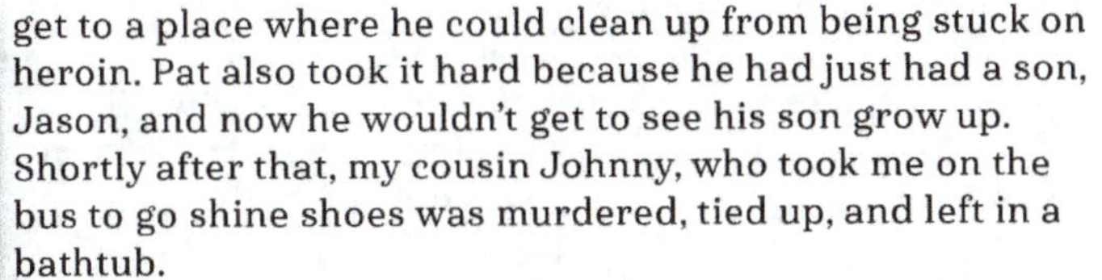

get to a place where he could clean up from being stuck on heroin. Pat also took it hard because he had just had a son, Jason, and now he wouldn't get to see his son grow up.

Shortly after that, my cousin Johnny, who took me on the bus to go shine shoes was murdered, tied up, and left in a bathtub.

My cousin's death hit me really hard because we had a pretty tight relationship.

The hustle life got him killed. I remember what my grandfather said: "There are many ways to be a black man." I had to find out what type of man I was going to be.

*Cousin Johnny*

## Time to Meet the Family

During the time that we were going out, before our marriage, I would take Pat regularly to see her grandfather. He was in a care facility. Her grandmother's birthday was coming up, and Pat asked me if I would go. That meant to me that I would have to be eyeballed by the whole family, so I went. It was Granny's birthday. Pat said it was time for me to meet the queen. There were at least 150 people there. I never

**Pat's Grandparents & Dwayne's brother & sisters**

**Granny**

saw a family so big; Granny had 13 kids, and 90% of them were there. A really big family! It blew my mind. The love that Granny showed me over the years made her one of my favorite people. She commanded love and respect; there was no bullshit around her, and she didn't have to open her mouth to say a word; just her look at you would stop you in the middle of whatever you were doing. Pat wanted to start a family and know that she could be loved just like her grandmother, and she succeeded. Granny would be proud of you, babe.

## On the Road

I can't hold the booking agents off. They want us, one of their top bands, to travel out of the state. Laticia is around 11 months old. It is time now for us to get ready to go on the road, and I'm at a turning point. I just had my daughter and wanted to be with her.

The agents had gotten a deal with the Holiday Inn, and we had to decide whether to take it or not. It was time for me to talk to Pat. She told me I should do it. "This is what we've been working for—to be recognized." It was one of the hardest things to leave my baby girl and my wife after all that we had been through. Yeah, I know that it's only three or four months, but it seemed like it was going to be forever. A week was too much. The band persuaded me to sign the contract.

Now it's time to get ready, and we have a lot of things to do before we hit the road. We had to get a new practice room because we were only going to be in town for a couple months. We had to let the other one go because our lease was up. None of us knew what the future held and could not be tied to a one-year lease. The only practice place we could find to accommodate us was a small warehouse unit in East Palo Alto. It's time to tighten up the performance, get new songs, and buy new equipment. And also, make sure everybody's family is okay before we hit the road. There's no turning back now.

## Welcome to the Ghetto

East Palo Alto has a gang reputation. I had to reassure all the band members that it would be safe. The stories they heard weren't always true. I remember a story Razor James told me about our first rehearsal.

He was driving down the back streets of East Palo Alto. Between him and our practice place was a black motorcycle gang hanging out. He slowed down and considered turning around. He quickly decided not to let fear interfere with his goals and cautiously proceeded.

I also didn't know that the place right next to us was the clubhouse for the MC Soul Brothers Motorcycle Club. The Soul Brothers Motorcycle Club was officially founded in East Palo Alto, California, in 1967. Leading up to the founding, a small group of friends had been riding together for approximately 3 years. Making the club rather unique at the time was the fact that they were a mixed-race club from the beginning, with a mix of black and white members. Considering that this was the late 1960's, this was unusual for an outlaw motorcycle club. The club's first official run was on Labor Day of 1967, with a total of 57 members participating.

The Mother Chapter for the club would also shift over time, from the early years in East Palo Alto to Stockton and then Fresno.

I was kind of scared because the only thing I knew about a motorcycle gang was the 'Hells Angels' and I was very afraid. Don't mess with them is what I was taught in San Francisco.

One night we're practicing, and we hear the loud rumble of bikes, and we are all scared as hell. We hear a knock at the door. It's some of the bikers, and it was nothing but love. They believed in equality and wanted us to play for their party. They had black and white members, and the emblem on their vest was of a black hand and a white hand embracing one another. They became some of our biggest fans.

## Vicious Business

It's time that we make sure that all the members are going to be able to do this job. We've been on the road for months, and we're moving on up. Trying to keep a band together is a hard thing; players come and go all the time. People were making offers to our best members. It was a vicious business with lots of ups and downs.

When somebody leaves the band, you have to kind of start over again. He or she had to learn all of the songs, and we had to go through the songs more than we wanted to. It was something that you had to do to keep the performances consistent. When band members would leave, it would make me think I wasn't good enough. Always blaming myself, like I could have done more.

You just have to put that kind of stuff to the side because all things happen for a reason. We were lucky because we always had better people, and in this business, you have to believe in yourself or you'll never get anywhere. In this business, you get more no's than yes's.

Well, as the leader of the band, I had to go and talk to some of the younger band members' mothers. Now I have this responsibility. To me, they are grown men as far as I am concerned. I had to assure mothers that everything would be alright. I didn't know if it would be safe or not. I was praying that my family would be all right. That was the only thing on my mind. For years, it was our pursuit to have a child.

I'm having to make one of the hardest decisions I've had to make in my life, but Pat wasn't making me question anything. "You've got to go," she said. She reminded me that it was our vision and look at what we've created. All I could do was listen to what she was saying and appreciate the confidence that she had in me.

## In My Feelings

In writing this, I see how much I depended on her. Being without her shakes me to my bones. Looking back, she gave me the confidence that I needed for this whole journey. She believed in me, and I believed in her. Though the hardest thing is for me to believe in myself, In my life, I've always needed to be alone to create. Now there's something strangely different. She was the person that I always wanted to impress. I rushed to show her my new poem or new song. Whether she liked it or not, I always valued her opinion. Always.

## She Got This

It's almost time to get on the road, and I'm mentally messed up. The stress of leaving my wife and my daughter was getting the best of me, and I wasn't dealing with it well. Pat sat down and talked with me. She recognized my mood swings and reassured me that I could go on tour and not worry about them. 'She got this.' Somewhere in my mind, I didn't want them to learn that they could make it without me. It may sound silly, but think about it.

## Proud Mama

Over the years, Pat and my mom have become pretty good friends. My mom could not deny the love that Pat had for me. She put her feelings to the side and joined in instead of being left out. I remember the look on my mom's face when Pat brought her to one of my performances. The smile on her face is something I'll never forget, and Pat never forgot it either. She said that my mom was glowing and that she couldn't wait to tell everyone that I was her son.

I can say that she never disowned me as her son, but when you're a kid, you sure can feel who the favorites are. I said to Pat, "You're kidding." She looked at me like, "Dude, why would I make that shit up?" Once I took it in, I did feel some of the healing from the anger that I held. Don't get me wrong, I loved my mom. I just didn't agree with the way that I was raised.

When I got a little older in my life, I realized after getting some information that our family had escaped from the Black Wall Street Massacre. She told me she was from Tulsa, Oklahoma. She never told me about Black Wall Street. From what I understand, the family had a little store. My mom always wanted me to be docile - "Don't make a scene. You don't know what could happen to a black person."

## Growing Up in Prejudice

I understand it now and remember that desegregation didn't happen until 1965, and I was born in 1953. My mother had witnessed black men being treated like dogs and hung from trees; she didn't want the same for me. I had a white stepfather. They had four kids together. She might have thought that my light-skinned brothers and sisters may have it easier in this world.

When I was a child, I could definitely feel the amount of fear that my grandmother and grandfather carried around with them because they were so in love. My grandfather made sure to let me know that the world wasn't right and that I wouldn't get the same respect as a white man no matter what I did. Though he had hope that one day it would change.

*Dwayne's Grandpa*

He always pointed out the fact that we were both standing right here and that we loved each other. This gave him hope. One of my aunts was also married to a white man, 'Uncle Chuck'. He was pretty cool, and his kids were my cousins. My cousins were mixed, you know, black people with light skin; they had that good straight hair, and I had *nappy* hair. I was like the black sheep, and I felt like that was the way I was treated sometimes. Talking about my grandfather reminded me of one of our adventures. He went to the desert to collect rocks that he would polish and make into jewelry, and along the way, he taught me survival techniques.

We're coming back from the desert on one of those long roads, and there's like a 'last chance' mom-and-pop store. We go in and get something to drink. We're sitting on a log when all of a sudden a fire truck goes by, and I say, "Pops, can I be a fireman?" He says to me, "You can be anything you want to be."

At the same time that he was saying that, a white man said to me, "Niggers can't be firemen," and before I knew it, my grandfather was punching this guy in the face! The cops were called, and they let them both go. I knew that when I was with him, I was safe.

## Baby Black Panther

A number of strong men had been assassinated in my young years: John F. Kennedy, Malcolm X, Martin Luther King, Bobby Kennedy, and various members of the Black Panthers. I had been a member of the Black Panther Youth Corps.

We would serve breakfast to the kids who were younger than me. At the height of the movement, there were some comments made that I couldn't agree with; they said, "Kill the white man!" To me, that meant killing my grandfather. Something in me shifted, and I never went back.

I knew that being a black man in this world was going to be tough,and I better learn everything I can to make it through life every single day. My grandfather told me that. "There was no bigger test for a man than to have a family that would test you. You can measure how well you did by the love you get back. That's all you can really expect in this world—the love you receive from the love you give."

When I was a kid, I used to dream about who I would be when I became a man. As early as six years old, I was listening to 'The Wolfman Jack Show' on my transistor radio. The Temptations were my favorite band. I wanted to be just like those guys so bad. Now my dream is right in front of me. We have created a band called Midas Touch, and here I stand, fearing the unknown.

## Learning the Business

I read everything I could about the music industry in those days and was sad to find out that the Temptations and other groups in those times didn't really make any money unless they were performing.

They didn't own any of the rights to their music. Performing was their only paycheck. I knew I didn't want to end up like them. Over the next few years, I hired a music attorney, Ned Hearns. One of the best in the business at that time in the San Francisco Bay Area.

He gave us a crash course on how to preserve the rights to our music. Look over the contracts and explain what they were talking about. Through Ned, I met a couple of popular artists at that time: Sylvester and Lydia Pence of Cold Blood, and they gave me advice about the business.

I'm doing my homework, and over the years, Pat and my mother have made a tradition of cooking for the band on Sundays. The Sunday before we leave is coming up, and we have a feast. All the guys really bonded and tried to shake the cobwebs off, realizing the task ahead of us. It's what we've all been waiting for. Going on the road. Another step up the ladder. We sounded good, we looked good, and it's time for us to go. The Soul Brothers MC were our audience for our last performance in East Palo Alto.

They threw a party and invited all their friends and family. When we got ready to go, they rode in front of us for a few miles and gave us a proper send-off. One of the first times I realized the saying, "You've got to see it right to get it right." The MC Club helped me grow by being the genuine people that they were. Yeah, they were a motorcycle gang and could mess you up, but most of the activities they did were charity work.

The many forms of Midas Touch did a lot of gigs to prepare for what we were getting ready to do. We played in Santa Cruz, Hayward, Belmont, Fremont, Redwood City, and in a couple 'Battles the Bands' competitions. We didn't win; we came in second, and the audience loved us. We did some radio contests to try to win a contract. It wasn't a recording contract; it was a performance contract. We were hoping a recording contract would be in our future.

We had gotten pretty hot in the Bay Area. We were 'in the mix' as they say. After all the work that we did to build an audience in the Bay Area, we had built up a great following no matter where we played we had a packed house.

It could all be lost because we were taking ourselves out of the scene after years of work. There was no social media. We put flyer's on cars, and we created a mailing list.

The guys were really feeling good—no more weddings, no more high school proms. We played a lot of things we didn't want to. Remember, we had a practice room that we had to pay for every month, so we went where the money was.

**Dwayne Hall , Larry Beck, James Lewis**
**George Glover, Ray Cordoba, Rasan Samson**

'77 BAY AREA '77
BATTLE OF THE BANDS
$3000 PRIZE MONEY
11 BANDS
1976 WINNERS!!!
ALL THESE PEOPLE
MAKING GUEST APPEARANCE SAN JOSE
MONGOOSE SALINAS
SELF EXPRESSION SAN FRANCISCO
STRIDE RIGHT HAYWARD
BRASS HORIZON SAN FRANCISCO
CLEAN SLATE WEST SAN JOSE
MIGHTY MIGHTY SAN JOSE
MIDAS TOUCH PALO ALTO
C.P. SALT SAN FRANCISCO
KICKING EAST SAN JOSE
IMAGE FRESNO
$3.50 ADV.
$5.00 DOOR
FUNKY SOUL NITE
SANTA·CLARA·COUNTY·FAIRGROUNDS·
SAT.
FEB. 5
5:00 P.M.
2 STAGES, 2 SOUND SYS.
OVER 100 MUSICIANS
#2 ROCK BATTLE FEB 12
#3 FINALS FEB. 26
TICKETS AT: ALL BASS OUTLETS, PACIFIC STEREO, TOP HAT
MUSIC STOP, (STORY & KING ROAD) FOR INFO.
DIAL T.E.L.E.T.I.X OR 295-6050 or 295-3060
PLEASE NO BOTTLES CANS OR ALCOHOL

## The Middle Man

This musician's life had its ups and downs; luckily, me and Pat had a side hustle. Selling weed has always bailed us out of a jam. The guys that I used to move pounds for moved to Oregon and started growing. In the hustle game, I was known as *the middleman*. I knew a lot of people, and I knew where to get anything you wanted. People were willing to pay for a connection.

It was less risky to get two connections together rather than driving around with a trunk full of weed. We just made introductions. Me and Pat did a lot of that to make ends meet while she was pregnant and the first year Laticia was born.

I knew all kinds of people. They would come into the club wanting to show off in front of me for some strange reason. I was the lead singer so they just wanted to brag about how cool their lives we're. Making *bank* and big deals. I took note of these connections. In the dealing business there's a whole lot of trust involved and for some reason I was able to get the trust of people. Me and Pat had found a 'sweet spot' where we weren't intimidating. You know black people can be intimidating.

We were just a loving couple and it earned us a lot of trust over the years. People told us about the energy they felt when we were together. They used to call us "The for real couple."

## Childhood Friend

Growing up as a teenager, I was kind of a loner, but I did have a few friends: Kirk, Howard, and Billy. Those friends would play different roles in my young years. Kirk was the kind of guy who, if you needed to *do some dirt* you went and got him. He was incarcerated from a young age, and our friendship would be broken up by his visits to *juvy*, the local jail, and then prison. His family was well known in East Palo Alto. The city was broken up into different parts. I lived in 'The Village' and Pat grew up in 'The Gardens.'

In my teens, there weren't a lot of gangs. Fighting was the measure of a man. Someone pulling out a gun was unheard of. It wasn't the honorable way and I could hold my own with them. I had a ghetto pass because nobody wanted to fight all those brothers and sisters in Kirk's family. If someone was older than me and had a beef with me, I would go to them. They said I was their cousin.

People knew not to mess with me. They knew not to mess with their family. I understood the culture because it was similar to San Francisco and my family. All the streetwise cousins I had If you mess with one, you've got to go through all of them. I fit right in. I understood the dynamics. I was the oldest in my family. I had been in plenty of fights protecting my brothers and my sister from being called all kinds of different names by our own people, black people. Calling them "Piss Color" or "Half and Half." They said our family was a bunch of "Oreo Cookies." Really hurtful shit for kids back then.

I got into a lot of fights and knew how to handle myself. I know it's going to sound cruel, but in the streets of San Francisco, The Pimps used to put on little kid fights. I was one of those kids, better known as, "The King of the Little Kids." The first title I was given said that I was proud of.

My whole family called me by my nickname, which was, "Pee Pee." Don't laugh! My grandfather gave me that nickname because he said that it looked like I was 'peeping' at him because my eyes are so tight. I don't know how many bloody noses or bruised faces I've had, but I've got money to buy myself something to eat and a lot of respect. The first time I ever heard applause for me was from pimps and ho's. It was addicting to see the smiles and cheers from people. I have to admit that getting applause from singing a song instead of fighting is the way to go.

Dwayne & Kirk

Pee Pee & Baby Bull

## Stole My Name

Let's get back to Kirk. He ended up going to prison and using my name throughout his whole prison sentence. He used my name because he knew I didn't have a criminal record. That meant that it looked like I had gone to prison. I lost a good job because of it.

In those first years, Pat and I both worked electronic jobs. Pat was a quality control expert, and I worked in the warehouse and became pretty good as a shipping clerk. Over the years, I became a warehouse coordinator.

I had just landed this bomb job. They gave me a beeper and gave me a car to drive, and three months into the job, they walked up and asked me for the keys and told me that I had lied to them. I asked them why, and they told me that I had a criminal record and would not give me any more information.

I had to research it, and that's how I found out that it was Kirk. I was even arrested and thrown in jail for three days because he had used my name. I don't know all the stuff that he did in his life, and they put me in the 'Red Zone' for high-risk inmates.

Violent? Inmate? I was neither one. I just sold a little weed. After three days of telling them that I wasn't who they thought I was, I finally convinced someone to go and look at a photo, and then I was released.

You have to remember that there weren't a lot of computers like there are now. Things took a little longer to, "See it right to get it right." I never got that job back, and Kurt and I were no longer friends. I guess he felt he could do that to me because of what had happened on the second day that I knew Pat.

He came by my house, and I was bragging as we do about this beautiful, fine-ass girl I had met the day before. Pat showed up, and he tried to *jump in my lane*. He tried to make his moves on her, and Pat made it very clear that she was only interested in me and that he had no chance. Our relationship soured after that. Me and Pat were boyfriend and girlfriend. After three weeks, I got the courage to ask her, "Would you go with me?." She said, "Yes." She didn't know she was saying 'yes' to fifty years.

## Brother From Another Mother

My friend Howard, who I've known for fifty-five years, we both had similar upbringings with headstrong mothers. We bonded over the stories of our domineering mothers. He was the one who encouraged me to make relationships in the white world. We did a lot of things that we would call 'white people things.' He moved to Monterey, but we always kept in touch.

Howard & Pat

Our first apartment was in Palo Alto, where Pat used to bring her little brother every week to go swimming. During those times, Howard and I did some deals to make a little money. Then he went on to be an executive in the electronics field. It had been a few years since I had seen him. Sometimes me and Pat would work through a temporary agency, and they would send us to the same job. We walk into the place, and guess who's sitting in the office: Howard. We worked for him for a couple months, and he was one of the people who encouraged me to get into the music business.

We had moved to Sunnyvale, and we lived around the corner from him. I would chill at his house and play all of his African percussion instruments that he had collected. It's where I gained my love for the congas, timbales, and other percussion. He was that guy that I could talk to about all of my insecurities. As we say, "Chop it up" without any judgment.

He later became a big executive at the Coca-Cola Company and parlayed that into his own restaurant in Oregon, along with many real estate investments. I still talk to him to this day. He's still giving me encouragement, and he has a great relationship with my kids. Pat called him her brother.

## Billy the Kid

Now, my friend Billy, I can't remember exactly where we met. I do remember we were always at the auto shop buying parts for our cars, and we started chopping it up and became good friends. He had the baddest Volkswagen in East Palo Alto—the first one I ever saw like that. I haven't seen one since.

It was off the showroom floor, fully stocked with every extra option that you could put on a Volkswagen. We loved each other's tailpipes. We would go down the road, making that awesome roar, and I had my pretty T-Bird. We both appreciated each other's hustle. We both had beautiful cars and had worked hard as kids to save money to get them. We hung out a lot at the park where I first started playing congas in a conga circle, which would take place on the weekends. He was the other half of my weed business before I met Pat. When I couldn't go to pick up the weed, he would go.

We never went together because that was the way to get stopped. Two black guys in a nice car. We had been stopped before together, and the first thing we were asked when we got stopped was, "Where did you guys get this car?"

I had East Palo Alto covered, and he had Menlo Park. We had it on lock. Looking back on it, I guess we were serving a wide community. Forty pounds of a variety of herbs come into town every two weeks. I don't remember all of the details, but we introduced him to Pat's sister, Tobina, and they fell in love. From friends to brother-in-laws. They were married, and he went to the military and gave me three amazing nephews that I have a relationship with to this day. Unfortunately, he left us all way too soon. It's beautiful for me to see that a relationship we created years ago still lives on in our kids because they are down for each other. Loving cousins. You would be proud of your boys, Billy! Rest in peace.

These people helped me grow into the man that I became. When we were youngsters, Billy, Howard, and I would always talk about what we wanted for our futures. We wanted to make a difference, and we knew we couldn't hustle forever; either jail or death was the outcome. That wasn't who we were. All that our peers talked about was the next score, and did we want part of it? They used to say, "You guys think you are too good to work with us?" They called us "Stuck up." We wanted no part of their image of success: chasing women, drinking, and hustling. We knew that they could get us into big trouble. Living that kind of lifestyle meant we weren't going to live very long. It was very dangerous. They both knew Kirk was in jail more than he was on the streets. We knew what he and his buddies were into, and we didn't want any part of that. Heroin is a man's game. Kirk had tried to get me to shoot up, but I refused. I'm so glad I have a fear of needles. I never went down that road. I watched him disintegrate into the young man that I had first met. He wasn't the same person, and I promised myself that I would never mess with that stuff, which I never did. I've never tried it.

I knew that Pat had gone through her own version of hard drugs with a person that she loved. If I ever did heroin, I think that would have made us break up.

## She Don't Play That

Pat did not tolerate heroin. One time we were having a party and someone *shot up* in our bathroom. She saw something that let her know someone had done that. Pat asked very politely, and no one would tell her the truth, like it was no big deal. She kicked everyone out of the house. She didn't tolerate that drug at all or being irritatingly drunk; she'd kick you out of the house for that too. We had seen a lot of people take heroin. It took our whole community down. It took all of the community leaders down who were trying to get improvements for East Palo Alto. There wasn't even a grocery store in East Palo Alto. There were only corner

Kevin, 'BJ' Billy Jr. Dwayne & 'Ant' Anthony

stores and liquor stores. If you wanted to get some meat, you went to the barbecue place. They were fighting to get a store, a small clinic, better educational opportunities, and to change the name to Nairobi, California, seeing that it was a black town. All of a sudden, heroin came on the scene, and money got stolen from all of the contributions to get things done. It was a mess. I don't know if it was all the Vietnam vets coming back with *habits* or the government. I will never know. History shows that kind of crap went on in different towns that were inhabited by black people.

## Should I Stay Or Should I Go?

Being in the band has made both of my dreams come true. I have a brand new baby girl, and here I am sitting in the car on my way to Oregon to play music for people. I'm realizing that the music business is going to bring separation from those I love. My life as a father had only just begun, and my mind was racing with all the thoughts of what I was going to miss out on. Pat and I had only spent a few weekends apart.

Of course, me and Pat have a weed deal brewing. Once we get to Oregon, the guy I'm introducing to my connection will be there. I will make an introduction. I'll make some money, and my family could be provided for. Pat would keep the weed business running while I was gone, *hooking up* the connections. We still had people bringing us our deliveries every month.

At this point in time, because the music was extremely demanding, Pat had become the face of our business. She made all the phone calls and promised to only work with the circle of people we had been working with all along. There are no new customers. We made rules early on. We would not sell to teenagers. You had to be grown up. We kept to that policy no matter how much pressure we were under. Pat would not give in on that.

I called Pat about every four hours when we stopped to rest. Remember, there were no cell phones? She's working the connection and giving me updates when I call, letting me know what I have to do.

At the same time, I'm not trying to let everybody know my business in the band. We made a couple stops, and I made a phone call. Now everyone decides that it is time to eat, and I have to call Pat. I wanted to go to someplace that I could call.

They were hungry. I had to do something. I needed to get this information from Pat at the exact time. I let them know that, "None of y'all got babies, so you don't know what I'm feeling!" They all agreed to go somewhere where I could get on the phone. I'm trying to get this deal together and check on my family at the same time.

## Sweet Potato Pie

We open the care package that my mom has sent us. Inside, there are five sweet

potato pies, three whole fried chickens, and a macaroni salad. Before my mom's, the white members of the band had never had sweet potato pie. It quickly became their favorite, and they became critics of anyone else's sweet potato pie. They would say, "It doesn't taste like mom's." My mom had arranged that when we got to Portland, which was going to be early in the morning, like 3:00 a.m., we would arrive at my cousin's house. She would let us crash there until the morning came.

This is a cousin that I didn't grow up with and probably had only seen once before in my life. She tried to be nice and make us a pot of spaghetti. I appreciated her hospitality and could make my mom happy by dropping in on her. The spaghetti made the whole band sick. The first night that we're away from home, we all get sick from food poisoning! We were all throwing up. It was the hottest, spiciest, and greasiest spaghetti meal ever to this day.

My call to Pat made a deal with the person in San Jose for our Oregon connection. I *scored* then met up with the band at the Holiday Inn to start our next adventure. We got set up in our rooms, and everybody slept until the next day. I also picked up a big bag of weed for the band—around a half pound. The next day comes. We all felt better and began our five-night-a-week journey in the nightclubs and hotels to follow.

## Can't Let It Go

Hustling has always been in my life. Looking back, I thought this hustling thing would get me into big trouble one day. I was always trying to put a deal together. I don't know how I had all the energy to hustle and be in the band.

I didn't want to hustle anymore. Pat and I had talked about quitting the business, but it was the only thing that seemed to bring in money. We worked hard together as a team, which kept us living that middle-class lifestyle. Now it was time to concentrate on the music. I was eager to see what not having that pressure to deal with would feel like. Just being a musician and a dad. Dealing always gave you a sense of paranoia. Giving up a connection was a big deal for me. I have been working with these people ever since I was 16.

They made enough money to move to Oregon and start a weed farm. To help set them up, I introduced them to some long-time business associates. Now they dealt directly without a middleman, they would be able to get a wholesale price. It cost him a nice *chunk of change* in order for me to hook him up with my associates. Pat would receive shipments once a month, and because we were friends and long-time partners, I was able to set a price for the customer, allowing us to get a *cut* and roll over the shipment all at once. When I got back,

I would still be able to pull him in as a customer. I hoped that everything would go smoothly. He makes some money, and they make some money because that's the name of the game. The price that he was paying me was market price, and the growers agreed not to tell him how much I was paying for it. Since I was paying below the market price, my customer didn't need to know how much I paid for the weed. If you lived in that world, a reliable connection was good business.

It took a lot of hustle to make these connections, and it took only one mistake to lose them. I had been pretty lucky, and people just loved my wife. Working with us kind of took some of the danger out of the whole process of *copping a bag*. The sweetest couple. We hadn't been busted, and nobody that we ever dealt with had been. And that was very important. I just appreciated that people trusted us. Now back to the band.

## Cali Boys

Our band, Midas Touch, played in Portland, Eugene, and Medford, Oregon. Things are going pretty well. Making money performing nightly for energetic, beautiful audiences. We were known as the 'California Boys'. "They're from California", the people would say. Some people thought that everybody who lived in California lived like they did in Hollywood!

Now we're on our way to Coeur d'Alene, Boise, and Nampa, Idaho. I think we've been on the road for about a month and a half now. It seemed like a lifetime to me. The phone calls weren't enough, and I missed the hell out of my family. I have worked just as hard for my family as I have for the band. I'm still torn, but I'm dealing with it.

I keep hearing Pat's words, "This was a thought a few years ago; you got to do it." I would have my moments. I would push on, concentrate on the business of the band, and keep moving us forward. It's difficult when you are carrying other people's dreams.

## Get to See My Baby

Pat and I couldn't take it anymore. We made plans for her to meet us somewhere along the way. We talked about it and decided for her to hop on a plane; a bus would be too difficult with the baby. I didn't want her traveling like that, but she insisted on coming as soon as possible.

Well my wife always had a flair for adventure. She told me she had her ticket, and I asked her what time I would have to pick her up at the airport. She tells me, "No, you have to pick me up at the marina. I'm coming on a boat; I'm taking a cruise."

Luckily the timing was perfect; she was arriving in Washington the day after the band got to Seattle. We're in Idaho and I'm counting down the days I'm going to get to see my baby and my wife, oh yeah!

## Can't Get Away From Prejudice

Throughout our tour, racial stuff hadn't been an issue. We've been in many towns and met a lot of beautiful, caring people. We were getting a little taste of what being a star was like because, when we were in these towns, we were a big deal. People were treating us like we were movie stars or something.

When we went to eat at restaurants, people knew we were part of the band and sometimes gave us meals on the house or things like that.

They were happy we were playing in their town. We're living the life, and then, you know, ugliness always rears its head. Now I have to say there was a twist to this prejudice.

They called the other members of the band, "Nigger Lovers" while I was standing right there. They didn't insult me personally but I was pissed off because they insulted my band members. I knew the nigger they were talking about was me. They threatened the white boys in the band, yet they already knew what to expect from having two black guys in the band.

Once we were stopped in Santa Cruz and made to 'pile out' of our vehicles. They put all the white people on one side, and they put all the black people on the other side. Well, it was very cold out there and we had our hands in our pockets. They made the two black people take their hands out of their pockets with the threat of pulling out their guns, and they made us sit on the ground.

The cop asked the white boys in the band if they were all right and if they were in any danger. That really *pissed them off.* After questioning them and us and getting patted down and searched, they let us go. That was the first time some of the members had to actually deal with the police and that type of prejudice.

They had attitudes and talked about them the whole way back home. They asked me, "This is what you deal with?" I told them, "My whole life so far." They witnessed the difference in how the police dealt with black people versus white people. It showed them how we lived in two different worlds and gave them a quick education. They got called that kind of name, which blew their minds. They had just had their outlook on the world changed in those moments.

## We Have A Stalker

Over the weeks, we noticed that a certain number of women were following us from town to town. Back then, we called them groupies; now they're known as stalkers. We had one crazy woman who had been put out of the club several times for saying that she was my wife.

When Pat came, there was a certain amount of tension. This crazy woman would sit on the stage and just stare at us. She took the horn player's horn one night. She always used to try to grab my attention until it got out of hand, and she was *86'd* from the club in the week that Pat and Laticia came to visit.

I am in heaven, as far as my family goes. Laticia called me Daddy for the first time, and she hadn't said Mommy to her mother yet. I was feeling really good, and Pat's feelings kind of got hurt. She loved that the baby had recognized me.

Pat wants to come to the performance because it's her last night, and I'm scared that this woman might attack her, so I didn't want her to come.

## Who Mistrusts?

I may not have handled it in the right way but something changed in our relationship that would take us to a place that we had never been before: mistrust. It created a couple of weeks of pure hell for me. Pat thought that I didn't want her to come to the performance because I had another woman coming, which was totally ridiculous. It was the first time she thought I was lying to her. I understand why she may have felt like that because when we were playing in town, she would have the ability to come see us play, go into the bathroom, and listen to what the women were saying about me. She would let them know that I was her man so they could quit thinking about getting with me.

Now she was thinking that I was cheating on her, that I was lying to her, and unfortunately, saying goodbye was like a knife in my heart. I could not convince her that I wasn't doing anything like that. What she didn't know until later was that the band had her back. They had gotten mad at me for just talking to a girl. They thought that I was betraying Pat, when the truth was that she was a photographer and I was setting us up to get live pictures taken.

After talking to this woman one night, the next morning I go to breakfast, and certain members of the band have an attitude toward me. I asked them what was wrong, and they told me about their seeing me talking with this other woman and that they didn't think it was right because Pat was such a lovely woman and that they had lost respect for me because of those actions. I explained to them what we were talking about and got back on track.

It taught me that the respect they had for me could be lost if I treated Pat with disrespect. She was not aware of that at the time, so her mind ran wild with what I could be doing. In reality, I wasn't interested in any other woman. I truly loved Pat and my daughter and wanted to have my family be as real as I could.

Another woman in my life would have made our relationship less meaningful than what I believed it to be. I hadn't prayed and wished for what I and Pat had for years to get out here on the road and fuck it up. That wasn't in my heart. I can't lie and say that I wasn't tempted, but I didn't want to have to carry that lie. I loved Pat truly, and I didn't want to mess it up.

## Prove My Love

When I was a kid, I was molested by an older girl over a couple years and then seduced by an older woman who happened to be a professor at college. My attitude toward women was a little different than that of my band members, who were going crazy with these women.

I didn't like aggressive women because of my past, so I never took the bait. I like chasing, and I didn't have to do that anymore. I found the one that I cherished.

Pat gets back home safely and she's got a whole different mindset about our marriage. Now we're on the phone, arguing all the time. She has no more trust in me, and I don't know what to do. I'm frustrated. She's frustrated. She makes up her mind that she needs to look and see if there's somebody better than me. She goes out with some dude a few times, and she says that she never had sex with him.

Well, I didn't believe that, and I acted like a fool for a little while. She told me that she realized that she really loved me and that everything would be all right, but my heart was broken; I was destroyed. I felt like she had lied to me, and even though I wanted to forgive her, I couldn't let myself believe her. I kept harping on the stupid little things that she did early in the marriage.

Like, whenever we went somewhere and I got up, another dude would come and sit down. And when I came back, she wouldn't tell them to get up or that I was her 'old man.' I ended up getting into a couple tussles with these dudes.

During these tough times in our relationship, like a kid, I would hold that over her head and try to get her to give me another answer about what she and this dude had done. I didn't want to hear that she may have slept with somebody else. Thinking about it would send me into a rage.

## It Changed Me

There was some kind of strange comfort in thinking that nobody cared about me; it was something I was familiar with, and that's how I grew up thinking. We had a lot of happiness in our marriage, even though we had the ups and downs of miscarriages. We had learned to love each other more in our marriage.

I had been on a 5-year high, and now it was gone, and I did not know what to do. She could have lied to me and said that she never went out with anyone, but that wasn't her way. She was honest, even though it hurt. Her honesty was one of the things that I eventually loved about her. You could believe what she said.

She told me years later that she wished that she would have lied about her going out with the other guy because she felt like it changed me. It changed us. She felt like I didn't trust her anymore, and she could feel it for years.

That incident caused me to regain all of my insecurities all over again. Jealousy has found a home in me once again, but this time on a different level. It's like the first time I've ever experienced jealousy to that degree. My 'daddy issues' came back, and playing music and being applauded became very important to me. Music has become my comfort. She had been my guiding light and my confidence. Now I felt like I had lost part of her and part of me. During this time, I wanted to go home and straighten out my marriage. The band was counting on me. The show must go on! We played in Seattle, Spokane, and Tacoma, Washington. Now we are on our way to cross the border into Canada.

## Smoke It or Lose It

We are worried about the laws in Canada because we have all this weed. The band has a meeting, and we decide that the best thing to do is to get rid of it because we don't want to be in jail in a different country. We all agreed to throw out whatever was left before we crossed the border. We started smoking joint after joint as fast as we could.

Then I had to throw the stash out the car window about a mile before the border. It was a sad day to see it go to waste.

I remember being so high while sitting in the waiting room as they thoroughly inspected our suit cases and car. Then they opened the back of the equipment truck, took a quick glance, and just shut it. I was paranoid, and it seemed like they took forever because they did such a good search. In my eyes, I was glad that we threw it away.

James remembers them not searching the equipment truck. It was about 5:30 AM, and the sun was just coming up, and they did not want to hassle with all that gear. James thought, "Fuck! I could've put it in my guitar case or inside one of Doc's congas, and they would have never known." We were confident we could get more. We thought.

Our first stop is Vancouver, Canada. We set up and got ready for the next night's gig, and we wanted to party a little bit. It's time to look for some weed. We could not find any. The people over there like to drink more than they smoke.

Unknown to us, we had one member of the band, saxophone player, 'Cool Breeze' Ray Cordoba, smuggle some tiny *pinners* in his sax case over the border. Ironically, he was the one making us even more paranoid about getting busted as we approached the checkpoint! So he rationed it out. We could only have a few puffs at a time in order to stretch out our small supply. And believe me, the band was mad as hell!

He put all of us in danger of being locked up, and we didn't take that lightly. Now he couldn't get away with not sharing it. Oh man, the arguments that we had because he wasn't ready to smoke. It was like high school shit; we were truly like a family now, arguing like siblings over the last cookie.

We just wanted to get high. We were hoping that the next town might have some.

## White Wonderland

We get to Canada during the winter of '78, and there is snow everywhere. I had never seen anything like it before in my life. I'm trying to drive, and I put the brakes on, and the truck just keeps going. I didn't know what to do. I didn't know that there was a technique to drive on the snow, but I found out soon. The next day, we had to take a crash course on how to drive on the snow.

If we thought we were going to drive across Canada, we needed that information, or we were never going to make it. People were already laughing at us when they asked where we were from. As always, we said, "California." They would laugh and then wish us luck. It was kind of eerie driving across Canada in the middle of winter. Oh man, the chuckles that we created. That little bit of fear started to creep in. We didn't know what was ahead of us; it would test us. The gig in Vancouver went on without a hitch. We moved on.

## Caution Brothers

We practiced how to drive in the snow while we were in Calgary, Canada. It  was a challenge, but it was something that we had to learn. The journey we were taking was long and dangerous. We had never been in this type of weather before. It was cold, way colder than Lake Tahoe. We're in a different country, trying to get used to the things that are very different. The food was different, and the language was different. Many people spoke French as well as a Canadian slang that they used. The people were great and friendly, and treated us with the highest regards. We couldn't wait to get on the road to our next city, Edmonton.

After that, Saskatoon, and then Regina. Our last stop on our journey will be Winnipeg. We take off, and I've been trying to shake the feeling that has come over me. Pat and I aren't seeing eye to eye, and the band knows something's wrong with me. We push on, and things are going well.

All of a sudden, we run into freezing rain that hits your window and makes a sheet of ice over your windshield. We would all share driving shifts. To the driver, the view would narrow, like a lens, until they could only see about a 4-inch circle. The defrosters on top were useless. Every 10 minutes, we were jumping out and scraping the ice off the windows so we could see safely. All we had were some flathead screwdrivers, and we tried not to scratch the glass. We battled those conditions for hours, and we were worn out. We thought that would be the worst of what we were going to see. Unfortunately, it wasn't.

Rason was starting to act a little strange. Different members of the band told me several stories that were disturbing, and he showed signs that he was losing a grip on reality. I was really concerned, and I started seeing it for myself and was concerned about what to do. I'm in Canada, miles away from home, and this guy is starting to lose it!

I told you earlier in the story that he Rason started slacking off from the duties that he had once done. The band was listening to me more than him, and he never could come to grips with him not being the leader of the band. I was, and he couldn't handle it. He came to me with the weirdest proposal in the middle of a road trip. He said, "Let's break up the band, fire the horn player and start rehearsing with these new girls." I told him, "You're out of your mind, we are not doing that."

I go to my room, and I'm confused. Pat and I are arguing every other phone call because I'm jealous now, and she has proven that she can get a man at the snap of her finger. The same way that I could get one of those girls that came to my shows. Why were we playing this emotional game? I don't know. We took shots at each other for the rest of the time that we were on the road. Being insecure makes you more controlling. We were trying to control each other from afar. Now I'm trying to figure out what my next move is, and I have to inform the other members of the band. I call a meeting. I lay out what Rason's plans are. I leave and let them talk amongst themselves.

Eventually, they came to my room one by one and expressed their feelings. To put it in a nutshell, they all told me that they were in this band because they believed in me and my voice. We all agreed that our plan was to move forward without him. I told them that I appreciated their trust in me. At that time, I let Rason know the band's decision. This was his last week, and he wouldn't get paid until the week's gig was done in order for us to complete our tour.

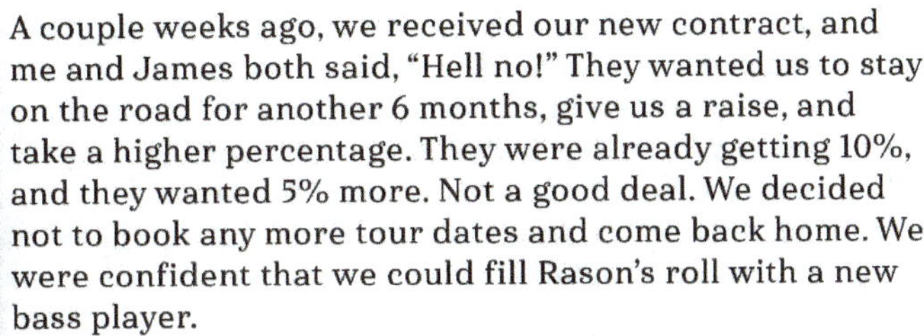

A couple weeks ago, we received our new contract, and me and James both said, "Hell no!" They wanted us to stay on the road for another 6 months, give us a raise, and take a higher percentage. They were already getting 10%, and they wanted 5% more. Not a good deal. We decided not to book any more tour dates and come back home. We were confident that we could fill Rason's roll with a new bass player.

The vehicles that we took on this road trip were as follows: a Chevy Step Van that was an old bread delivery truck with suspension not designed to handle the weight we were carrying. A green plywood trailer is attached to a tow bar behind it. We had a big Chevy Impala that band members would ride in. We all rotated the driving shifts.

In some cases, we drive around the clock to reach our next city. We're now headed to Edmonton, Canada. Traveling on a narrow, winding, icy road up a big ass mountain. We could even see over the edge of the cliff. Looking down, it seemed like it went on forever.

I'm driving the Impala, and James is in the passenger seat. All of a sudden, a big gust of wind hits our equipment van, and it begins to sway back and forth. We were shocked as our plywood trailer hit the railing and came flying apart in pieces as our equipment began to spill out onto the road. I see my congas rolling down the highway with some of our equipment. If they go through the railing, they're never coming back.

On the other side of the mountain, there is a small town. We had traffic all blocked up. We were still hours away from Edmonton, and to my surprise, people on the road from the town picked up different members of the band and some of our stuff and then took us to their homes.

The family's home that I went to had three boys and a little girl, and I got a chance to enjoy Canadian culture. I don't usually drink, but I felt it was right to accept. They gave me a shot of Canadian whiskey to warm me up and tried to feed me some moose meat. I passed and had a hamburger. It might have been moose meat, I don't know. It sure was good after being in the cold trying to retrieve our equipment.

The boys had a hockey rink in their backyard that they wanted to show me. They swore to me they were going to be the next great hockey players in Canada. I shook all the kids' hands, and the little girl looked at her hand and then rubbed my hand to see if my color would come off. She had never met a black person in person before. We spent most of the day with them, and the townspeople arranged for us all to meet back up and assisted us in fixing our trailer and getting us back on the road to Edmonton. Luckily, no one was hurt, and my congas had a small dent, but they were okay. We could continue on our way with an abundance of caution!

We finally made it; our last gig is in two more weeks, then I can go home.

The next town is Winnipeg. We have to get ready for this journey. The fears had settled a little bit, and everyone was feeling some kind of way. You could cut the tension with a knife, and I'm praying for just two more weeks until New Year's Eve, and that will be the end of the tour.

We were driving all night. Larry Beck, the drummer, was driving the equipment truck. James was in the passenger seat. I was driving the Impala behind them. It was a long, straight, flat stretch of road. Elevated about 6 feet above the flat land to allow snowplows to clear it when necessary.

We drove cautiously at about 35 miles an hour because we knew there was a thin layer of ice on the road. The sun was just beginning to rise. And through my eyes, I saw what made my brain say, "Oh no, not again!"

The truck began to slide off the road. It's almost as if in slow motion. It went off the road, down the embankment, rolling 360 degrees, and landing back on four wheels. The ice chest flew open, covering Larry and James with ice, milk, and pancake mix!

Eventually they jump out of the truck and get sucked up by the snow, and we can't see them at this point. The two members that were in the truck are trying to get to the car to warm up; luckily, it kept running. They make it to the car; everyone seems to be all right.

I immediately started shivering like I had never felt before. It was deathly cold. We couldn't even get to the other members that were in the truck. Our stuff from the now-destroyed trailer is scattered all over the road, and we're trying to see if our other members are hurt or not.

With all the fear and adrenaline running, I remember us all sitting and laughing

about them covered in pancake batter. This was very serious; the drummer was bruised really badly. There were no broken bones, we hope, but he needed medical attention. We had to figure out how to get our truck going again. Would it even run again? Would the drummer be able to play?

The first thing that came out of my mouth was, "Okay, we're going home now!" I wanted to get home and save my marriage, and distance was the problem. People came by who had CB radios. There were no cell phones back in those days. They radioed their emergency personnel and got us off the road. Now we have to find a doctor.

We found out from the locals that there is a phenomenon called 'black ice.'
When the sun comes up, a thin layer of water appears on top of the ice, making
travel treacherous. No wonder there was nobody else on the road. The truck
was totaled, and we rented another one.

I'm losing my mind. I'm split in two because we're in danger now. Our first
time out on the road caused the first real problems in my marriage. I'm thinking
we just survived; will we survive the rest of the trip?

Transferring the equipment between two trucks butt up against each other
left a channel of freezing cold air whistling through. It was a -40 degree wind
chill factor. Every inch of our exposed faces felt like pins and needles piercing
our skin. I remember James saying, "I will never be this cold again in my life!"

Everyone told us that there's more snow and bad weather ahead of us.
We were all being put to the test—was it all worth it? We were in a different
country and on a different terrain than we were used to.

It's December, and we've never been in this type of 'hellacious' weather
before. Remember, I told two of the members of the band's mothers that they
would be all right, and I didn't want to break my promise. I'm scared. We find
the doctor, and the drummer is okay. We get ready to keep going. I'm not having
it; I'm ready to go home. I need to go home. My wife and I are not doing well,
and I wanted to be home anyway! This was the excuse I needed. And looking
back, this is the first time I felt this kind of desperation about any relationship.
I was truly in love, and I was scared that our whole world would be gone.

I tried to use it. Seeing what we had been through with Rason, the band
was counting on me to see this through, and I was at the end of my rope. The
thought of losing Pat and us getting killed out here in the snow and never
seeing my daughter again had taken me over the edge.

The visit I had with my daughter showed me who I really was: a dad. I
finally broke down. They had never seen me like this before, so they were very
concerned. The whole band consulted me and brought me back down to earth.
As we put our hands together and said, "The show must go on!"

We were a little shaken, but not broken. We continued on to Winnipeg. We
try to pull ourselves together and have a pretty good show despite the drama
that we were getting from the bass player and the two girls he wanted to form
a new band with, who followed us from Saskatoon. When we saw that they had
come, we knew he was losing his mind. We thought that maybe he would come
around, but no! Here they were, and he felt like they were his future. It didn't
make sense in our minds. He had practiced for a year and helped me put this
whole thing together. And now he's willing to throw it away because a couple
girls couldn't make sense of it. I crossed my fingers and prayed that we could
get through this. One more town, and then I can go home.

We couldn't find any weed in the last couple towns. We were hoping our luck
would change.

THE
Paddock
NOW APPEARING
MIDAS TOUCH
DANCIN G9 TO 1.30
LICENSED DINING &
COCKTAIL ROOM

Midas Touch

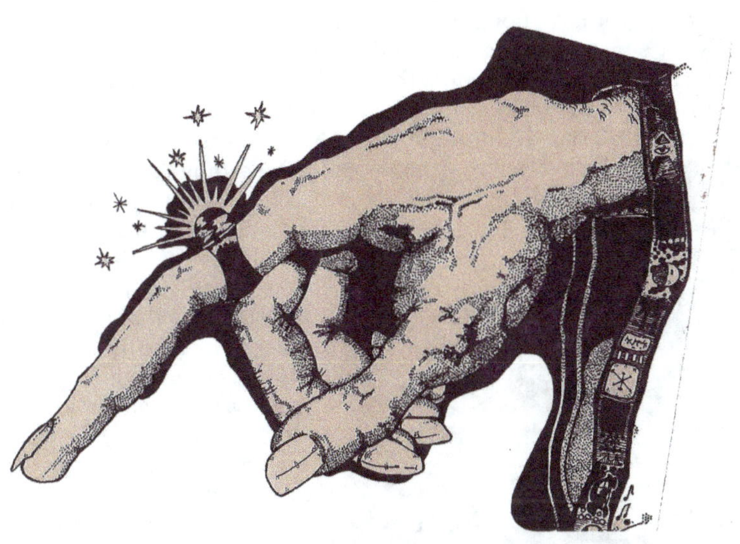

What we found was worse than dirt weed and expensive as hell, and we were desperate. We bought it and didn't complain too much. You can see it on everyone's faces. Get me back to California weed.

During this trip in Canada, the band started drinking a little bit more because we didn't have any weed, and it was taking a toll on everyone.

I remember one night at the club. The waitresses and bartenders wanted to

do something for us. They made us dinner, which was great and really made us feel like family. That night, at the beginning of our fourth set, they made us what they called "Zombies", and it made us turn into zombies. What it was made of was a little bit of everything behind the bar; with some juice on top. If I remember correctly, that was the last time I ever got drunk and wasn't trying to.

The zombies came in a big pitcher with straws, and they cheered us on until it was completely gone. "Drink! Drink!" The whole club was chanting. It's all I remember because I don't remember the rest of the night. All I know is that the whole band was drunk, and I believe I couldn't even sing anymore. They basically played instrumentals until our time was up.

The last time I got drunk was when I was 17, and my friend Billy had set me out in front of my house by the tree; so my mother would not know who I'd been with. I was so mad at him but he did get me home. Mom took the my car keys for that one. "Drinking isn't for you", Billy told me. I said and did all kinds of things that I didn't remember. I'm too much of a control freak to be like that often.

The things I do have good intentions; and when your drunk you don't have good intentions. I've never in the years that I the band, got 'shit-face' drunk like I did on that night. I don't like the person that people become when they drink too much. I couldn't have that going on with me. We had to deal with those types of people on a nightly basis. Great when they first came in, assholes by the time they left.

In my whole marriage of 50 years, I only saw my wife drunk once, and the same goes for her with me. Growing up, I watched my relatives drink themselves to death. They had all kinds of health problems behind their drinking. They could not stop, even to save their own lives. Smoking weed was our choice, and we used to joke that they could dissect our brains to get data on how it affects people who've been smoking weed their whole lives.

We had arguments. Trusting each other was the true test. We'd become a great team over the last 5 years, and now we were at odds with each other. When we planned this road trip, we didn't realize the amount of energy involved. And being a new mother would require a lot; she needed my help. She did not want to be a single mother. We as a team, had fought courageously to get to this point in our marriage. Our dreams came true; we had our baby, and now she's all by herself. I tried to understand her frustration. I really did.

I could not just hop on a plane to be there. I was realizing the vision that she had encouraged me to achieve. We had never dealt with separation this long, and it was taking a toll on both of us. We loved each other.

What we did not know was if we could get back to the trust that we once had. Only time will tell. I had to ask myself, "What was our definition of success?" I thought I had it in my hand. At this time, both of my worlds are crumbling through my fingers, and I am searching for answers. I'm only about 24 years old; I just celebrated that birthday on the road, and I'm dealing with a lot, as is Pat.

I would have to man up to get things right again. What would it take? With patience, understanding, and determination, I would have to see it right to get it right. I would have to figure out what my definition of success was.

## Out of His Mind

Over the months that we have been playing, the band has been purchasing a lot of new equipment. We had to figure out how we were going to settle things with Rason. At this point, he's out of the band. We took an estimate of the money we had spent on the equipment and gave him his share of the money, and the band took the equipment. He's still playing every night, but things will never be the same. His mental stability was fading from the realization that no one believed in his vision; it was eating him alive. He had those two girls, and that's what we would leave him with. In some ways,  I felt abandoned by him. He was the one who encouraged me to get the band in the first place, and now he was flipping the script on me, and I couldn't trust the things that were coming out of his mouth.

His mind was really going bad. He said some weird stuff to the band. I think the phrase was "The flies have eyes." On the last night, New Year's Eve, he pulls out a book of weird poetry and starts reading it to the crowd. We didn't know what was going on. The dancers on the floor just stood and stared. Larry kicked into a beat to quickly get him off that book and back into playing music. Back then, people weren't diagnosing themselves on Google. I believe, looking back on it, was he bi-polar?

New Year's Eve was our last night. We put on a damn good show! People loved us. I was ready to go home. I just have to get the band back home, and then I can concentrate on my marriage. After Canada, I didn't see Rason for about a year. When I did see him, he was now practicing some weird religious cult-type shit! Something about women being evil. That's the last thing he could say to me? My little baby girl is evil? I never contacted him after that. I wish him well.

## Going Home

Ready for another adventure? Not really! We had to figure out how we would  get back to California. Rason would drive his car, the Impala. The band bought an old Chevy Suburban, which James and Ray drove home. The rest of us would have to ride on the Greyhound bus.

James, the guitarist, and Ray, the horn player, were driving the truck back. I believe they told me that they stopped off in Denver for a couple days and had a jam session with some friends of Ray at a nightclub. The only thing I remember James saying was that Nebraska doesn't have many people; he kept waiting for a town to pop up over the next hill, but it never would. They made it back safely.

Now on the other hand, my trip was a bus ride from hell. If you were driving yourself, it would take you about 24 to 36 hours. On the bus, it took us like three or four days. It was funky and nasty, and my patience was running out. I couldn't wait to be in my own bed back home. I knew that me and Pat had a lot of things to work out, and I wasn't looking forward to it. Our relationship has been shaken to the core, and I prayed that we could get back on track.

When you break a woman's heart, it's like shattered glass. Can you put it back together? Can you hold it together? Did I have the strength to deal with the fragility of our relationship? Do I have the patience? I'm mentally beat up.

I am coming apart, and the uncomfortableness of the bus ride is only causing more stress. Three and a half days on the road and a number of bus stops later, we finally made it home.

## Shaky Love

All I'm thinking about are the missed phone calls. The unfinished conversations, the uneasy feeling that we were in a bad place, and how we will react when we see each other. When I step off the bus and my feet touch the ground, you know how in those movies you see people kissing the ground? I felt like that, and I looked up and saw her face through the window, and my heart thudded. My body is going through weirdness. I have a lot to unload from the bus.

We give each other a quick kiss and a hug, and I unload my stuff into the car. She wouldn't let me drive. That should have been my first clue that she was in a different mindset. I always drove; I see it now. I didn't see it then. We made an agreement on the ride home that we wouldn't talk about anything. She said, "We had a lot to discuss." We agreed to just be a family that night, and I would get to enjoy the company of my daughter, whom I hadn't seen in months. Three months is a long time.

Laticia had grown so much in that time. Running around talking. Tears fell down my cheeks because I felt the loss; not seeing her go through those moments had changed me forever. *Lil Ma* would always be mad at me when I first got back home from road trips. She would get all the stuff I bought her, but she wouldn't talk to me for a while. Until my presence would melt her heart, and then it was on. My baby girl and her daddy—this is what my heart has been craving—the love of my daughter.

I ate and played with my baby girl until she fell asleep, and then Pat and I enjoyed each other. It felt strange; it wasn't as deep as it had been before. Or was it now my mistrust that was starting to come to the surface? I know what she told me—that she did not sleep with anyone else—but my mind couldn't let it go. Had she been lying to me? It was like we were marking our territory (you-my man, you-my woman). It wasn't the loving way that we had developed over these seven years. It was just lust.

'I'm going to do it to you so good you don't want anybody else' was what was going through both of our minds. Insecurity runs through both of our veins. For the first time in our relationship we didn't know what each other was thinking.

I can only tell the story because we talked about it over the years and discussed what we were going through. Pat had grown in ways that I wasn't aware of. Me not being there, her with the new baby, and her running around taking care of *stuff* (our weed business). I had put all that on her. It became obvious that she had to change and become more of an independent woman.

She was living the life that she said she never wanted—to be a single mother. That was one of her red flags: "If you don't want to have a baby, don't have one with me because I need you to be a father." Her words from early on in our relationship. Which made me ask myself, "What happened?"

## You Are The Father

She knew how badly I wanted to be a father because it was so important to me not to be like my father. To experience someone loving me as much as I had loved him, and he was never even there. I could be there to watch them grow but that's just it: I had not been there. I had a lot to accomplish in a month.

**Willie Hall**
**Dwayne's Father**

**Ray, James, George, Larry, Dwayne, Chris**

We were booked in Arizona the following month. I had to find a bass player and get him ready to do the gigs. We found a player who had road experience just like us, Chris Chaney. He was an excellent bassist and had a van! Things went pretty smoothly. We all worked together with him to get the music *tight*.

I was able to spend a lot of time with my family before I hit the road again. About a week before I was going to leave, tensions started flaring. The pressure of me leaving again was showing the cracks in our relationship and that we hadn't come to any type of agreement. I think it was the first time that I realized that I wouldn't be able to do the music business.

## Either / Or

I wouldn't be able to be a musician on the road. What would I do after spending all this time making this happen? With her encouragement over the years and now we both could not handle the reality of what the job took. The separation was palpable.

My heart is split in half. I want to be a father and I also want to be a musician. Would I have to choose one or the other? It wasn't fair. The sayings of old people pop into my head: "Life isn't always fair. Now what are you going to do about it?" Everything we had dreamed about seemed to vanish, except our trust in each other's well-being. I'm going to be gone for a month and I don't have a clue what's going to happen. I have been burning the candle at both ends for a long time  and it was starting to take a toll on me physically and mentally. I was starting to get cysts growing along my fingers from playing the congas five nights a week and they would have to be operated on. The plans were to have it done in the next two months because we were booked closer to home. Fresno, Bakersfield, and Tulare, California.

Pat would be able to come and see me once we got back to California. I wouldn't be home, but at least she could occasionally come to our gigs. I'm hoping that will take some of the jealousy that she has away because she could be there. It's time for us to take off, and me and Pat are not doing well at all because she has to wait a month before she can see me. At this point, nothing I do is good enough. For the first time since I left, we were not talking!

## On the Road Again

We started off on the road to Arizona, and we used to call it the road trip from hell because when we started out about 200 miles away, we got a flat tire. Well, we have a spare; it's no problem. We put it on and go another couple hundred miles, and we get another flat in the middle of nowhere. Two flats on the same day, and I mean, we really were in the middle the desert. Finally, we got a ride to a truck stop. We are close to Arizona; it's over 100 degrees. They have another tire that would work. We have to spend way too much on it, and we make it to Arizona. We do a great job. The bass player, Chris Chaney, was a good fit, and they wanted to book us again. No way.

Not with the way that my marriage has been going. Did I accept it? No. It's the first time I turned down a booking that paid good money like that. Arizona was nice, though I had never been in 113° weather, and it was overwhelmingly hot. I only went sightseeing in the evening and purchased Pat some turquoise jewelry from the native people in Arizona. Turquoise was her favorite stone at that time, and even though we might have been *at odds* I still wanted to please her. We finish up in Arizona, and we're headed back to California after three stops there.

## Best Friends

What I do remember is that she came to see us in Fresno—her and my mom. Francine, my sister, took care of Laticia. They drove down and got lost for 2 hours, which had everybody tripping out. She didn't make it until the second set. You have to remember that there were no Google Maps or cell phones. You had to find a pay phone. They finally made it.

My mom was saying, "This is my girl." They became great friends. Laticia was the first granddaughter, and that alone created a great bond between them. My mom is who she turned to when I was on the road. Laticia loved her grandmother very much, and Pat always nurtured that relationship.

## Club Jealousy

We finish the set, and the night is over. Time to get my mom set up in her room. Me and Pat want to fall into each other's arms and make love. It's been five weeks since I've seen her. Unfortunately, in the middle of it, she said three little words to me: "You're the best," and I lost my mind.

George Glover, Chris Chaney, Dwayne Hall, Larry Beck, Ray Cordoba, James Lewis

# Midas Touch 1978

I got up immediately and said to her, "Why are you saying I'm the best if you haven't been with anybody else?" In five years, she had never said that. I felt like that was a clue that she was not telling me the truth. What I did was wrong because of what it did to her— not letting her come to the show. That wasn't my intention; my intention was to protect her. The way I felt was that she was doing this to get back at me. I really showed discipline out on the road. I never took it there.

She did not want to believe that because of the conversations that she had heard from different women over the years in the bathroom at the clubs I play at. Talking about what they would like to do to me. I felt like I was being punished because she didn't trust me anymore. I didn't feel like I gave her a reason not to trust me. I made a mistake. To bring somebody into our marriage, I couldn't deal with it. If she did that, the thought of it would send me into a rage.

The most beautiful thing about a relationship is that you give yourself to each other and create a loving thing instead of just a humping thing. How could she take that sacred thing and give herself to someone else? The images a jealous mind can make up are the stuff of nightmares. Now I was doing too much thinking and not enough listening.

## Hindsight 20/20

What she told me years later was that at that moment she had been thinking about how close she had gotten to sleeping with that dude. Her mode of operation before she was with me was, "You hurt me, and I hurt you back double." She knew if she did, it would destroy our marriage. She was convinced that I could get another woman at the snap of my finger and was so happy that I was still with her. That wasn't what came out of her mouth: "You're the best, and I don't want anybody else."

It took me a long time to let that go. I loved her so much that even if she had done that, I would probably still have been with her. I loved her that much, and I was hoping that she loved me that much.

I had never known a love so deep, to feel pain so deep, to be so confused, so heartbroken, so disillusioned, and I don't know which way to turn. The business of the music kept my mind occupied enough that I didn't go crazy. Slowly, the jealousy started eating me up inside because, in truth, she could get any man that she wanted. Laticia was our bond, and she was the thing that pulled us together—the thing that didn't let our jealous behaviors take over. Even though it was rocky, we were stubborn people, and we were going to make this family work one way or another.

I saw the way men looked at my wife, and her personality would just suck you in. I knew the value of what I had, and I wasn't going to let it go. I thought, "What are we doing, Lord? It's not supposed to be like this."

We finished up the tour and spent a couple months in the Bay Area doing nightclubs and hotel parties, New Year's frat parties, and a bunch of other stuff during those times. I felt disillusioned about our marriage. I believed in the family and the love that we once had and still have for each other to some degree. It was not like our first five years, and both of us knew it.

Pat had, over the past couple years, acquired some new friends that I didn't know too much about. They started going out a lot, which triggered my jealousy even more.

I could be playing a job, and on the same night, she would go somewhere else with these girls, and when she would show up with them, they would come in looking to beat somebody up. I didn't really like these girls. I knew they were telling her there's no way he's not messing around looking at those thirsty girls trying to holler at him and things like that to keep her on this jealous trip.

## The Player's Mind

My heart felt like it was broken, and my mind was fragile. I was looking for some type of relief. I started talking to girls just to pump up my ego. I never slept with any of them. I just enjoyed them gassing me up knowing that I was desired, and just knowing that somebody wanted you and you didn't want them is power. It got really boring, and it wasn't fixing the problem.

I started to feel bad that I was using these women because I knew they didn't have a chance to be with me. I didn't want to play with people's hearts because they create great wounds. My desire was to have Pat back the way that I had her six or so years ago. Or at least that's what I thought... What I had to get through my thick skull was that she wasn't the same person anymore, and I wasn't the same person anymore. Whatever was going to come out of this was going to be new. The girls that she was hanging with, her 'work buddies,' fell by the wayside after their enthusiasm about talking about me went a little too far. Pat didn't allow anybody to talk shit about me; if you knew her, you knew that. They didn't.

## Free Base Anyone?

She got one friend out of it, Debbie. They were friends for years. She was all right, but she was really sneaky. She had some stuff going on. Pat would come with different clothing items that were brand new with tags on them and stuff like that. Me and Pat started going to a lot of parties. Back in the day, we called them "Coka Cola Parties." Everybody brought a little bit, and you would snort all night.

That's when we were first introduced to what we called 'freebasing.' Back in the day, black people didn't know about freebasing at this time, at least not any that I knew. Freebasing is smoking cocaine.

I'm still curious to this day about what changed everything. Here's my theory: They called it freebasing when they discovered that you could smoke it. Well, some chemists got together and made it directly hit your pleasure and craving senses and override your impulse control along with all the other sensations that you get from snorting it, turning it into what we all know to be *crack*.

It was totally different high from freebasing because of the added elements that the scientists created. Going to these parties, of course, brought out the hustler in us. We knew where to get the cocaine cheaper, and we were both good at spotting opportunities. That's when I got introduced to the Mexican Mafia because my connection could not supply the amount that we were needing.

Now this girl, Debbie, has become pretty good friends with me too. She owned a limousine rental service; later on in life, I'd be able to use one of her limos to chauffeur Pat's brother out on graduation night. She had a Corvette that me and Pat would drive, and it was part of our cocaine business. We knew the connection to the Mexican Mafia, and because of that connection, Pat also learned how to make Mexican food from my connection's wife.

## Just Living Life

A lot is going on. Pat is working back in electronics and being a great mother. I'm getting to spend a lot of time with my daughter because I can work temporary jobs. We were trying to get the money anywhere we could at this particular time.

My friend, who owned a temporary agency, was the reason I could just get a job at the drop of a hat. He wanted to start investing in real estate. What me and Pat did was, after a house had been gone through and everything was fixed inside, have landscapers come and do the work.

Well, I became a landscaper in two years. Pat and I lived in four different houses. I would do the landscaping, and then he would sell them. We will move into the next place and then on to the next rent-free place. We were saving money and living in beautiful houses in white neighborhoods. Our relationship has gotten better because we were always busy trying to get stuff; we didn't have time to argue.

When Laticia started in school, she was the only black student in the class. We were trying to make sure that she had a better education then we did. We were able to get Laticia whatever she wanted.

We would throw theme parties, take her to Bullwinkle's, Great America, and the Santa Cruz Beach and Boardwalk. Laticia loves the ocean. I think because her mom spent a lot of time there when she was pregnant. I would take her to the beach because Pat had to be on bed rest. We gave Laticia anything that her heart desired.

We loved her, and we made sure we gave her plenty of our love. It was a happy time in our lives, though we still had jealousy issues. Me and Pat were growing into good parents— at least that's what we thought. We didn't get cocky with it; we were always conscious of the impressions that we made on our daughter. We had learned how to live in those two worlds: our businesses and our family's middle-class lifestyle. I knew that the music side of me wasn't going to work, and it saddened me daily.

The band is still playing a few nights a week. I'm working a temporary job sometimes, basically when I want to. In this period of time, you could quit a job in an hour and find a job in the next hour. Silicon Valley was booming. Pat stopped working. Yet she kept coming up with this money—a few hundred here, a few hundred there.

## A Little Bit of Forgery

One night I got home, and she had a couple thousand, and I asked her what was going on. She didn't tell me all the details. She told me some story about flipping clothes or something, so I believed her. Pat didn't lie, and then a couple weeks later I came home and she'd got like $5,000 on the bed, and she was so amped up because she said that she got away with it but almost got caught. My mind is saying, "What the fuck! What are you actually doing?" All I can tell you guys is that there was a little forgery going on, and I let her know the same thing that she told me.

"You have to stop because I'm not going to have you go to jail, even though the stuff we were doing every day would send us to jail!" Whatever she was doing scared the snot out of me. All my insecurities were on full display when I even thought that she could go to jail. Whatever she was doing was going to be federal time, and how would our family make it through that? I didn't want to find out.

She had accomplished by herself the biggest score that we've ever had. Looking back, hustling was really taking over our lives. We knew we were getting in way too deep. She stopped doing that forgery stuff, and we continued on with the rest of our businesses.

## Best Weed in Town

At this time, we're still selling weed from our connections in Portland, Oregon, and cocaine from our connections with the Mexican Mafia. Weekly deliveries from them and pounds of weed every 2 weeks. The weed that we sold came from Oregon.

It was a specialty item because most of the weed that you could get came from Mexico, full of seeds. Me and Pat had the sen-simian connection: no seeds, green weed, beautiful buds—that's why we stayed in business so long. I'm playing music and writing. We're doing well, and then I get the news.

## De Coming

Pat is pregnant. 'Whoa, stop the train!' Immediately, mentally, we get back to the team that we were with in the first five years. We have something to accomplish together. We gave Laticia the news, and she said to us, "I know that's my brother; he's coming." We didn't think anything about it until after he was born. How did she know it was a boy?

We knew that something greater than us had given her the heads-up. We had to get in touch with the doctor and inform him that we need to get the procedure done in the proper amount of time. It was important to have it done at the right time, so we set up an appointment. We also knew that she would have to be on bed rest for the next nine months, and things were getting ready to change. I had gotten the band to a point where it wasn't so demanding of me.

We only played a few times a week. Just enough to keep the band going, and interest shifted to becoming an original band. We only wanted to play our own music and make money that way.

## Biracial Blues

Remember, I was born in 1953. Segregation was still legal until I was 12, and the stench of racism was always present in our lives. My family was unique; there weren't a lot of families like mine. Our family back then looked like the family you would see now—a multi-racial family, and all of us came up with different problems because of it.



I remember being jealous that I wasn't biracial. I was just a little black kid; there were plenty of those in the world. Until I heard my brother and sister's side of life. My brother said to me that he didn't think it was fair that he would have to go through his whole life explaining who he was. He said people would always ask him, "What are you?" He really let that eat at him all his life. I don't know how many fights my sisters had because people would ask, "What are you?" When they would answer back, "Black," they would try to convince my sisters that they weren't black enough to be black. "What are you?"

After hearing that from them, I wasn't jealous anymore. I was like, "Cool, I'm the little black kid; you can look and see who I am." I didn't have to be bothered with those questions. It was asked a million times, "Is that your grandfather? Is that your stepfather?" Like it was something that was foreign, that was strange, that was weird; it was my family, my life, and the people that I loved.

## Mr. D'Lamont

A few months before we found out that Pat was pregnant with De, Pat had made a friend at one of her electronic jobs. She insisted on me meeting her new friend's boyfriend. I didn't have any time for that, then she talked me into it. I have practice going on, and I have to entertain someone that I don't know, Mr. D'Lamont.

The house we were living in was big enough, so I had the band practice there. We were introduced. I really did have to practice, so he sat down and listened. At that time, I didn't know what part he would play in the rest of my life.

All through practice, the one thing that I did notice was that Laticia acted like she had known him forever. Kids and dogs could always tell good people from bad people. Laticia just didn't go to anyone. Over the month, we became really good friends and had intense conversations about religion, the world, and how we felt about being black men in this world.

The amount of energy that we would create by just having conversations led us to write songs. He played the piano and the keyboards. At that time, I don't think he believed in himself enough to attempt to be in a band, even though he had skills. I have been doing this for a while, and I could see the raw talent.

**Dwayne, Larry, James, Ron, D'Lamont**

## Earful of music invades festival

Musical Director Manuel Romero of ASAP Staffing assembled 11 of the Bay Area's best groups to provide music for the Milpitas Corn Festival.

Manifest Destiny is a band that blends emotion with song and rhythm with rhyme. It is a locally developed act whose musical statement of truth and quality of relationship is delivered by strong male and female lead vocals.

By uniquely blending various musical styles, Manifest Destiny successfully creates beauty that has often been called "The

I saw in his eyes that this was a really big thing to consider. He had never considered playing with a band. He was a person who played the piano for his own satisfaction and didn't have dreams of playing with other people. I started breaking it down bit by bit. He had a lot to overcome. He was a real trooper and got down to business and became the keyboard player for what was now my new band, *Manifest Destiny*.

I believe D'Lamont's first show was in Milpitas, California at the Corn Festival. You could see the nervousness on his face. He had overcome a lot to get ready to play this live event. I can see the confidence though and the show went great.

After the show as we were packing up, you could see he had a little more bounce in his step and a big old smile on his face. He had done it, and I was proud of what he had accomplished. I was grateful he let me pull him into this crazy music life.

D'Lamont and James worked really hard to get him ready for performing shows; and before he knew it, he was in the band. I know he really enjoyed finding that part of himself and I was happy that I could help him discover that. He was brought up in the *black church*, which I didn't have a clue about. He educated me on how black churches were necessary pieces of our history and how they played an integral part of where we as black people are in the world today.

## Look to Your Dreams

Back when I was a kid, there weren't a lot of black people to look up to. We weren't on television that much. What I could see was that to be on TV you had to be good at sports, be an athlete, or an entertainer. I did not want to be a janitor or a garbage man so there was not a big list for me choose from. I wasn't good at sports, so I could take that one off the list.

In the years that I worked, I ended up being a garbage man and a janitor, and I hated both of those jobs. But I had to feed my kids and I was a man now. I don't ever remember being taught that college was even an option. I lived in Hunter's Point near the baseball stadium. After hanging out, trying to sneak into the ball bark, they offered me a job.

In the old days, stadiums had wooden seats and they would rent cushions for fans to sit on. I was a cushion boy at Candlestick Park. My job was to stay after the game and pick up those cushions off of the seat. I would be paid in hot dogs and tickets to the next game. Of course, I would sell the tickets sometimes. I was luckier than others because of the men in my life who gave me some nuggets of wisdom and encouragement.

Willie McCovey and Juan Marichal of the San Francisco Giants used to sit and talk with me, play catch, and give me guidance for the future. They were well aware of the racial challenges of the era we were living in. Willie Mays, told me, "You just have to get over this childhood thing and then you can plan your future."

Over the years, I have come to believe that everyone has a special talent. I started at a young age looking for mine and what I discovered was that I could sing. That was my superpower. Everyone can do something special.

Do you even look for it, or do you even take the time to look for it? Do you listen to the adults in your life because you think they know better? I'm so thankful that I found my superpower. It filled in a lot of gaps for me. When you find something that you're good at, it gives you a certain amount of confidence to walk through this cold world.

## Watch and Learn

One of the other jobs I had as a kid was working at the barbershop, sweeping up hair, and it was always interesting and educational. Because who came in could be a businessman, a pimp, or just a father bringing in his son. A variety of different people. I could see the different levels of respect for what they may have achieved and the disrespect for those who they felt did even try. I learned a lot from that experience. I started to understand what my grandfather had said to me, "There are so many different ways to be a black man in America," and I wasn't sure what kind of black man I wanted to be.

## I'm Black and Proud

Back then, black people were pressing their hair, making it straight, and wearing the hairstyles of white people. And then the late 1960s came. Black people had been assimilating into another culture, and we were finally getting our own. Now that we were starting to be people, the colors of Africa came into our lives. The beautiful afro hairstyles are *naturals—* no chemicals. The jewelry was from the home continent for the first time in my life. There was some pride in being a black person. When you walk down the street, people throw their fists in the air and say, "Black power to you, young brother." I remember how I felt the first time I heard James Brown's song, *Say It Loud, I'm Black, and I'm Proud.* It's hard to explain the way it made me feel to be one with something because, with my family as a kid, I always felt like the odd man out.

The pride I had now meant more than just the family; I was part of a tribe. We were trying to create a village. What I felt was fabulous. I took pride in being a black person, and I wanted to be a good representation of our people. I'm not an *Uncle Tom*, not a *Step and Fetch It*, and not just another nigger that ain't worth nothing.

Pat's sisters weren't having any kids at this point in our lives, so Laticia was attached to my nephew Nate. That was her big brother for those years. I spent a lot of uncle time with Nate, my sister Francine's son. I was figuring out the dynamics of a boy and a girl. I was getting ready for my son to come.

De is coming. My heart is in my throat. I'm scared Pat is in pain. I know that it's part of the process. Standing there helpless takes everything out of you. De arrives! Me and Pat are standing in the glory of having our own son. At this time, I could tell that we had gotten our love back when she found out he was a boy. His birth was similar to Laticia's. Her blood was 'pooling.' They got it under control quickly. She said, "I want my tubes tied, please." I agreed with her. We had a boy and a girl. She would never have to go through that type of suffering again.

## Rainbow Hawk

D'Lamont stayed the whole time at the hospital with me. No one else was there.

I remember standing at the window and giving him some *dab* (a handshake). He tells me, "Look up." We witness a hawk flying through a rainbow. At that moment, he gives Dwayne the 2nd, the nickname, "Rainbow Hawk." It seems that he was destined to become an uncle to my kids. We had become brothers. He would have kids in the years to come, and I would become 'Uncle D' too. My two beautiful nieces. One of the things that our friendship has created is a beautiful relationship between our kids. They call themselves cousins, and they're *down* for each other.

## Disbeliever

In one of our talks he told me that he wanted to be a teacher. I wondered how he was going to be a teacher if he didn't go to college. I asked him if he was going to go to college and he told me, "No." I didn't think that he would be able to make that dream come true because college was the way that you became a teacher. I didn't discourage him but I didn't encourage him either. I also didn't know how he was going to make that dream come true, over the years' after the band he studied and worked hard and became Head Chess Master D.

He was the head chess master for up to thirty schools, tutoring up and coming chess instructors. I nicknamed him in the band, 'The Professor' and now he really was. One day we were talking before he went to class, and he forgot to turn his phone off. I got to listen to him teach. What I did hear was enthusiasm and confidence, his tenderness, and the joy that it was bringing him. I could hear the kids responding with the same type of energy. I've seen his enthusiasm before on stage, but this was different. I knew he had found his superpower; he knew what he was supposed to be doing. He made his dream come true. There's more than one way to skin a cat!

He coined a phrase that I use to this day: "You've got to see it right to get it right." He also taught, "Be true to who you are." And, "Believe in yourself; anything is possible." I'm thankful for him letting me be that shoulder to cry on and encouraging me to write this book.

## Ticket Problems

Over the years, I've gotten a lot of tickets for driving without a license. I got a lot of 'Fix-It' tickets for driving with an outdated registration, and for some strange reason, I really didn't give a damn! They started catching up with me. Over the next couple years, I would go to jail for 1 to 3 days over the tickets. The system back then would allow you to take a certain amount of money off of your fine for every day that you spent in jail. I ended up getting into a program called *Work Release.*

If I went to work for the county, they would consider that I was in jail and deduct a certain amount of money from the fines. I referred to it as a modern-day chain gang. Over these couple years, I paid off all of my backdated fines, which were a couple thousand dollars. It felt great to get that *monkey off my back.*

We had slowed the business way down. We were only selling weed enough that we didn't have to pay for the weed that we were smoking. After all the years of being 'major players' in the business, it was really hard for me and Pat to just go by an ounce for ourselves. We knew how much it cost and sometimes couldn't even afford it.

## The Simple Things

I'm playing locally in the band. De is still a baby. I make up some rules for being a good father. Every weekend, I take Laticia somewhere. I give her true 'daddy time', because when I was a kid, that's what I was craving. Everything that we didn't have when we were kids, we tried to give to our kids, and love was the biggest priority.

I used to make them so mad at me because, ever since they were babies, I would say to them, "You know I love you, right?" They would answer in their sarcastic, sweet way, "Yeah, Dad, we know."

From day one I practiced taking those moments to say, "I love you!" Every day, even when I was mad at them, I would tell my kids. "I love you; I just don't like you much right now."

Pat and I sat and approved of all the rules that we were giving our kids. We gave them lots of room to grow, and they were allowed to question things. It wasn't mandatory to respect adults if the kids felt like they were being disrespected.

As parents, we did a lot of things differently. As the saying goes, "Kids are meant to be seen, not heard." We didn't believe in that because that's what was pounded into us all of our young lives. I did mess up on a few things.

My kids were able to tell me where we went wrong. We listened when they were kids and when they got older. We allowed them to express their feelings about their discipline or a decision that we had to make for them. I made mistakes, but those mistakes came from love. They were everything to us. It was very hard, but we managed to do it. Let them be kids and enjoy their lives in spite of the responsibilities that Pat and I grew up with. We didn't want anything like that. Laticia was never made to feel like she had to watch her brother or that he was her job. She was his big sister, so we did expect a certain amount of responsibility towards her little brother. We knew that it was our job. We were his parents, not hers.

## Stay At Home Dad

Both of our kids were very intelligent. Laticia was already spelling and reading at three and a half. De was intelligent, daring, and curious, which could be a bad combination. He was into everything. Just as adventurous as I was when I was a kid. I had my *mini-me*.

My son and I had a different relationship than what I had seen. We had formed a bond when I was a stay-at-home dad because he trusted me. I could take care of all his needs. He depended on me to do that, not his mother.

For a couple of years, he would come to Daddy to fix his 'boo-boo' until I went back to work and she became a stay-at-home mom. Don't get me wrong; no one comes before his mother; he was and is a mama's boy, and I wouldn't want it any other way.

Laticia is remarkably like her mother. Though she's a daddy's girl and a mama's girl, it's like she has half of each of us. Which makes up the unique character, which is Laticia. She will always be my baby girl. Because of our childhood experiences, we were very serious about our kids' education. I created different games before she even went to kindergarten. I found different colors of material and wrote the names of each of the color squares. I would lay them out on the floor and play it like a hopscotch game. You would have to identify the color and then spell it to move forward.

We taught them how to count with real money; it had greater importance to them than just counting. We always made special time for the kids. I would take Laticia; she would take De. Me and Laticia would go to petting zoos and things like that.

I would take him, and we would play video games at the 7-Eleven or the arcades before you could buy consoles to have in your house. We were always at the park in the summertime a couple times a week, where our kids would feed the ducks and learn how to ride bikes and skate. It was a wonderful time in our lives.

Then at night, we would talk about what we learned about our kids and adjust the way that we dealt with them based on the information that we had learned; during those special times.

The one thing that really haunted me and Pat was that we felt like our parents never knew who we really were. We were going to make sure we knew who our kids were. We weren't going to repeat the mistakes that we felt our parents made. We were going to treat our kids like people. Because of the rules that we gave the kids and their ability to communicate with us, lying was not permitted, and they knew that they would get double the punishment.

If the kids got in trouble and came and told us the truth and why they did it. If the reasoning was good enough the fact that they came and told us the truth was a plus. A lot of times, we understood and let it go. When we were kids and made a mistake we had to try to lie our way out of that ass-whipping; no matter the reason we did it.

If you lied to us you created a whole different thing. We developed our golden rule: Never Lie To Yourself. If we are one; then never lie in our home. As long as we're communicating with honesty we can't be broken by the outside world. The outside world is anybody except the four of us. We are the *Halls*, and that's the way we roll for each other.

The memory of us all hugging with our foreheads pressed together saying "We the Hall's and no one can come between us." We would then end with what we called the 'Hall Kiss.' Recalling those moments of loving energy still helps me through life even to this day.

We taught our kids that the whole world is a stage, and when you're in the world, you're an actor. People are always watching you and judging you, but when you're at home, you're free to be who you really are. I hoped that being comfortable at home with themselves would one day allow them to gain the self confidence to be the best version of who they really are in the real world.

Laticia had many questions when she was young about race because of the makeup of her family. She now had cousins who were mixed kids. From a young age we taught her that she was just as good as anyone else. No matter if her skin was light or dark, she was still a black woman. Her mother used to say she was her caramel-chocolate baby, the perfect blend of me and her.

## *Shirley Temple*

I thought it was very important to talk to my kids about race because, in my day, they did not. It took a long time to figure out how to move correctly in this world. I needed to make sure that my kids could see all the different angles.

And race is one of them. I had a lot of different activities that I did with my kids on a regular basis. One of those was watching Shirley Temple. One day we were watching it, and a scene in the movie showed the little black girls with 'Picin' Nanny Braids' in the backyard saying happy birthday to Shirley Temple. They couldn't go inside; they couldn't go to Shirley Temple's birthday, which was in the house.

There was a big, table with cupcakes and beautiful sterling silver candelabras, and sitting around the table were all the little white girls. She asked me, "How come the black girls couldn't come inside?" And "Why they couldn't go to the party?." I'm her daddy, and I kept it real and told her, "Because they're black." Laticia's face was saddened. She took it in and said, "No way, that's not right!"

We never watched Shirley Temple after that day, and I knew that she had suffered discrimination at a very young age. She understood it and adjusted her approach, knowing that there was prejudice in the world. Dealing with color barriers just like I had to.

She couldn't wrap her head around why people acted like that. All I could

do was tell her we don't act like that and ask her to pray for other people not to act like that. It was hard for me to explain to my little girl that certain people didn't like her because of her color.

How do you explain this to your kid when you're trying to make them confident in themselves while other people point out the color of your skin and hate you for it? It took a lot of conversations, and I explained to her that it was about who she was and not about her color.

We talked about my relationship with my grandfather. She had seen our relationship and knew how much I loved him. I told her what he had told me: "It's only about good and bad people, not a color, and love is all that matters."

Over the years, we taught her how to deal with people who hate and deal with prejudice, and considering who she is today, we did a pretty good job of that.

## *Good Lie, Bad Lie*

We talked to our kids about not lying. One day, Laticia came to me with a sad face. I asked her what was wrong, and she told me, "I lied."

I asked her what she was lying about, and she said that one of her friends showed her their new dress, and she was bragging about how pretty it was. She asked me if I liked it, and I told her, "Yeah, but Daddy, the dress was ugly!" I started laughing, and she stared at me as I was laughing and she told me, "It wasn't funny."

I asked her why she didn't tell the girl the truth. She said that she didn't want to hurt the girls feelings. I told her that when she got older, she would realize that there were good lies and bad lies, and that was a good lie, and it showed that she had a good heart. Sometimes the truth hurts, and you didn't want to hurt her. Just to explain something like that to my daughter or my son was everything to me. I knew this was why I was put here on Earth. I was erasing some of my childhood pain every time I did something like that with my kids. Because when I was younger, I just wanted to know why people were so cruel to each other. Our parents made everything seem like a secret, and older people would say, "You'll find out when you're older."

## Don't Use That Word

*Stupid* was a bad word in our house; they would get in just as much trouble for saying that word as they would for saying the word shit. They knew not to say that word around their mother because she would *pop them upside the head* so quickly. My kids probably don't even use that word to this day. Not being identified for your intelligence kind of meant that you were stupid in the world that we grew up in.

We just wanted a strong family, and we received a lot of *slack* from people about the way we were raising them. And we didn't care about what anybody said. We had an idea of what we wanted our family to look like, and we weren't going to let anyone mess that up. Pat and I had spent five years observing people raising their children and had a long list of things not to do.

## Bye Jealousy

I believe the early health issues that we had with De when he was a baby

brought us back to love. I have been working on my jealousy for a while. I remember one night Pat went out with her friends. I let my jealousy get the best of me. That little voice in my head was haunting me, telling me lies until I got to a point where there was nowhere else to go and no more made-up scenarios to work through. That is when I realized the truth, and the truth was that if Pat wanted to do something behind my back, she could do it, and there would be no way that I could stop her.

I knew who Pat was, and she had not done anything to me to have me think like that. When I realized that, a calm came over me. I had found the key to turning it off, and jealousy was never an issue for me again. The truth can be painful at times, but it can also be revealing as well as healing.

## Who Are You?

At this point in my life, the question looms over me daily. What was my definition of success in life? I didn't know. I knew that I was a good father and husband, and I knew that I was a good entertainer. I just didn't know how I was going to make the two work together. Success in the music industry meant separation from my family. I had a couple years left before I had to make a big decision.

Manifest Destiny had played a bunch of gigs and had gotten really good at writing original music, but it was just too hard to maintain the band and my family. Something had to change.

## Wrong Move

We had calmed things down on the hustling side; all we did now was sell a little weed to our customers that we had known for years. We didn't have time for all the socializing and partying with people like we did in the past.

We were serious about being parents, as we were about to make the biggest mistake of our lives when we started selling more cocaine. Over the years, the cocaine industry had grown by leaps and bounds—at least that's the way it appeared to us. There were opportunities to make money in that business, and my hustler side of me wouldn't let me ignore how much money I could make. Along with the industry's growth, the danger grew. It was dangerous now to be in this business; it was nothing like the weed business, and we learned that quickly.

There was a different motivation that people had smoking weed: it was good times; "Let's party a little bit." Now it's, "I have to have it no matter what I have to do to get it." What was unsettling was, even though the amount of money that we could make had my nose wide open in more ways than one. How far would I go to get ahead in a system that was built to hold me down? I had gotten caught up in bad decisions, those which I had experienced all the way up the ladder. Now I'm going to deal with it all the way down.

## Meet the Mafia

I have a friend who is now a real estate agent, and he tells me that if I can get $15,000, he could get me into a townhouse. We hadn't been thinking about it. Was this the next logical thing for us to do? We had our kids, and now you know we're trying to live that American Dream in order to get the $15,000.

Me and Pat put together a couple of big cocaine deals, at least for us. I hadn't

really purchased that much before. We were getting a lot, and the guy that I normally got it from didn't have enough of what I needed. He took me to his boss's house, and immediately I knew I was in way too deep. There were armed guards roaming in and around the house. Like in the movies, a sense of paranoia flows through the air. I look to my side when he opens the closet door, and I see pounds of cocaine stacked to the ceiling. My heart started beating fast, my hands were sweating, and I'm thinking that if the cops came in right now, I would never see my family again.

Was this all worth it? Oh my God, I prayed and prayed and prayed, "Please let me get home." We left the place, and I had never transported this much cocaine before. I had to get this money to buy our house. You know, that hustling thing. It's running through my blood, along with adrenaline and fear. I've got to make it home.

I make it home. We do the deals, and we start the process of getting the house. I find out that because I don't have any credit, my credit is bad, and I can't put the house in my name. I reach out to my cousin, who is a cop, and one of my friends, who has been an entrepreneur and has started a couple businesses. I persuade them to put the house in their names because they could both benefit from having the house in their names, and down the road, they would sign the house back over to me and Pat.

We all agree on the game plan. Soon, me, Pat, and the kids move into our new townhouse. I felt such a sense of accomplishment. I had finally gotten all of my tickets paid off, and I had spent about 15 days in jail. Like I said, for three or four days at a time.

This whole thing had plagued my life for the last couple years, yet I managed to keep the band and my family together even through all of this jail time. Jail had never been on my list of stuff to do; in fact, it was the thing I consciously tried not to do.

I have made it through, and I have promised myself I will never go back to jail. I had my license back, all my tickets are cleared up, and I'm thinking it's smooth sailing from now on. (That's what I get for thinking.) What is my definition of success? This question keeps coming up, and I don't have an answer for it.

D'Lamont, Larry Beck, James Lewis, Dwayne Hall, Ron Bistolfo

# Manifest Destiny

MANIFEST DESTINY

Represented By:
American Syndicated Artist Service
P.O. Box 501, Freedom, CA 95019
(408) 280-7625

**Larry, Ricky, Lisa, D'Lamont, Dwayne & James**

**D'Lamont, Felicia, Ken, Dwayne, Larry & Ron**

Manifest Destiny has been gigging locally for about three years. I needed to raise my kids, and I figured out that music, at least playing cover tunes in the Bay Area and on the road, wasn't the way to go. We needed to throw a *Hail Mary*. One more shot to make it big. We had played in the minor leagues for almost a decade and the time had come.

We took $3500 from the band account to record two original songs, *Sad Eyes* and *Knock Down the Walls* at Ayre Studios in San Jose. As the budget ran out, we we're not satisfied with the results. James thought, 'this is way to expensive, we can't afford it'. So he hung out at the studio as a *Go-for*. Getting food, alcohol, weed or whatever else the artists, engineers and producers needed. He watched, listened, and learned the art of audio engineering and music production. After a while he was doing sessions for a variety of artists and record labels. Eventually earning the rank of Chief Engineer/Studio Manager.

Now we could use the studio without paying the hourly fees during the grave yard shift and other hours when the studio was idle. This gave us the opportunity to write songs using all the pro equipment available to us.

At the time (1980's) synthesizers and drum machines were exploding onto the scene. Many of the manufacturers were in the Silicon Valley where we lived. We were like kids in a candy store with all these exciting new sounds to chose from. Creating inspired and imaginative music.

Meanwhile, I was working warehouse jobs, becoming pretty good at

that business, which led me to become what they called a 'warehouse specialist.' I would go to a new warehouse, read the blueprints, and set up how they would function efficiently. I was working four to five months on a job, and then I would move to another warehouse, and I did that for a couple years. It was okay money, and I'm still selling *coke* because I have a mortgage and I got to have those extra things that the kids wanted, and we made sure that we got them for them. The other important thing is that Pat, through her life, got to choose when she wanted to work, and that was something that she really appreciated. She lived with the fears that dealing brought.

## Cop Hustler

The kids knew nothing about our dealings, and none of our family knew. What was going on except for a couple people in the family who were in the business? My sister Francine, was dating this guy, and he wanted to sell some pounds of weed. I told her I would buy some. They were at a good price, and I could make a nice amount of profit off of them. She gives me the time and the address, and I show up. I'm talking to this guy. We make the deal. I'm drinking a beer. He tells me "I've got to get ready to go to work, but you can stay and talk to your sister." So I do. A little bit later he comes out of the room in a San Jose Police Department uniform. My heart stopped. They're laughing, and I don't think shit is funny because I think I'm getting ready to go to jail. Well, it happens to be that he was a hustler too, and a cop. I couldn't be mad at that, but it sure did blow my mind.

## Betrayal

We're doing pretty well in the townhouse. We've been there for a couple years; we've got a nice neighborhood; the kids know all the kids on the block and are doing really well in school. We get a letter from the mortgage company, and the letter states that we are in default; we are 10 months behind. Our world is rocked, and we don't know what could possibly be going on. 10 months behind? We paid the house note every month. That's right, we've been giving it to Tommy every month, and he hasn't been paying the house note.

Now I am furious, and all I want is blood. I'm pissed. I know it's got to be some kind of mistake. This guy's my friend; he wouldn't do that to me. He supposedly loved my family, and that's why he did it in the first place.

It's got to be a mistake. I contact him, go have a talk with him, and ask him what is going on. He convinced me that night that it had to be a mistake and that he would get things cleared up as soon as possible.

I cross my fingers, calm down, and wait for him to get back to me. Tommy was the boyfriend of Pat's cousin, and that's how I knew him. They were a couple and had *fallen out*, but he was still good friends with me and Pat. We trusted him. I trusted him with one of the biggest goals that I wanted to accomplish, and now my faith was disappearing, and my fear was that I had been hustled. A day goes by with no call. Three days go by, and he won't answer his phone at this point. I've been reaching out to the mortgage company, trying to get the full story. The house isn't in my name. They won't give me any information. I go to my cousin; he's the only one who can get the information. What we find out puts a knot in our stomachs about how the house note has not been paid. I have receipts now, so I got my gun and tried to track him down.

## Fool Me Once, Fool Me Twice

I'm out of my mind. Pat is worried; she's never seen me like this, and all I want is revenge. I feel like he spit on my family, and I wasn't going to let anybody do that. And this anger is being fueled by my cocaine abuse, so Pat starts digging and finds out that he's been having parties, spending money, and stuff like that.

And the papers that I was able to get from my cousin (the cop) showed that he paid for the first couple months, skipped the next couple months, and then caught up. He started off well and then just said, "Fuck me and my family" and never paid anything else.

Because of the way that we had set up the deal, me and Pat couldn't pay the back mortgage because the title would have still been in his name. We spent another $1,000 just to find out from an attorney.

I staked his house for a couple weeks, and he never showed up. One day I went over, and he had moved out completely. I had got 'played'. It was hard for me to swallow. We had an eviction notice, and I had to shift my energies to where we were going to live now. We moved in with my mom. She's going to be moving out of the place, so we managed to be able to take it over.

Every day, I'm looking for Tommy. Every time I see a white Porsche, I speed up to it and look inside. I'm disappointed that it wasn't him. If I had ever seen him, I don't know what I would have done—run his car off the road or something. I wanted revenge, and I hadn't felt this type of anger since I was a kid and didn't know how to deal with it. Anger, hate, and animosity burns the one who holds on to these negative emotions. We will meet again.

## Salary Job

Luckily for me, I got a great job offer at Hitachi. It was the first time I ever took a job like this, and I had to wear a tie every day. I was now an inventory control clerk, and my responsibilities included ordering all the parts needed to make the computers. Handle all of the outgoing shipping dates and deliveries, making sure all the parts are in stock.

It takes a lot of parts to make a computer, and I had to make sure all of them were in stock. And having to talk to Japan every day wasn't easy. You had meetings every day, and in those meetings, everyone would shift the blame on someone else, so you always had to watch your back.

It wasn't the world that I was used to; it was the first salary job I ever had. I used to work 8 hours a day; now I am working more like 10 or 11 hours and am taking reports home at night to complete for the next day. It is really cutting into my dad's time way too much; there was one silver lining for me. The hustling side came out, and before you knew it, we were supplying all the executives every Friday with their *Coke* for their weekend. Here we go again. My mother moves into her new home.

## Bad Idea

Me and Pat take the apartment. Things are going well for a while until we get more ideas in our heads about making money. We agreed to do some deals because neither one of us could deal with the loss of the townhouse, and we wanted to get another house. It was the only way we knew how to get that much money. Things are really getting bad in the cocaine industry. *Crack* is running wild, and we see how we could make more money. Now remember, we've been selling cocaine for the past couple years, not crack. We saw the profit margin, and with our connections, we could make tons of money. Hustling is addictive and it gives you a false sense of accomplishment. Because we did not know what we were getting ourselves into we called ourselves smart. We were getting ready to bring other people into our day-to-day business; now we had to use our trust again. During this time I've been working at Hitachi for about a year and a half. I'm really burned out on this job; all the paperwork was driving me crazy. I was trying to prove to myself that I could do this type of work without realizing that I saw no future in this career.

## This Is America

De had gotten sick; he had a cold that turned into pneumonia. Pat called me at work one day because she had taken him to the hospital. I left work immediately and went to the hospital. I asked for the next day off because he was still sick. Well, when I got back to work; I was told by one of my bosses that it was the woman's place to be at the hospital with my son, and it was my job to work and take care of them. That's the way it was in Japan and that's the way he was going to run his company here. Well, I held my tongue and didn't show him the anger that I had for him saying what he had said. In that moment I handed him my badge and told him, "I quit." Pat had been telling me to quit for months and was happy that I did. She didn't like how much time the job took from her and the kids.

## Double Duty

Now, I had to figure out how to keep my family going. Hustling is my crutch; so that's what I turned to. At the same time, *Life on Earth* is playing a couple gigs a month. We opened up for up-and-coming artists such as Kenny G and a number of other artists. We were trying to get to the level they were at. We were now functioning as a warm-up act for those types of artists. We had climbed up the ladder a little bit, but it was only for the exposure; it wasn't a money-making opportunity to play those types of gigs.

The recording sessions are going well and I am going to the studio most nights. From midnight until 6:00 or 7:00 in the morning and then I would go to work. I even played a couple instruments on the album including percussion and string lines on the keyboard.

I had never done that before, and my musical abilities are growing. We are producing an album, and I am full of joy inside. The recording process is exhausting and demands a great deal of attention to detail. We do our best to get every line right by repeating the same part over and over. Choosing instruments and adding tracks was a whole new world. I was in heaven with that part of me: which is the musician. We're thinking that if we can just get this album out, it may change the course of all our futures.

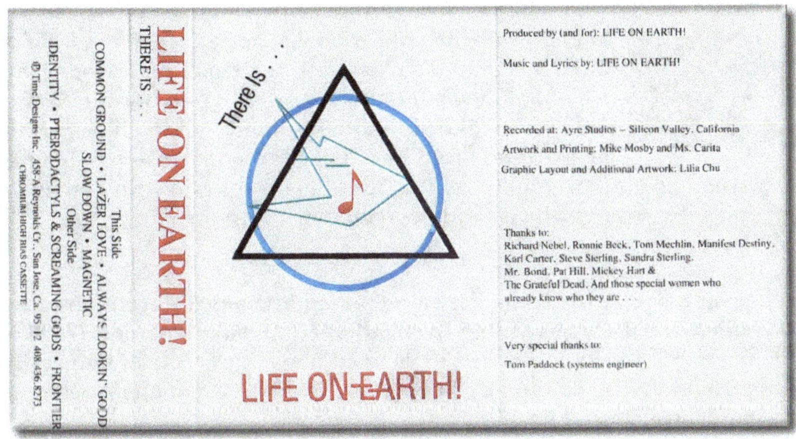


## We Did It!

The album is finally finished! To save some money, we decided to get hundreds of cassettes pressed instead of doing the album on wax. Times were changing, and this way was much cheaper and more in line with the times. We got all our cassettes together. We've done the artwork for the album cover, complete with lyrics on the inside. We're selling the tapes at shows to anyone who would buy them. We probably sold a few thousand of them. It's just not going how we expected it to go; we hadn't figured out how to get our stuff on the radio.

It was kind of shaky from there. Without signing to a record label, you can only go so far. So, here we are again! Now what do we have to do to get noticed? Neither one of us has the energy to reboot everything again. I have been doing this music thing for over 13 years. Do I start all over? Do I keep writing music and spending money to produce it? I didn't know what to do. I'm also scared that I may not have the courage to keep the promise that I made to myself and Pat about quitting by the time De was five.

### In The Grip

It's time for the listening party and that night I did a little bit too much coke. Me and Pat had always been very cautious about our use; I had just stepped over the edge. I was not only snorting it but I had started smoking it more than we had over the previous years. I could feel my decline into substance abuse. My connection in Oregon got out of the business of growing weed; they had made enough money to open up an antique shop. The years of growing weed had burned them out. Now all I had was the coke to make money off of and I did more and more of it. We were getting deeper and deeper into the use of it. Pat reminded me of what I told her the first time I had ever smoked it. I told her that, "I didn't like it." She asked me why and I told her, "I like it too much." Even during this time, we managed to be good parents. Our kids meant everything to us and I think that's the reason why we didn't go all the way to the curb.

### The Big Decision

A decision had to be made. I'm being pulled in many different directions; it's very challenging. De was turning five, and I had to make a choice. We made the decision to shut the band down. I have been playing the role of entertainer for most of my adult life. A vision had become a reality. I had made it real and now I'm walking away from one of my biggest dreams.

### Slipping Into Darkness

I have done the album. I thought I almost achieved success. I'm walking away. The sadness would creep in over the next couple months to such a degree that I couldn't recognize it back then. I didn't know anything about depression. In retrospect, I now know that's what I was going through. I was getting more and more depressed. Which had me doing more and more cocaine; which would open me up to making some bad decisions.

Me and Pat had only sold grams, eight balls, and ounces. With this new epidemic of crack it was more of a street thing. This business was getting more and more dangerous, and dealers were getting robbed all the time. We knew that if you sold on the street, you could make twice as much money.

I knew there was no way we could be out there on the street slinging crack. Our bright idea was to get somebody who could sell on the street for us. We hired a couple that was into that street life hard; we knew that they were strung out. We exploited them to hide our guilt, though we also tried to take care of them. We let them eat dinner with us, come in and take showers, and when they lost their apartment, we let them sleep in Pat's truck.

I bought Pat a little red Toyota truck with the camper shell on the back, and I put a great sound system in there for her. We could pile all of the kids into it and take them to the drive-in. During this time, my brother had a son, and my sister had some more kids. Laticia and De had plenty of cousins to play with. We paid the couple (our employees) well and they were able to get a place to live. They did all of our street sales. We were making double the money that we had made dealing grams, 8 balls, and ounces.

The kids knew them very well and had no idea what the four of us were up to. Me and Pat should have been actors because we sure did act our way through this part of our lives. People thought we were this *straight-edge* couple raising their kids. Little did they know what was really going on, and for years, no one knew. Those that we did business with were the only ones that knew.

## A Little Deeper

Through the couple, I met a guy who dealt in stereo systems stolen out of people's cars. And my dealer, the guy I got my coke from, a member of the Mexican Mafia, would take as many stereos as I could get. Now that my smart-ass is dealing with stolen property, he would bring them to me and I would have them out of my house within an hour. I'm depressed, I'm snorting too much coke, and I'm making bad decisions. I have the eerie feeling that I'm being watched.

Money is my motivation. And I'm getting those weird feelings suggesting that we get a safe. We put one in because now our dealings are generating a couple thousand dollars at a time. The safe was camouflaged, and it ended up saving me a lot of years of jail time. I had just gotten home from work. I have a deal set up to sell two '8 Balls' and I never did business in the house. I had the guy meet me in the apartment parking lot because I never brought anyone into my house—one of our first rules when we started in this business. It was very important to us that the kids know nothing!

## Close Call

He meets me at my car, and we're sitting there doing the deal. I look up, and the cops are pulling up. I tell him to get out of the car quickly, and I stick the two *8 Balls* into my gear shift rubber. I did have a stash box built into my bug. There was no time to put the stuff in there, so we got out of the car and locked it. By that time, the cop approaches us and asks us to empty our pockets. Well, the buyer had just given me hundreds of dollars, and I have it in my pocket. The cop does all the questioning and runs our names. Fortunately, I've gotten all the tickets cleared up, and he tells me to prove that this wasn't dope money just because it happened to be all $20 bills. Luckily, I had a check stub from my job. He let us go reluctantly. That was too close; I could have spent years in jail.

Nothing would stop me. Not even that close call, and I didn't tell Pat how close it was. At this time I'm going crazy. Putting all my energy into working every day and trying to fill the void that not having music in my life has left. Laticia is going to be 12 in a couple months, in August, and if I remember correctly, me and Pat are looking forward to our anniversary in July.

## Honest Truth

Now this *crack game* is intense, people are constantly begging you. They would sell their stuff out of their houses: TVs, kids Atari games, anything that they could sell quickly. People are starting to really go crazy. Me and Pat were shaken by the way people were acting behind this crack; but still it wasn't enough to make us stop selling it. Women were selling their bodies and giving blowjobs for a piece of crack. What would it take to make us stop? We felt like the world was going crazy, which me and Pat didn't want any part of.

We realized we were part of the problem. We couldn't watch people destroy their lives anymore. We set a date for when we would have enough money for our next house. We carried a certain amount of guilt about selling crack; we felt beneath ourselves. We were stuck in this cycle. We've got about $5,000 saved; we have $15,000 more to go. We are stuck. What would it take to get us out? We didn't have the weed connection anymore.

## I Didn't Ask To Join

The Mexican Mafia were happy with the amount of business me and Pat had brought them; they kind of trusted me; there weren't many black guys that they would even deal with.

On one hand, I'm lucky. I can't see the other hand yet. They felt like they had invested in us, and we were part of their *family* now. I never asked to join. I would have never joined the mafia! I knew what that meant and the danger that it would bring to my family because if you try to cheat them, they mess with your whole family. They felt like I was a member, even though I didn't fly their colors. I was in too deep.

I'm running on adrenaline, fear, cocaine, and depression—not a great combination. How I manage to still be an attentive father, I don't know, even though I'm doing this stuff. Being a father and a husband is still my priority. I would *get high*, mostly after they went to sleep.

Okay, it's two things: what I want and how the world is. If I can get both of those to line up, that would be happiness. That's what I'm searching for. Happiness is to feel as important as I did when I had all the band duties. Ever since I was a kid, I've always wanted to be appreciated. Now that I don't like myself anymore, I have fallen into this darkness that I did not understand.

# Missing Her

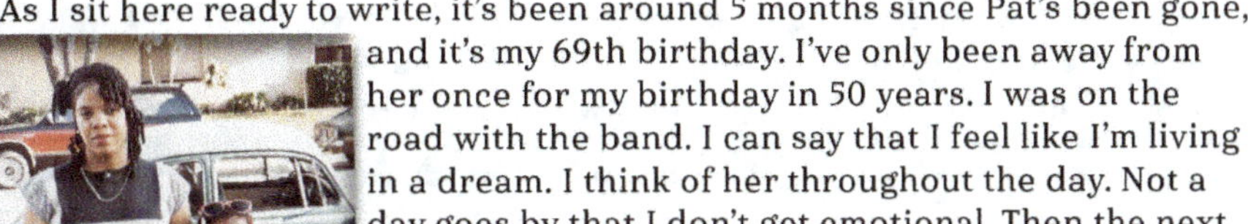

As I sit here ready to write, it's been around 5 months since Pat's been gone, and it's my 69th birthday. I've only been away from her once for my birthday in 50 years. I was on the road with the band. I can say that I feel like I'm living in a dream. I think of her throughout the day. Not a day goes by that I don't get emotional. Then the next day, I feel guilty because she wasn't on my mind every moment.

I hope all of this will pass, and there will be a room in my heart to keep her cherished memory and love. A calm place that allows me to remember, appreciate, and feel grateful for the relationship we shared for so many years. Pat gave me the experience of being loved, which is the thing that everyone is looking for—to be loved. Well, I have been loved. Will I love again? I'm not talking about the love for your kids or the love of your mom or auntie; I'm talking about the love of another person who chooses to be with you.

They love you so much that they wouldn't want to be anywhere else. Someone with whom you can build telepathy together. Who would finish your sentences? They knew that something was wrong with you before you could even express it. That's what we had. It's hard to think about the future moving forward. There are things that I'm going to have to continually work through.

Looking back, I see so many different ways that her love plays out in our romance. The encouragement, the support when things are going bad, and her constant belief that I could accomplish anything I set out to achieve.

When I struggled to make sense of it all, she saw the strength in me that I didn't see in myself. We didn't have to prove our worth to each other; we respected each other's point of view. Love is the greatest challenge for us humans. Hopefully, you take the commitments with your eyes open. If you take on vows, you're going to have to fight for them harder than you can imagine.

And since she's been gone, it's been kind of strange when it comes to people and family's or just acquaintances. It could be my grief. I noticed that people avoid me so that they don't have to talk about the awkwardness. Try to figure out the right thing to say to me. While they're avoiding me, they should realize that they're leaving me alone. And being alone is something I'm not trying to be or should be. I understand the human condition is full of sorrow, pain, and tragic events. My thought pattern is only from the point of view of that insecure kid who thought nobody loved him. There are not enough words to express what I've been going through. I had the security of my woman, and now the question is asked, "What is left for me to do?"

We had so many things left to do; there are things that are coming up that I never had to explore because of her companionship. Now I have to deal with the whole new world without my favorite partner. It's vital to love, and I don't want mine to dry up like a raisin. This life has been a constant search to find out who I am. With her, I always knew who I was; her husband.

## All About the Kids

At this time in our lives, the kids were starting to get older, and it was getting harder and harder to keep our dealings a secret. Laticia is 11 turning 12 in a month and a few weeks and De is going to be 6. Since the kids have been in school, Pat has volunteered for every baking event, field trip, and even was a teacher's assistant for a while in our daughter's class. We stress education constantly because of the guilt that we both carry for not being good students. Our kids were going to be different; they were going to have the confidence that an education can bring.

And we were feeling pretty good about the way we were raising them. They were both highly intelligent kids who advanced in most of their classes. De had played in the marching band on the xylophone, and Laticia was offered to go to a performing arts school. At that time, she had finally become comfortable in her school and really didn't want to switch to a new school.  So we allowed her to stay where she was.  We were looking at this as an opportunity for her future. In the end, her happiness was the most important consideration.

I couldn't stand the thought of Laticia doing all of that training, stepping out into the world, and receiving all of those *no*'s. Because you get way more no's than you do yes's in the entertainment business. I didn't want her to have to suffer through that. We decided to let her stay at the school that she was in. We figured she had time. If that's what she wanted to do with her life, we would fully support her when she was old enough to make a decision for herself. Now my son has got me a little wary because I came home from work one day

and there were a bunch of kids in front of our house. I was walking up, wondering what could be going on? I looked down, and my son was running a craps game, throwing dice and winning everybody's candy. I figured out that outside influences were going to always be there. I would have to teach good lessons so they knew how to make the right decision. I don't gamble. What do I tell my son? They were living in a different world than mine (a middle-class lifestyle.)  He's still seeing the things I saw on the streets of San Francisco and East Palo Alto when I was a kid. One of my friends was stabbed over 10 cents, so I never went down the gambling road. I told him the story, and we also talked about how black men were always *dogged* in America.

Pride is the most important thing, and the way black people treat each other is very strange. I don't know how many times in my life I've heard, "You tryin' to punk me?" Or, "Why you tryin' to make me look bad?" The insecurities we have among our own race are really crazy.

We should be united and not criticize each other or pull each other down. You've heard the saying, "Crabs in a barrel." I guess it's part of the growth of humanity. Our job is to raise adults. You don't want to wait for them to grow up. In our case; no one taught us how to be grown ups. We had to figure it out, and we were going to make sure our kids knew more than we did.

## The Fight

One day I get a call while I'm at work, and they tell me that Pat is fighting. I

know it's serious, and I leave work immediately and get home. When I get home, she's still all hyped up. I have seen her this mad a few times, and I had to pull her back and hold her from whooping somebody's ass earlier in our relationship. Though nothing like this since the kids have been born. My brother Tony was there. I asked him what was going on, and he began telling me the story. He said things had started earlier in the day; it wasn't one fight, it was two. He told me, "Your daughter was fighting too." This is how it happened.

Laticia went outside in the morning, and a girl, whom they called Munchie 'the bully of the neighborhood,' pushed her down. She skinned her elbow and ran into the house, crying for Pat. Her mother told her, "I don't care how big the girl is, I ain't raising no punks; we don't back down from a bully. Now you better go find a stick that you can hold, and the next time she comes outside, knock the shit out of her, or you're going to have a problem with me."

Laticia did as she was told and went and found a stick. Later that afternoon, Laticia was washing the dishes, and she could see Munchie leave her house, headed to the carports. Pat had just run to the store. Laticia wasn't about to let this opportunity slip by. As Laticia followed Munchie to the back, Pat pulled up, got out of the car, leaned on the side of it, and gave Laticia the nod. Munchie was leaning over a station wagon in the window, talking to the driver. Laticia hit her once in the back. Munchie stood up, looked at Laticia, and went back to talking. Laticia hit the girl again; this time Munchie turned around and snatched the stick. Munchie then hit Laticia once in the hand.

Pat yelled, "You better get it back!" Laticia got the stick back and *flipped out*, beating the girl under the car. Pat had to pull her off of her. At that point, Pat took Laticia into the house and then proceeded to change her top. Tony asked, "Why are you changing?" Pat told Laticia and Tony, "That bitch is coming over here," as she put Vaseline on her face. "If my daughter got her ass whipped like that, I'd be headed over here too."

And true to Pat's word, Faye walked her ass up the walkway, talking about how Pat and Tony had held Munchie while Laticia beat her up. Pat told her, "I didn't have to hold her; your daughter is a bully, and she ain't going to bully my daughter anymore. Munchie asked for that ass whooping by pushing Laticia earlier." Faye then tried to slap Pat. Pat blocked it and then proceeded to beat her down. So proud of myself to have taught her that blocking move. The talk in the neighborhood was that Pat had shown the whole neighborhood Faye's breast.

Faye didn't change her loose blouse before fighting, so Pat ripped it off. Faye's dude ran over while they were fighting, and Tony grabbed the stick that Laticia had earlier and told him that, "You better not touch my sister!"

Tony didn't have to use the stick, and the dude just pulled Faye from under Pat. They say he caught a couple of Pat's punches too. From what Laticia tells me, that fight gave her a reputation that didn't get tested again until high school. Her mother taught her that day, "Don't start the fight, but if somebody starts it, you better finish it."

## Little Bruce Lee

My son's first fight was a little different. I have been training him since he was 3 years old. In the first five years of our marriage, I had taken Taekwondo and almost got a black belt, but the music got in the way. I taught him everything that I knew, and by the time he was 6 years old, he was pretty good. I enrolled him in a Taekwondo course, and he excelled and moved through his first three belts very quickly. Talk about a proud dad to pass some knowledge on and see your child use it for their accomplishments. It was one of the greatest highs of being a parent and one of the happiest times of my life.

His first fight had me a little scared. One of the boys on the block had broken a bottle and started running towards him with the intent to cut him. He says he remembers being frozen for a second. His whole world kind of slowed down, and in that moment, he said that fear came over him. Then his training kicked in. I know it sounds like a movie, as he kicked the glass out of the boy's hand and delivered some blows. Yeah, I was a proud papa, a little shaken.
No matter what we did, our kids were vulnerable to our society.

## Give Them Everything

I knew when I got married that it was going to require me to be better than I was. And that's what I've always tried to do for my family: provide and be better than I was the day before. I came up short sometimes. Selling drugs wasn't something I dreamed about. I always felt bad about doing it.

I don't know what I would have done if the kids had ever found out. Like a race horse, cash has a way of putting blinders on you. All we wanted for our kids was to do better than we did. To go farther than we did. Selling dope gave us the ability to get the things our kids needed to expand their minds. We all know education costs money, and we made sure they had everything they needed to succeed by giving them three rules.

Rule 1: Do well in school. (No C's or D's.)

Rule 2: Listen to your parents.

Rule 3: Don't lie to us.

If you follow these rules, we promise to make sure you have as much fun as you can before you turn 18. Laticia had been to Disneyland twice before she was 11, and De had been there once.

Thanks to Pat's parents, I think they've been to Disneyland five or six times all together. Pat went most of the time. I was never able to go with them when they were younger. It killed me inside that I couldn't go. I was always working; it was all for them, not me. My satisfaction came from knowing that they were getting the opportunities I wasn't given as a youth.

## What You Do For Family

Me and Pat were tested. Pat's sister Margo had moved to New York to chase her opera career, and she hadn't seen Laticia in a long time. She begged us to let Laticia fly out. It was a hard decision, but eventually we let her go. She was very young. The airline pinned a note on her clothes, gave the kids an escort, and kept us informed along her journey. It was a lot safer this way; at least that's what we believed. It was a big step for us to overcome because we kept our kids close to us. It was one of the hardest decisions that we had to make. Pat felt it was important for Laticia to have that relationship with Margo because of how close those two were.

**Margo & Pat**

The stuff that they went through and the promises that they had made to each other as kids. When she first asked, I said, "No." It was really hard to keep that paranoia off our backs, and we were emotionally sick while she was gone.

We didn't want to smother her but it was very important not to lose the only daughter we will ever have. Or live in fear that God will take her from us. We did have that fear deep inside, and we constantly reminded Margo to take care of her and that God had given her to us. We prayed, and all went well. She got back home safely, and she had grown up a little bit more because of the experience.

## Boss Baby

There were a lot of themes for birthday parties, and De loved the Ninja Turtle cakes that we had specially ordered for him every birthday. I don't know how many years we went to Bullwinkle's Pizza; he loves pizza! He always wanted his birthday there.

Laticia was a lot fancier; she would always have a theme party as well. In Laticia style. From an early age, she always knew what she wanted for herself and knew how to organize it. It would always be a three or four-course party. First we're going to play games and have fun, then we're going to have a birthday cake, then we're going to bust the pinata, then I get my presents, and then everybody can go home! Pat and I used to laugh and say, "That's a kid that knows what she wants."

## Crack in the Family

Things were getting a little weird, even though the family was doing great. I was getting a little spooked out, and I had every reason to be at the time. I was collecting unemployment and working *under the table*.

Me and my youngest sister had gotten into several disagreements; money was stolen, and she was a prime suspect. Pat's wedding rings got stolen, and I found out my leather coat had been traded for crack. I loved my sister, but enough is enough. Her addiction was bad; she was really out there. She would abandon her kids, and I would have to break into her apartment and take her kids to my house. I took my duties as an uncle very seriously, so we were always butting heads. She always wanted the focus of attention on her, no matter how good or bad. She had to be the center of attention. Our arguments were heated.

## Truth Matters

I'm waiting in line at the unemployment office. Back then, you would have to go

to the unemployment office to get paid. Two guys walked up to me, put their hands on my shoulder, and asked me my name. Then they proceeded to put handcuffs on me and take me to a room in the back of the building to inform me that I was being charged with unemployment fraud. I was pretty lucky not to have to go to jail. Luckily, no charges were filed, and I didn't get a felony record. Instead, I got suspended from unemployment for 3 years. I could not file for it, but there was no jail time, thank God.

And it wouldn't affect my criminal record because I didn't have one at that time, so they gave me a break—at least that's what they said. They interrogated me for a while and I knew they had caught me. I told them the truth and admitted to it. Case closed. I found out later that it was my little sister who turned me in.

This *crack thing* was really bad; unfortunately, it had gotten its grips on our family members, and we wouldn't sell it to them. We created a lot of anger, to the point that my sister let the whole townhouse complex know me and Pat were selling, but people didn't believe it. We played our part as *straight lace*, which wasn't true. We were good at not letting people know about our business. All they could see was that we were good parents. 'We wouldn't do anything like that?' Little did they know, I wasn't a victim. I knew what I was doing, and I was sure that I could be more than the worst version of myself.

## Warning Before Destruction

One of the street guys gave me a kind of encrypted message, "Keep your head to the sky." I didn't know what that meant at the time. I felt like I was being watched. Something weird happened with the couple that was selling for us; they went missing for two days, and when they showed up, they told us that something had happened in their family. We believed what they told us. Suckers! They weren't there to party with us. They turned my ass in!

The next day was our 15th anniversary, and we were going to do one of Pat's favorite things. Go to a fancy hotel and sit in the jacuzzi, take bubble baths, get high, watch HBO, and just be with each other. We had always used these special times to unwind and reconnect. We could recharge ourselves and get ready for the next battle ahead.

This day felt really strange to both of us, and we talked about it. We tried to push the feeling aside and continue on with the rest of our day. The kids were scheduled to go over to my mother's house to spend the weekend while we celebrated our anniversary together. Pat's Uncle Shorty was over at the house playing with his favorite nephew, De. Laticia had gone to the fair that day and was over at a friend's house.

## Busted

Pat tells me to get the *party favors* so that we can go; she's ready. I get the stuff and close the safe, and at that moment we hear a knock on the door. We were in a townhouse on the second floor. We look out the window; it is the police. I hand Pat the stuff and tell her to hide it because I don't have time to open up the safe again. I go downstairs and answer the door. As soon as I open the door, they rushed me and said, "We have suspicion of child abuse," because they could smell marijuana. Which wasn't true. We hadn't been smoking. That was their way of getting in.

They pushed me up against the wall and handcuffed me while the other officer ran upstairs and brought Pat, De and Shorty down to the living room, where they had me handcuffed. Now they're asking me, "Where is it?" I keep saying, "What are you looking for? I don't know what you're talking about." One of the officers says, "Oh, he's a smart ass; we're going to have to find it for ourselves."

They began to search the closet closest to the front door and started pulling everything out and asking me, "Where is it?" In my arrogant way, I kept saying, "I don't know what the fuck you're talking about." I kept asking them why they were here. They asked me, "Where are the stereos? We know you've got them. We sent two in here today. Where are they?"

In that moment, I knew that someone had set me up. I was caught up in the moment, along with the cops. They were trying to get me, and I didn't want them in my house. I wasn't shocked that I was handcuffed and that they were going through my stuff. I was shocked when I saw my wife and my little boy's face and the fear that they had come upon them. That's when I knew I had really messed up. I knew a little bit about my rights. I informed them as they were searching that it was required that I be there and present for their search. I got really mad and started to swear at the officer. They had to shove me back into my seat. As they tore up my kitchen, they went into the freezer, the oven, and the refrigerator. They poured all the cereal out into the sink.

They picked me up and marched me up to the bedroom because I insisted that I be in every place that they searched. Now remember that I had given Pat the party favors—an *8 Ball* of cocaine—before I answered the door.

I had no clue where she had put it. I'm sweating bullets and getting more scared with everything that they search for. They searched the closet underneath the mattress, and they kept walking by the safe and never even saw it. I'm sweating it every time they walk past it. We have a half-kilo in there with some cash and our gun. The combination of those crimes would give me a lot of jail time, and then it happened. They opened up one of the dresser drawers, and I heard infamous words, "We got them."

Now I don't know if the cop stuck it in the drawer or if the couple that we were working with put it in there. Cause Pat and I were unaware that it was there. Me and Pat had one spot where we were obsessed with making sure our kids never saw any of that stuff. We know we did not put it in that drawer, and the piece of crack that they found was in a plastic bag that we didn't even use.

We didn't use that type of plastic bag; we used Saran Wrap because we never sold $20 pieces; the couple we had working for us did use that packaging method. We knew that bag wasn't ours, but the cops wanted to pin it on us. The piece that they found was about as big as a diamond earring. Now I'm listening to everything that they're saying, and I'm wondering why there aren't more cops at this "crime" scene.

If this were a real raid, there would have been 20 cops there by this point. I knew these two were *going rogue* and trying to get some *brownie points* to move up in their careers. They let me know that they'd been watching me for a while, and they kept asking me, "Where are those car stereos?" They were really

**Uncle Shorty**

agitated because they couldn't find them. What they didn't know is that I got rid of them earlier in the day so that I could have money to go on my anniversary. The officers questioned Pat's Uncle Shorty briefly, and searched him down. I insisted that he had nothing to do with anything because he was De's uncle and he was over where playing with him, so please don't mess up his career. He had been working at Lockheed Aerospace for, like, 20 years. I didn't want to mess that up for him. They didn't arrest him, though me and Pat were aware that we were about to go to jail. I am running through a million different angles to try to get out of this. They finally got me. They took me back downstairs and sat me down in the living room along with Pat, Shorty and De.        I can see the fear on Pat's face, and that makes me angry all over again. All I could do is pray, 'Please don't go back upstairs and find that safe.' I'm running all of the scenarios in my head. I was caught by the one thing that I had feared all of these years. I will not shut up. I keep pondering, "That little, tiny piece of crack you snitches planted in my dresser drawer, messed up my whole house, scared my family and destroyed our lives. The cops keep pushing me back down in the chair because I'm irate.

Their response to me was, "You did it to yourself," and all I could do was bow my head and admit under my breath that I knew they were right. As I sat there in handcuffs during the time that they were in our home, Laticia was across the courtyard, looking out of our neighbor's window at the whole scene, crying and scared.

In those moments, her childhood, I believe was taken away. We had made arrangements that if anything ever happened like this, the neighbors were to call Pat's mom or my mom. They called Pat's mom, and she was on her way because we didn't want the kids to end up in child protective custody.

The cops were fed up with me and my attitude; they told me, "Shut up!" Their attitude towards me was like I was an abusive husband. Luckily, they had some empathy for my wife. With our ability to read the situation, Pat got them to agree to let her mother take the kids. Though they arrested us they could also have taken our kids, just to be assholes. Me and Pat are still afraid that they might discover the 8-ball that she had hidden. I didn't know where she put it. By this time, they'd been there for around an hour and a half, hovering like vultures. They get some other officers to come transport us to the jail. What I didn't know then was that this would mark the beginning of a 5-year nightmare that would intrude on my life and my family's life for a long time.

Pat got the two officers to agree to lock our house up. Now it was time for the *Walk of Shame*. Pat's mother is there, trying to get information on what

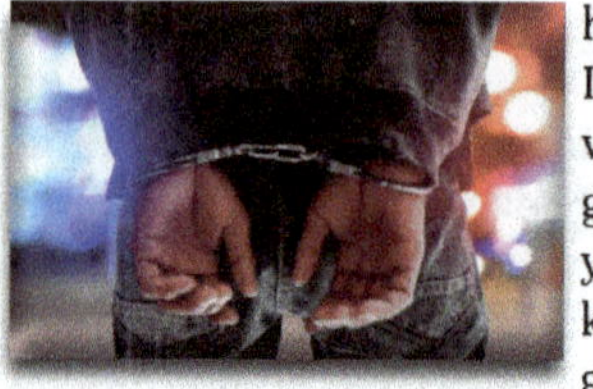

happened as they walked us out of our townhouse. I look up and see Laticia crying in the neighbor's window. My whole world shifted when I saw my baby girl's fear on her face, and then she asked, "What are you doing with my parents?" It broke my heart, and I knew it was all my fault. I told Pat, "I am sorry" that I got her into this before they put her in the squad car. Then they put me in another police car. This wasn't our life; this was the first time I was actually arrested for something that could get me some jail time. I have been busted for fix-it tickets, and you just pay them off and spend a couple days in jail. That was nothing; this was different. My whole body knew this was devastating; this was a felony.

## Broken Promises

I have broken my promise to my mother. I have broken the promise to myself and my family. I fucked it up. That's how I felt all through that car ride to jail, in disbelief and not knowing what to expect in the future. We get to the jail, and we see each other briefly. I'm dealing with so much guilt that I can barely look at her. They take her to the woman's side and me to the male side to start the paperwork for our incarceration. There is no respect from many of the officers; "You're a piece of shit dope dealer now."

## Little Snitches

Which gave me another clue that I have been set up because they couldn't find enough dope to call me a dope dealer unless they knew more than what they told me they knew. The cops come that night, just because I had given our dealer couple their supply to sell that day. They knew I had *scored* that day. Don't get me wrong; I knew that dealing crack was wrong. But there's nothing right about setting someone up. Catch me if you can; the cops shouldn't lie about not having an informant. If they had been smart, they would have waited for us to leave the house and catch us with the weed that was in the car and the coke that I was preparing to take with us. They would have caught me with a lot more, but that's not what happened.

## Humiliation

They're doing all the paperwork to put me in jail, and I gather that Pat was going through a similar process. After the paperwork, what comes next is standing in the room with about 15 other men, and they command us to get naked, spread your cheeks, open your mouth, and do all of that degrading ass shit that they do. Next comes the interrogation; they admit to me that they have been watching me for over a month.

They have been on the roof with binoculars and swear that they have seen my activity. They told me these different things because they wanted me to believe that they had me *dead to rights*.

The thing that they wanted to know was, "Where did I get my dope?" I told them some bogus stuff; if I remember correctly, I told the cop that, "I didn't know." All I had was a phone number that was written in the phone booth. I would call, and someone would drop it off.

They weren't buying my bullshit. I wouldn't give him the info they wanted, so they went down the road of telling me that my wife said, "He's a junkie. I'm living a life of shame, and I'm happy that it's over." Hearing that made me pause in my tracks, and I had to tell myself that they were lying. 'Don't believe their fuckin' lies.' Through the whole three and a half hours, they were really trying to put this rap sheet on me.

They were using how much I love my family to *guilt-trip* me. I didn't break. I was really worried about my wife because she had never been arrested before. I *did time* for those tickets, so this part of this journey was familiar to me.

I knew my kids were in good hands. I was very concerned about them. I didn't know how she was going to react to my incarceration. I just prayed for the best and waited for 3 days until they transported us to the courthouse and we saw the judge.

## She Didn't Do That

We see each other there. They brought us together for a short time because we were arrested together and we were supposed to talk to our attorneys together. Little did I know Pat's mother had gotten Pat an attorney only to represent Pat. I had a public defender at that time. I told Pat that I was pleading guilty, and she blew her top. "No, you're not." I remember her telling me as I whispered in her ear, "I need you to be able to take care of our kids; that dope that they found is mine. We'll talk about it later. I have to do it. I am the man of this family, and it is my responsibility to take care of you and my babies."

She wasn't trying to hear that. She wanted to share the responsibility. I told her, "No." I got advice from my public defender that this was the way to protect my kids, and that's what I was going to do. If she had committed a felony, then Pat's mother could take our children. We weren't going to let happen! Dorothy had already threatened to take our kids in a random argument she and Pat had once before. She didn't agree with our marijuana-smoking lifestyle and felt like we were unfit parents. She finally calmed down and agreed with me.

## First Impressions

Now it's time for the judge. He asked us a couple questions. I let him know that the drugs were mine and that Pat didn't have anything to do with it. Because she didn't have a record, they agreed to let me take the blame.

Now the judge is reading a report that was written from the interrogations of me and Pat. That's all the information that he has. His opinion of me is that I'm an abusive husband and a drug dealer who had his wife caught in this dope nightmare. I was abusing her because that's what the cops wrote, so the judge knows me by the words on the paper. The judge also saw that we did not have prior offenses and accepted my plea of guilty for possession. He then took Pat off of that charge. Pat was charged with being under the influence, and he made us both go to a drug diversion class that was, I believe, about 8 weeks long.

I was pleased that Pat wouldn't have any felony charges and that our kids would always be able to be under her protection. I never understood why Pat had an attitude toward me of taking all of the blame. In my mind, that's what a husband, a father, and a man should do: protect his family at all costs, even if it costs him his freedom. The judge also informed us that the district attorney is not filing charges at this time. They have up to 3 years or something like that to file. Pat and I were released following our court appearance on our own recognizance, with our commitment to complete the drug diversion classes.

## Lying Eyes

I remember the anger that Pat carried with her. She said that those cops made up all kinds of stuff. They tried to convince her to give me up and to admit that I was an abusive husband.

That's what the cops were telling the judge. Pat needed to know whether I believed any of those things. I let her know right then that it would take more than cops and their lies to make me believe that she didn't love me.

I don't remember who came to pick us up from the jail. I do remember the anger that Pat had. She said that she wanted to go and get Laticia from her mother because she felt that her mother was wrong in her meddling approach. Only getting Pat an attorney and *hanging me out to dry* with the public defender?

I asked her to please calm down. For Pat, it was just another act of disapproval that she felt in her heart, and these were the times when Pat felt that her mother should help instead of emasculate the father of her grand children. I felt like it was a very strange relationship. Pat's mother would pull her in and then disappoint her over and over. Pat just wanted her love, or for her to say, "I love you, Pat."

This was the dysfunctional relationship that they were both used to. Pat didn't want Laticia to stay at her mother's house because of the anger that she felt about her attorney only representing her.

I begged her to leave Laticia at Dorothy's home because we had unfinished business. We had to get rid of that half kilo that we had in the safe, and all I could think was the police were going to come back because they didn't get what they were after the first time.

## One More Deal

The case that was presented in the hearing told me with all certainty that I had been set up. The informants were mentioned, surveillance was mentioned, and the story that the prosecutor was spinning to the judge was that I was a big-time dope dealer, but they only found a little piece of crack.

The judge informed me that I might be charged with possession of crack cocaine and being under the influence. I believe that's why the judge saw through their bullshit, and that's the reason why it went the way it did, no jail time, this time. I wasn't going crazy; it was my *spidey senses* going off when I felt like somebody was watching us, because they were. The information that I got said that the couple had gotten busted and gave me up after I told them my whole operation, and that's why the cops weren't believing anything that I said. I've always wondered if the police got information from them that I was some kind of abusive husband. Pat and I wondered about that for years.

## Alone

As I sit here thinking back on the things that we went through, it's been six

months now, and I've been swimming in that ocean of loneliness and drowning from missing her. Only her memory is what gives me strength. I hear her whispering to me, "You have to keep going. I need you to keep going." Remembering our love is the only thing that I have now. I am trying to find where I go from here. 'Where do I feel that heaven? Her warm embrace?' I was a whole person with her, and that part of her is missing in me. This world is a two-player game, or at least it's always been for me, and finding a new direction is going to be incredibly hard.

I don't even know what the future looks like right now. We were two children trying to be adults in this crazy world. I have never been alone in all these 50 years; it's always been a *we thing*; now it's a *me thing*.

I push that grief to the side. Sometimes it catches up with me. Whispering and taunting me to fall back into the arms of sorrow. I can't believe I got so lucky to love somebody, and they loved me too. I always knew that love was important, but not as important as I do now. It has changed my life forever. Everyday seems just like another day without Pat, lonely. 'Will that change? I'm asking the question, God, and looking for your answer.'

## Walk of Shame

We get home and are horrified because we walked up to our door, couldn't get in fast enough, slammed the door, and left the rest of the world behind us.

The last 3 days in jail had taken a toll on both of us mentally. We were shocked by the shape in which our house was in. With all the stuff that was going on the night that they arrested us, we did not realize how much stuff they had tore up. Pillows, all kinds of different things. Even some of De's stuffed animals. Anything that you could possibly conceal something in was ripped apart! Pat was devastated and instantly broke down. I did my best to comfort her. We had to pull it together so we could go see our kids and let them know that their parents weren't just snatched out of their lives.

The kids were happy to see us, and we tried to put our shame to the side to enjoy the visit. Trying to avoid the disapproving look from Pat's parents. The look on their faces. "I told you, so he was no good." We tried to ignore all of the disapproval that was being directed at us. We focused on the kids and told them that we were working on a plan for when they could come back to the house. Pat had made it perfectly clear to me that she could no longer stay there. She did not feel comfortable there anymore.

It reminded her of the time someone broke into our house. You feel violated and unsafe. I knew I had to get her out of there. I asked her, "Give me a couple days, please." I had to get rid of the coke. I made some phone calls to some of my connections and made a deal for the next day. I went and used the telephone booth because I didn't know if they were listening to our phone calls. I made a deal. I just wanted to get rid of it, so I gave them a really good price.

The next day, I got on my bike. That way, nobody can really follow me because I can cut through alleys and things like that. I make the deal and head back home. Pat has packed our bags and is ready to go. I had one more thing that I had to do. I received the phone call from my cocaine connection, and he said it was urgent that he talk to me. I'm carrying a certain amount of fear as I approach the meeting spot.

He asked me if I'm all right and if Pat is all right, and he seemed to be sincere with his concern. He slipped me a wad of about a thousand bucks and told me that he was happy that I didn't give him up and that $1,000 was from the boss's Mexican Mafia connection.

I was a little scared now because they were looking at me as maybe a loose end. I hope not. 'Do they still have confidence in me?' I guess my head is busting with all kinds of different scenarios of what could happen, and I pray that they really did believe that I didn't give them up (snitch).

## Bad Cops

I get back to the townhouse, and we pack up and go to a motel for about 2 weeks until we can secure another house. Luckily, we had the cash. Getting another house wasn't that hard. The day that we were moving out, two cops showed up just to harass me a little bit. They were standing in the courtyard as I moved items back and forth to the truck, taunting me with phrases such as, "Guess the landlord found out what you were doing," and other ludicrous statements, coming from supposedly the protectors of the people. One of the asshole cops told my 6-year-old son that he would be locked up next. I lost my cool immediately, walked up to the cop, and shoved De behind me. I put my face right up to his face and told him that if he ever talked to my son like that again, we were going to have a problem and that I would whoop his ass right here.

He steps back and puts his hand on his gun. His partner had enough sense to escort him out of the courtyard as he kept hollering, "Don't worry, I'm gonna get you, I'm gonna get you!" I guess I could have been another statistic like George Floyd and dozens of other black men in similar situations. God was watching out for me. I never saw those cops again, and I never saw the couple that was selling for us again, and I told myself no more dealing.

## Who Are You Really?

I felt like this person who I really trusted in my life had completely bamboozled me, and that person was me! I struggled with really low self-esteem for a really

long period of time. In a way that made it difficult for me to function. I felt like the entire world was looking at me in a negative way. You were the *drug dealer*. I have to figure out how to survive with my new title. I knew I could be more than this life I'm leading. I was carrying so much guilt, and Pat was like my therapist through that time. Our ability to be vulnerable with each other is what makes us strong. Even though we have been shaken up by that whole experience. We concentrated our energy on bringing our kids back to a normal living situation. I told myself, "I don't feel guilty about my past because I'm making better decisions today, and because I'm making better decisions today, I will not worry about tomorrow; I just have to reach for it."

It's time to start another journey. I have to get my family right with the money we have and getting our kids' minds back to being comfortable again. We rented a motel room. I was still afraid that the cops were going to bust in and take us away. I live every day with the fear of the police filing charges against me, still I continue on.

Over the couple weeks that we were in the motel, my mom had been trying to convince me to move into her apartment complex because my brother and my sisters all had apartments there. We took that opportunity and moved out of San Jose to Mountain View. We felt that after having that experience, being around their cousins would kind of ease the kids minds from the traumatic events that they had gone through.

Watching their mother and father being put in a police car. We got to be Uncle D and Auntie Pat a little more; it wasn't the best experience.

For one thing, the family never lets you have a moment by yourself; that was different for us. We couldn't take it, plus, living on the second floor, the people downstairs were always complaining about the kids playing too hard.

In the years that Pat and I have been together, we have never lived in an apartment, so this was going to be different. The kids being around their cousins helped their spirits; it hurt me and Pat's spirits, and we found ourselves getting high again. We do not like who we are at this point, and we are trying to avoid it during this time. Our self-respect was at an all-time low. The only good thing about that time was that I wasn't dealing anymore.

We were basically just going through the motions of living; I hadn't worked for a couple months, so things started to get really tight. At this time in our lives, we had monster hospital bills that we were still paying for.

We've paid for years for the care that she got for the miscarriages; it took us like 15 years to pay them off. We got a break on Laticia and De's birth because of its experimental nature. We also had credit card bills, and it seemed like everything was catching up with us financially. I gave in to the hustle and did a few deals; things were not the same, and I couldn't make any money.

I was just wasting time and getting high; it wasn't like it was before, when we took a lot of time to build up our clientele. I didn't have the confidence; I promised myself that I was going to get a job. Things weren't like they were when we were young. Jobs at this time were very hard to come by, and I still couldn't get unemployment benefits.

Pat made the decision that we were going to apply for welfare because she found out the only way that she could get it was if I wasn't at home. She knew how badly it hurt my pride; she would have to remove all of my personal items in case she got an inspection. I stayed at the house but lived 'out of the bag' for a couple months. She was looking out for her kids, and I was going to have to eat my pride. I wasn't happy about this at all; we had nowhere else to turn. We argued back and forth about this decision, and she was right—we had to get out of this hole we were in.

A couple things happened while we lived in this apartment, including a big earthquake that took half the water out of the pool and knocked over a couple TVs. The biggest one I can remember being in.

The lowest part was when the social worker showed up and I had to hide in the closet so that Pat wouldn't be violating the welfare laws. That visit took all the pride I had left. I felt like a nobody, just another no-good black man who couldn't take care of his family.

Me and Pat's spirits were crushed and broken; we had never felt this low about ourselves in our whole relationship. All we knew was that we loved each other, and that was our strength. At this point, we thought we had lost our way.

We agreed to discuss our future. I agree that we aren't in the place that we want to be for our kids. We promise ourselves we are not going to get high anymore on cocaine, and for me to get back to work and to save our sanity, we must move out of these apartments. We save up our money and return to San Jose.

## A Slice Of Hope

Luckily, I still had a good reputation in the electronics world. I was hired to put another warehouse together. This job was going to last about 8 months. I used to bring De to work with me on Saturdays, and he would play in packing peanuts. They had a picnic for the families every month. We were allowed to go on the roof for the 4th of July and watch the fireworks display put on by the Great America Amusement Park. My kids both had season passes to Great America through the company. The memory of those days will always be with me.

We were feeling a little better about life. Their school was great. De was playing the xylophone in the marching band. Laticia was getting good grades, and we were getting things back on track. Looking back, I was frightened of what I might do, even though life was going great.

After I finished putting together the warehouse, the company hired me as a shipping and receiving clerk. And it gave us a little hope that things would get better. I can't let go of knowing charges might be coming my way. It's haunting me like a ghost. I had that fear on me every day. I was going out of my mind. This is something I didn't want to have to face.

I prayed that I wouldn't have to face the penalties for what I did. Life was going better for me. And I continue to try to blame the cops for setting me up. Inside, I knew it was my actions that caused them to be able to do that. I try to accept responsibility for what I did in the past and make better decisions now.

I have to remember that my family depends on me. The last thing I would do in this world is let them down again like that. I had built up a good reputation in the drug world, and that gave me a certain satisfaction that people wanted you; they needed you to get something that they could only get through you.

I don't know; it's hard to explain. Sometimes, the life you know is all you need, and I had to find another way to live this life. (The past is a place to learn from, not to live in.)

A few months have gone by, and people are still trying to get me to do deals for them. I resist because, with the job I have, I'm making good money. Time is going by, and I'm getting more comfortable with life. We were *making it* off of our paychecks. All together, I think I've worked there for about 2 years, and during this time I had a janitorial job that I worked 4 hours a night on. We paid down the credit cards, and we paid down the hospital bills. I believe at that time in our lives, we cut up our credit cards and never had any until we were over 60 years old.

## Parenting

Life is good during these times, and me and Pat were doing our parenting thing and creating ways to communicate with our kids better than our parents had with us. For instance, one of the things that we did when they got into trouble was make them write a letter. My kids had to write an essay about what they did, why they did it, why they shouldn't get in trouble, or why they would not do it again. In doing that, we had a lot of good conversations come out of their letters, resulting in a better understanding of us and why we did not want them doing whatever got them in trouble. A better understanding of them and why they did the thing in the first place.

Sometimes letting our kids face the pain of things is the only way to help them learn how to cope with it. When they were afraid to attempt something, we would encourage them and let them know we believed in them. If we trusted them and allowed them to trust in us, then they would get over the fear. Conquering fear is a great feeling, and it mostly happens when you're a kid. We always encouraged them to learn what we already knew about trust. It's a two-way street. We also taught them about trusting themselves and their parents, and they had to learn to trust their decisions. We also have to trust their decisions so that our kids are empowered to tackle confronting scenarios later in life.

When your kids and you go through life together, that's not something; it's everything. Me and Pat knew that there's a short amount of time that, as a parent, you can be effective in setting up the way that they look at themselves. We taught them that the word confident meant many different things and that you could achieve confidence in many different ways.

Over the years of miscarriages, me and Pat talked about all of the things that we wouldn't do to our kids and what we would do to help them deal with the world better.

## Pat the Therapist

Our love was strong, and Pat never let us slip too far apart. She knew I was depressed and blaming myself for all the pain that we have been through, and she convinced me that everything was going to be all right.

I still love my family, and she was confident that I would always try to do the right thing for my family and that I didn't have to be that perfect. "Nobody's perfect," she used to say.

She explained to me and asked me not to be sad about what happened anymore. It proved that she had the right man to be the father of her kids and the right husband. She said I proved that to her that day in court; for me, it was what I felt I was supposed to do. She told me, "You didn't have to do it; you could have chosen other ways to go, but you didn't."

She asked me, "How much do you think you can take? You're depressed from not playing music anymore, and now you want to be depressed about what happened to us? You have to get over it." I was trying to, but it's a long way down from people screaming your name and applauding, to you being naked in a jail cell. Knowing that might be in your future. It was hard, and I broke down many times and cried tears just thinking about it.

## Believe in Yourself

All we wanted for our kids was to do better than we did and go farther than we did, and I had thrown a big wrench in our future.

Life has been a constant search to find out who I am. It's my opportunity to restart and reinvent myself because you can't take back what you did. I was going to have to figure out how to forgive myself.

When you have a dream that comes alive, it's a blessing, and God blessed me with Pat, Laticia, De and the band. I was going to do everything I could to hang on to that. The warehouse job is over, and I get another job and another job. I'm working two jobs now to make up the money that I made when I was dealing. This was one of the hardest things that I had to go through mentally: trying my best to feel good about myself again.

I would be exhausted, and my kids would not understand if I couldn't get the things that I had been getting for them before. We had always provided what they needed. I wasn't going to let them go without. I worked my ass off; they used to joke with me, "Are you sure you don't have any Jamaican blood in you because you got way too many jobs?" That was a joke among our people. Jamaicans will take your job; you better watch out! Having multiple jobs is a sign of respect for their ability to make it in America.

## We're Only Human

We are living in San Jose on Peridot Street during this time in our lives. Our lives are pretty normal except for the fact that I may be working too much, but still spending a lot of time with the kids, and taking De to karate. I would take Laticia to buy the teen magazines of *New Edition* and all the other boy bands. Painstakingly cutting the pictures out to make her big collages, then hang them on her wall. She loved it!

She was growing up. I was trying to figure out how to get that 'Daddy Love' back somehow. For some reason, it didn't bother us to fight for our kids love.

We were so used to fighting to get love from our parents. This wasn't foreign to us; we felt like they had to know how badly we wanted them. We wanted them to carry our love for the rest of their lives and know that they weren't an accident; they're what we wanted because, as kids, we both felt like we weren't wanted or important to the family.

The other important thing that we did with our kids was let them know that we had made mistakes just like everybody else. We were not Superman and Superwoman, and we did not do everything perfectly. We wanted them to have a true sense of how the world really was. The kids have friends now. A lot of different influences are coming in fast and furious. Me and Pat are trying to negotiate this new world. Laticia is going to be a teenager pretty soon, and now my son seems to be just as mischievous as I was as a kid.

## Latchkey Kids

Pat is working at this time, and we both go to work in the morning. De said he wasn't feeling well. Pat told him to stay home, and she would check on him at lunch time. Both of them were capable of taking care of themselves, and we tried to teach them to be safe when we weren't there. My son is always messing with me, talking about how he was a latchkey kid because we wouldn't be there when he got home from school.

We go to work, and a few hours later, Pat gets a call from the San Jose police telling her that they have our son at the station. Let me tell you what he did: he dialed 911 and then hung up the phone. They sent the police out.

Seeing that he was there by himself, they didn't think that he was at the proper age to be there by himself. Pat had to go down to the station and pick him up. She was upset, so she explained the situation to the police. Let them know that she would have been there in an hour to check on him at lunch. They let her take him home.

Something good came out of that—these cops didn't have an attitude toward me. They treated him like a kid, like they're supposed to. He now had a picture in his head that all cops weren't bad, which gave him a middle place. Some cops are bad, and some are good, just like regular people.

Something else came out of it that he said to me later on when I got home from work: "Dad, I went to jail just like you," and that really hurt my heart and brought back the fear of what could be coming up in my future if the District Attorney ever chose to file charges. It is time to fight the fear again. It's always on my mind; I can't get rid of the thoughts and the fears.

## The Change

Laticia would start experiencing the things that would make her a woman. Now that I'm learning about all of this myself, I didn't know everything. Now it's my daughter, and I wanted to know what she was going through.

That was her and Pat's secret; she did not want me to know about what she was going through. Yeah, I'm kind of going crazy. My daughter is turning into a woman. How am I going to deal with that?

I want to enjoy the years while she's still a kid and hope that she'll always love me. My daughter is starting to get interested in boys; her little points are growing (her breasts), and I'm not getting those Daddy kisses like I used to. Pat explained to me in these words that she is transitioning from adolescence to womanhood.

## All About the Kids

Our time living on Peridot gave the kids a lot of different experiences. De and his little friend went to the store and got caught shoplifting. Pat went crazy; he got punished and had to write probably his biggest essay that he ever wrote as a kid. We spoiled them a lot. When we got mad and cut things off, they knew that they had done something wrong. In the streets where I was brought up, it is very hard for black boys to navigate feelings and emotions.

They feel, 'The world doesn't get me.' Pat really forced me to reconnect with the kid in me. Which gave me the ability to guide him properly. We found out years later, when they were in high school, about having to write those essays as punishment. The writing really helped them in school; writing a book report was easy for them. To thank us for that really blew our minds and gave me a proud heart.

Another thing that happened while we lived there was that the kids went 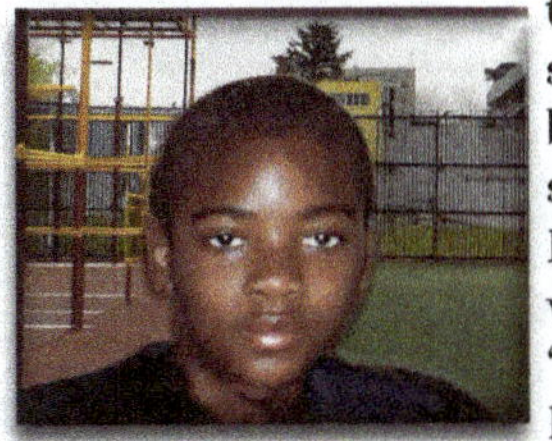 to Tahoe with the neighbors, and they were riding snowmobiles, and Laticia was letting De drive, you know, being a big sister. De ran into the rope on the course and scraped the skin of her neck down to the white pigment. Now, I would imagine that she was in a lot of pain; when we got the call from her, all she could tell me was Daddy, "I'm white. I'm white. Daddy, I don't want to be white." Even though we're freaking out we had to remain calm so we could calm her down. She still has a little scar on her neck to this day.

De got on the phone to try to let us know that he didn't try to hurt her; he was very emotional. We both knew he loved this big sister and would never do anything to hurt her. We had to calm both of them down, and they ended up staying for the rest of the trip.

My son was always mighty curious. I thought he was going to be a scientist. I built him a clubhouse in the backyard out of pallets that I got from work. I came home one day and asked Pat where he was. She said De was in the backyard with the dog. I go back there, and he is in his clubhouse.

I smell this weird burning smell, and I look inside his clubhouse, and he's lighting a 2-liter plastic bottle and watching the plastic drip into a puddle of flames. I explained to him that he had put his mother and sister in danger, and that wasn't right. I taught him from a young age that he was to be a protector. He took it hard and took his punishment like a champ. Just some of the stuff I had to watch out for with my son always experimenting. He was so into karate that he sat at the kitchen table trying to catch flies with the chopstick for 2

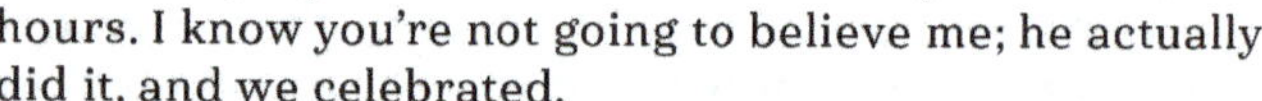

hours. I know you're not going to believe me; he actually did it, and we celebrated.

I remember the pride he had in accomplishing that feat. It warmed my heart as a dad to know that he had that much determination. He was a very focused and curious young man and could accomplish most things he tried. He was a kid, not like his dad. He had confidence, unlike I did as a kid. His attitude and skills were so excellent that his sensie's told me I didn't have to pay for his lessons anymore. He was so good that they wanted to take him on to help with other little kids.

During this time, he developed a love for movies. He looked at them in a whole different way than normal people did. He was the cameraman; he was the director, and it fascinated me. From his point of view, he watched tons of Kung Fu movies, and Bruce Lee was his hero. In the *Last Dragon* movie, he explained to me how a stunt would be done. I always wondered how he knew that.

What me and Pat did was look for their talents, push them in that direction, and help them identify their strongest attributes. They were both good students, and Pat made sure of it.

## Pay Attention to Mama

I remember them bringing homework home that I had no knowledge of. The math that they were teaching my kids, which I had never even heard of, was a whole new world. Their education was so important to us that Pat would take off work to go talk to the teacher to get the knowledge to help them with their homework. She was determined they would get a good education.

Pat went to visit college with Laticia. Laticia had failed a speech class in her

sophomore year of college, and she was refusing to retake the class. She told her mom, "We pay for these classes, so I don't have to take them again. Obviously, I'm not good at them." Laticia was stubborn at first and did not want to take the class again. She also didn't push her mother, realizing she needed to take the class again because she was going to be a boss and she would have to speak in front of people one day. Pat sat in her speech class with her for a little over a week until Laticia had her first speech in class. Laticia tells me that after the speech, Pat stood up and clapped, then gave her the nod, blew her a kiss, and said, "You got this Boo!" (Laticia's nickname), and she left.

## You Must Decide

The first time I saw my daughter give a speech in front of hundreds of

people was at her college graduation. I stood there, chest poked out, tears in my eyes, and ears tingling because of the pride she was giving us as parents for encouraging her to do her best. I looked at Pat and said, "We did it, baby!" Pat was proud of Laticia for standing so tall, eloquently speaking effortlessly, and looking just like her mother. All she could do was cry and scream, "That's my baby!" This was a day of celebration for achievements well earned.

We still had the bitter taste and some arguments that came from Pat's mother about the content of what Laticia would talk about in her speech. She wanted Laticia to praise her and her accomplishments and not talk about her parents. Laticia felt we were the catalysts for her accomplishments, not Pat's mom.

I watched my daughter have to decide who she was going to talk about in her speech. Me and Pat didn't really know how to take it; we also knew that it was up to Laticia. She wanted to honor us and not hurt her grandmother's feelings. She made a decision, and we didn't know until the day of the speech when we heard her decision. My baby girl talked about us and had us both crying and surprised that she gave us the credit. She had us both floating as we walked out of the graduation. With the amount of pressure that was put on her by her grandmother, she made the decision with her heart. I had always told the kids from the beginning, "Be true to who you are and never lie to yourself."

## The Letter

Back to the court date I get home, and there's a letter waiting for me from the county. I open it up, and it's a court date. The District Attorney finally filed charges for possession of crack cocaine and being under the influence. You know that knot that you get in your stomach? I had it for the whole two weeks until the court date. Now it's time to prepare for whatever happens in court. Will I go to jail? We don't know, and the pressure is crushing us.

## Judgment Day

I remember thinking as I walked to the courthouse how many other black men had walked this path before. I felt like I was getting on the auction block to be sold. It was out of my hands. I don't have a say in what happens to me. I had never felt this way before; I'm sure my ancestors did, and I called on their spirits to help me make it through this. For me this was on a different level. Superior Court was a beautiful place. I couldn't appreciate the beauty for the 'Doom and Gloom' that I was feeling.

It was the big court and the people piled in to take seats and Pat would not let my hand go since we got out of the car. We could feel each other's anxiety of not knowing what was going to happen.

They called order to the court and my heart starts beating faster. There are a dozen people before me and they're cranking them out like an assembly line case after case eventually my name would be called. I was noticing a strange pattern. People of color were getting sentenced to the most time, and the person right before me was a young white man who had been caught with an ounce of cocaine in powder form and a gun. They gave him probation and gave his weapon back. All those before him were people of color they got 6 months to a year or 5 years for less than what he had because it was cocaine and not in crack form. There was something really unfair about the sentences I witnessed. Now it's getting ready to be my turn and Pat tightens her grip in my hand. I have to pry her fingers off of my hand so that I can talk to the public defender before I'm called up. She did not want to let me go.

My moment was coming, and I was kind of disappointed in my public defender's response to my charges. He explained to me to take the plea deal, which was no jail time, if I pleaded not guilty and went to trial, I could spend two years in jail and three years on probation. The plea deal would give me two and a half years on probation, and it was up to the judge if I spent six months in jail or if he would give me work release.

That was the advice of my public defender, and I had about 5 to 10 minutes to think about it. Pat said no, "We'll get an attorney and fight it." I told her I couldn't go through that for all those months again. We just spent two and a half years waiting for this day. I wanted it to be over, at least this part of it. She told me that, "If this is what you really want; I got your back."

My name is called. I'm trembling as I walk up to the judge. He asked me my name, and I'm so nervous that I have to clear my throat. He reads my charges and asks how I plead. My reply is, "Guilty your honor." He asked me several times if I agreed with the plea deal, or if I was forced into taking it, to make sure it was my decision. I answered, and he looked at my file and contemplated for a minute.

He handed out my punishment, and in my mind, I'm thinking he has no right to judge me because he doesn't know me. He has the privilege because I've given it to him through the stuff that I've done.

He lets me know he's ready to sentence me. I'm weak in the knees as I hear him speak. I've already conjured up the worst-case scenarios, and all of those ended up with me behind bars. He tells me about a 3-month work program, two and a half years of probation, and a monthly urine test. This work program is modern-day slavery. How am I supposed to take care of my family?

I have to work at the jail for 8 hours a day, and they dug up some old tickets and suspended my license, so I'm angry now. How am I possibly going to be able to take care of my family? I shouted at the judge a couple times. The spectators in the court can feel my anger and frustration.

He bangs his gavel and tells me to shut up. He also lets me know that he hasn't finished sentencing me yet and that he can change it if I continue on with my outburst.

I hear Pat whisper at the back of my neck, "Calm down, baby." Life has been a constant search to find who I am, and in this moment, I'm lost. I have no idea how I'm going to make it through this. I asked myself, 'What if I was made for the bright lights? What if I was made for the stage?'. I let that go, and now look at me—stuck. On the car ride home, me and Pat don't exchange too many words; all she can do is slap me on the shoulder and tell me that we're going to make it through it, and I have to believe her even though I feel like this may be the lowest point that I've gone through in my life.

## How Do I Work Now?

I'm now a felon. All of those electronic jobs that I've worked for the last 15 years, I can no longer work at. I've always had to have a security clearance. My whole career was taken with this conviction. The realization that I was a felon now was hard for me to cope with. There was a certain amount of pride I took in not being a felon and never serving prison time. Look at me now. I can't undo what I've done; all I want is for God to help me. I don't want to dwell on the negative; I don't want it to define me.

## The Rules

I had to meet with the probation officer the next day to get the rules. The rules I would have to follow in order to get out of this would not be easy.

I didn't realize how hard it would be; I wasn't going to jail. That seemed to be what I cared about the most. I was determined to not let this drag me down, and Pat was happy I wasn't going to jail.

## Probation

I'm determined to make it through this so I can have my life back. And I'm hoping that the probation officer has a heart, not one of the kind that just *dogs* the parolee. I had heard horrible stories about probation officers. Some would harass you so much that you never made it through probation; they would pout on any mistake you made, and eventually you would be back in jail.

I was praying that my experience would be different. I met this guy, and he's acting like most of the cops that I've dealt with in the past. He's not letting any of his heart show through because I'm a drug person. He sternly laid out the rules and handed me a bottle to piss in on our first meeting. I knew my world had changed when he accompanied me to the bathroom.

And he stood there and watched me pee in the bottle. It's hard to explain the discomfort. Someone watching you pee as a total stranger. I'm beginning to understand that I am part of this system now. I am somewhere I never wanted to be, and he tells me that I have a week to report to the county jail to start my work release. I have to work there for 90 days. I asked him at that time if there was anyway that I could get out of this? 'How was I going to take care of my family?'

His words to me were, "You're going to have to figure it out." He explained to me that I could not get a driving ticket or any misdemeanor charges. If I did, I would be violated, which meant I had broken the rules, and the punishment was 90 days in jail. I left his office feeling really worthless; it had hit me so hard that I had to go in the bathroom and wet my face to hide the tears before I met Pat in the car. I explained to her what he said, and of course she was positive and told me that we would make it through it somehow. I just wanted to keep beating myself up. I really didn't want to hear what she was saying. She knew me very well and caught on that I was in that mode, so she let me soak in my sadness until we got home.

## It's All My Fault

I retreated to my room and contemplated how I had gotten myself into this position. Pat came into the room as I sat on the bed, grabbed my hands, and told me, "I know you think it's all your fault and that you're supposed to take all of the blame; It's that man thing." She says, "Nobody's perfect, and we will get past this." I wanted to hurt; I wanted to punish myself, and she would not leave me alone. She said that she wasn't going to let me dig my own grave and that leaving the music industry had taken a big piece of me away, and I was just starting to come back, and then we got the letter.

Pat did not like seeing me back in that depressed state of mind. She said, "Now that we know what's ahead of us, we can make it through this." I had to believe her; we had made it through so much other stuff.

It's time for me to suck it up. I was going to have to quit my job, and the saddest part was that I would no longer be able to work in the electronic industry any more. I have worked at Hitachi, HP, Intel, Ampex, Memorex, Sun Microsystems, Apple, IBM, Lockheed Martin Aerospace, and Gould Industries.

I even worked at the Stanford Linear Accelerator. I had worked in all aspects of inventory control for all of those companies and had worked my way up from being just a forklift driver to a warehouse specialist after 20 years in that business. All of it was gone; I could no longer pass the security check.

Pat had worked at Intel and Sun Micro Systems. At that time, I don't believe Pat really understood the change that was coming in our lives. She just knew that whatever it was, we could make it through. We were going to stay together and love each other because that was our strength.

## Bad Reputation

There was a mirror with a saying on it that Pat brought home from work one day years before this time, and each of the kids had one in their room hanging on their wall so they could look at it each morning. The words were, "Our Reputation Depends On You!" I couldn't help but feel like I had let my family down. The hardest thing was that I had to go and quit the job and give them an explanation of why I was quitting. I was filled with embarrassment and shame, and this is just the beginning of this journey. At this point, we can still hide our drug use from the kids; but I couldn't hide my depression. Laticia asked me constantly, "What's wrong, Daddy?" All I could do was promise her that I would feel better later. What bothered me the most is that I would be working for free. Pat was working at that time. That meant that I was going to have to learn how to ride the bus again.

I didn't have the money to get my drivers license back; they seem to always come up with more fines, which boggles my mind. I started working in their laundry for 8 hours a day at the county jail at Elmwood; it was an hour and a half ride on the bus, if I was lucky. Working here every day meant that they could pull me at any time and give me a urine test.

Me and Pat had to stop the drugs because the dirty test would put me back in jail, and the probation officer could knock at my door at any time. It was very controlling. One of our concerns was were we going to go through withdrawals because we had been doing too much on a regular basis. As much as we thought we were doing, it wasn't enough to make us go through the body withdrawals. Now the mental withdrawals were the hardest: fighting back your impulses and cravings and wanting to do it, pressuring you every moment. A constant throbbing of need.

An epic battle that would needed to be won by both of us. We won the battle and *kicked cold turkey!*

In our 90 days of work release, we have been very disciplined, and I passed all my urine tests. The kids are doing well in school, and I'm spending a lot of time with them because I don't have a job. I'm so confused; I don't know which way to turn. I've been doing the inventory job for a long time now. 'What kind of work can I find?' I didn't have the music anymore, and I didn't know what kind of work I was going to do to take care of my family. I'm pretty damn depressed, and I'm also beating myself up so bad that I don't recognize myself anymore. Who am I? That question always comes up over and over again in my life.

## Resistance Is Futile

And now that I sit here, that question comes back into my brain: "Who am I now?" I was the husband; I'm not now.

People say to, "Hang on to your memories." There's not a warm embrace, a kiss, or a tender hug. Her look of approval. How do I define, 'Missing her with all of me?' Grief is futile; I continue to fight to find my new normal. About the memories: the memories are what cause pain. Because I remember how lovely and loving our romance was.

Our relationship had been put to the test, and we endured. People say you have a love for raising your family; 'What are you going to do now?' For me, I don't know how to answer that. I do know that I need to finish this book, and hopefully I'll be able to figure it out.

Yes, I did those things. Now what do I have to accomplish, but to write this book right now? What I'm feeling is loneliness because she's not here with me. It's sad because I won't see her in human form again. I am frightened of not knowing what the future holds. Angered because I still want her here, and a sense of peace because she's not in pain anymore. Unknowingness of how to proceed in this world. Unfamiliarity with how to act. Alone frightened of the unknown hopelessness of what a future life could be.

## Follow Orders

We made it through the work release and didn't realize how difficult the rest of the probation would be. Things are starting to get tight, and me and Pat's patients are wearing thin. I don't know what type of work to look for because I can't work in electronics anymore; I'm a felon now.

Amazingly, the kids are doing great in all types of activities. Laticia is a teenager now and really getting interested in boys. She's on the phone all the time; that hadn't been a problem in her earlier days, and I would soon find out if it was a problem. Money is getting tight because we are not dealing anymore. Pat has been very patient and has started smoking weed again. She was very good about not smoking it around me; my patience has run out.

Now I am smoking weed in the first week of the month so that I can have time to clean up for the test at the end of the month. The probation officer had been pretty regular in testing me at the end of each month, and we knew that we were playing with fire. To be under this type of control was like being back under your parents supervision, even worse than your parents. We're having a tough time with these bills, and I have to borrow money from those who have my back. Such as D'Lamont, and some that didn't like Pat's parents.

Pat would ask her parents for the money. They would set up the terms for how I would pay them back. Since I wasn't working, they took full advantage of our situation and wouldn't give me what I thought I was worth for an hour. We always had more stuff to do than was reasonable for the small amount of money that they had loaned us. We were in a tight spot, and I was searching for a remedy. There was one time that I lost my shit. It kind of all came down to me at once. They had planned a family dinner and insisted that I finish up the painting job.

It's a really hot day. I'm very sensitive, and all I can hear is the enjoyment of the family. They're having a great time, and I'm out here. It was miserable as hell. The first time in our relationship, I felt totally alone and totally crushed by the weight of my responsibility for the family.

Me and Pat's parents didn't have a good relationship at all; they were always judging me and her. Since the arrest, they look down their noses at me, and now they are having so much joy in there, like they normally do.

When they got together, I could not take it. I left and went home. Pat was so mad at me because I did that. I explained to her how I was feeling. She told me that she hated that I felt like that. She promised me that she would never put me in that type of position again. It hurt so bad to hear all the laughter and them eating and drinking without even asking me to take a break and join them. It just went in really deep, and I reacted.

At that point, after our conversation, I knew I had to take a different approach to getting work. I am at this time doing a lot of different side jobs—a couple hours here, a couple hours there—just to make ends meet.

I'm working at my mom's house one day, mowing her lawn. There's a fence-building company down at the end of the block. I thought this might be an opportunity to try a new approach. I had always loved working with wood in my shop classes in junior high and high school. I didn't really have any professional carpentry skills, so I figured, 'What the heck?' I walked down and approached the head of the small company.

One guy was the boss and he hired Mexicans from Home Depot every morning for the jobs that he would book. He asked me if I had any skills, and my answer to him was, "No, but I learn quickly." He put me to the test; he showed me how to use the skill saw, and for the rest of the day, I cut two by fours down to the measured size.

That was the day I started on the road to being a carpenter. For the first couple months, the pay was shitty. I really felt undervalued. I have been at the top of my game in the electronics industry, and now I'm starting all over. Me and Pat are disgusted, and I agree to give it a few more months.

Randy was my boss's name, and he trained me really hard for the next 6 months. I was able to give him some tips on how to recruit employees. In six months, I helped him build a three-person crew with myself and two others. Now I found myself as the foreman. I had to discuss this with Randy, and how I needed more money. To my surprise, he knew that was coming and gave me a nice raise at the end of the year. Working with him, I was running two crews, and my day consisted of running back and forth across town from job to job to make sure everything was going smoothly and, if not, handle the problem.

I've gotten pretty good. Randy had told me one day, "I could actually call you a carpenter." But the long, physical shifts I worked, were wearing me down. This was a new type of work that I had never experienced before. When the weather is bad, you don't work. The summer months are the most important. You work really long hours. And when the weather's bad, you sit at home and don't get paid. I've never had a job like this before. For the first six months, Randy would pick me up every morning. Now that we have two crews and I am a foreman, I was going to have to start driving, and I don't have a license. Things are going well at work, so I'm willing to take the risk.

## She Knows What She Wants

At this time, Pat wasn't working. Every time they tried to give her a promotion

to a take a lead position, she would quit. The way she told me was that; she didn't want to be responsible for anybody else's life and if she were the boss, she would have to tell people the truth and fire them. She didn't have that in her heart. At first, I didn't understand. I said to her, "It's the way of the world, girl; Somebody gotta' be the boss." She said to me, "That somebody ain't gonna' be me."
She had learned to be; True To Who She Truly Was. I loved her even more for, "Always keeping it real." Even though that meant I was going to have to work a little harder. Pat also began to work for her mother and auntie May, who both had care facilities. So when things got tight, Pat would work with them. Pat loved her freedom, and not having to work an 8-hour job every week of the month was what was right for her. That meant that she could be there for the kids. Participate in different events that were going on at school, field trips and things like that. She was always into something. While Pat is getting more connected with herself, I feel like I don't know who I am.
That question continues to plague me.

Now that I'm a carpenter, I didn't see that one coming. It was taken care of by my family. I pressed on. Laticia is a teenager now and very interested in boys, and I'm losing my mind because my baby girl is turning into a young woman. It became more important to me to be a good male figure in her life. Pat was guiding me all the way and helping me not make too big of a mistake by saying, "My man's thinking."

## Look to the Future

The kids are doing really well in school, and at that point, we realized that we were at least doing some things right. Laticia was so bright that she skipped a grade. De could accomplish anything he set his mind to. Now it was time to make a decision that would affect the rest of his life, and that was his karate.

His sensei thought that he could go all the way to being a professional, but we weren't sure that we wanted that to be his main focus. Through my job as a carpenter with Randy, I introduced my son to many people. I met architects, engineers, artists, and writers who had home businesses. We were showing our kids that there were a lot of different things you could do in this world; with an education. Some of those people would even explain to De what they did and give him a glance into their world. They appreciated the work I did for them in beautifying their million dollar homes.

## Mini Me

De used to come with me to work. Randy hired him on the days that I would bring him. Randy saw him work circles around grown men. When De was like 9 or 10, he was interested in a lot of different things: music, movies, and sometimes just being a kid and a ninja. He wanted to be like his dad. You don't know how proud that made me. However, we all decided to not accept Sensie's offer.

During this time in San Jose, things were pretty normal for a growing family. Our parenting skills were *night and day* compared to our parents, and they never understood why we gave our kids so much respect. They felt like kids didn't know anything so they shouldn't be respected. We knew different because of our childhood experiences; we just wanted a little respect, to be loved, and to be appreciated just a little bit.

Over our years together, me and Pat talked about all the pain of our childhoods. We tried our best to not give our kids those kinds of memories. A few things happened to test our parenting during these times. Laticia asked us if she could go to Great America with her girlfriend and stay there until it got dark. Then they were supposed to have a sleepover at one of the girls houses. We had never let her stay out this late before; we wanted to trust her. Little did we know that they had cooked up this whole elaborate lie so they could go to Oakland and see some boys that they were interested in.

Things didn't go as planned, and they were stranded in Oakland. From what I understand, a couple of the girls parents told them they better find a way home; they had gotten themselves up there. They needed to figure out how to get back home. Laticia didn't want to have to call her mother; that's how it turned out. We got a call, and Laticia told us what was going on and where she was.

## Pushing The Limits

We hop in the car to pick these girls up. Pat is steaming the whole ride to get them. Saying things that expressed how pissed she was. We had both never been this upset with Laticia. She had never been this dishonest with us before, and Pat had a lot to say to all of those girls, so I kept my mouth shut.

I was incredibly disappointed. The only thing I said when we got home was, "Go to your room because I'm so mad I don't know what I might do to you." She told me years later that it scared her more than getting a whooping or anything else. Pat called all the parents and told them that they would be spending the night at our house.

The next day, Pat made all of the girls clean up the house, took each one of them home, and told their parents what they had done. Pat told me, "She's growing up, babe, and it's time to adjust our approach." Pat envisioned a different relationship with Laticia than the one she had with her mother; it was very important to her. She felt Laticia could be a daughter *and* a friend. Someone that Laticia would always trust. She encouraged Laticia to feel like her mother was there for her-no matter what. This wasn't the case with Pat and her mother.

## Never Learn

I'm still on probation when I come up with the *dirty test*, which means I'm going to be violated. I could get 3 months in jail. I didn't know how I found myself in this position again; I had been good for two and a half years. I played their game and never got a dirty test. Now I'm going to have to *face the music*.

I go to the probation office to hear what my punishment is going to be, and I'm scared out of my mind because I've just started to get things back together. For me to go to jail right now would totally destroy my family. Pat is working for her mother, and it never pays enough to live off of. I'm nervous. I walk in, sit down, and get the news that my probation has just been extended another year and a half with no jail time. Pat was going to be upset, and I was relieved that I wasn't going to jail.

## Keeping It Real

This whole probation thing has really been difficult to navigate. It had made Pat feel guilty because she wanted to smoke a joint when I couldn't. One good thing came out of me getting a year and a half more probation.

My probation officer said to me that he was confused because I had been
clean for a long time with no dirty tests, and now I have one. 'What was going
on?' I took a chance and kept it real with him. I told him about the difficulties
of putting my family back together while being on probation and not being able
to work in the field in which I had been employed for 20 years! In the two and
a half years of probation, I learned and created a whole new occupation. I was
a carpenter now. I worked 12 hours a day and ran two crews. I needed some
type of release. I didn't drink, and I wasn't doing coke anymore; I just wanted to
smoke a joint!

He chuckled and told me that he understood where I was coming from
because, when he gets home, he likes to have his glass, or two, of wine. He
agreed that for the rest of my probation period, I wouldn't have to worry about
having any more dirty tests because he was going to ignore the THC in my
system.

Pat was pleased that she could have her smoking buddy back with her, and I
was happy to not have to keep feeling like I was lying all the time. And we both
realized just how much we missed sitting down and smoking with each other.
A lot of deep conversations happened in those smoking sessions, and we were
thrilled that we finally got our chill time back.

## Daddy Don't Play

During this time, any free time that I had, I'd spend with my kids. There are a
variety of things that bring a smile to my face. There was a go-kart place I used
to take them to; from what they tell me, we went a whole lot of times.

My daughter was big enough to ride in the go-kart; De had to sit on my lap
to drive. They are fierce competitors, and they both wanted to be good at what
they would try to do. They both tell me that's how they learned how to drive a
real car.

I used to take them to the movies, and it was a place that had like six movies.
We will watch one and then sneak into another movie. We will also go to the
Aladdin's Palace arcade and play video games all day.

Me and Pat kind of lived our childhoods that we didn't have through our
kids. I asked my kids what they remembered about their childhood. And those
were some of the details that they gave me.

What I do remember is that they were getting a little full of themselves. They
were talking to their mother in a disrespectful manner. And I stopped them in
their tracks and told them, "I'd mess them up if they dis my woman. She was
my woman before she was your mother, and nobody's going to disrespect her,
especially not her kids and not in front of me." There were lines that shouldn't
be crossed, especially with your parents.

## Phone Magic

Me and Pat are working and trying to keep up with our bills, and one day I get a phone bill that is $800. Back in those days, a long-distance call was if you were calling the next town, and I believe they charged you for distance by the minute.

Well, Laticia had been talking to those boys in Oakland, and that's what this bill was: teenage conversations about what I didn't want to know about. I was pissed. Right now, after speaking to Pat, of course, I told the family that I wasn't paying the bill and we would not have a phone anymore. Laticia was upset and happy; that was the only punishment. And I was miserable for the next couple weeks. One day I came home and Laticia was talking on the phone.

Now, during the time that the phone was off, Laticia would be sitting there with it. I had asked her many times, "Who are you talking to?" She would answer me in that voice, "Nobody, dad, the phone doesn't work."

This day I came home and she was talking; she had prayed for the phone to be on, and I couldn't believe that it came back on with a different number. She said that the phone rang, she picked it up, and they asked for someone different. Laticia was clever enough to ask the person, "What number did you call?" She got that number from the person who called, and we kept it like that until I was able to pay the bill.

## Life Lessons

I knew it was going to take me some time to come up with that money because our rent was $1200 a month. The phone bill was a lot to pay, and I couldn't pay it all at once. I knew that I had to start teaching them more about the world and how it worked.

For the next couple months, I would bring my paycheck home and have Laticia pay the bills. It blew her mind when she saw how much money we actually had left to keep for ourselves even though we hadn't even bought groceries yet. Laticia never made phone calls that put us in that position again. She learned her lesson, and that's all that was important to us: learn from your mistakes. That's all we asked.

## Good or Bad Opportunity?

Randy, the owner of the company that I work for, spent a lot of time whitewater rafting. He would take a couple of us two weekends out of the month. We rode the rapids in every river in California and two rivers in Oregon. For the first year and a half, De couldn't go; he always helped us repair the raft. He set up everything for the trips, and eventually he was big enough to go. And it was great for him to conquer something new; it seemed like he had waited for years. When he finally got to do it, he embraced it and learned all he could about whitewater rafting.

It was a fun sport that was very dangerous, and I was worried about him and myself. It was a different experience for me; he got pretty good. I didn't have to worry so much. The more he learns, the more I enjoy the trips. That was something else that I and my son did together. We only got Laticia out there once or twice. My daughter does not like the outdoors; there's no shame in her game; she says she's *Bougie*, (Bourgeoisie). She's the one who would go *glamping*, not camping.

Pat loved camping and being out in nature. What both of our kids loved the most was spending time with us doing what they liked to do, as long as we were there.

One night we're sitting around the campfire after rafting all day, and Randy gives me a proposition: do I want to buy the company? The company had been profitable in the last two and a half years I worked for him; he had made half a million dollars in profit.

He said he had made enough money to retire; that's what he set out to do, and I had helped him do that. He let me know that he was proud of me and how I had learned the business. He said he wanted to do this for me and my family. He was a single man, and he loved the dedication that I and Pat had for my family. The problem was, in order to make him that money, I had to work 12-hour days on weekends; it took a whole lot out of me and took a lot of my family time.

I can't imagine taking on being the owner, which means that I would spend more hours every night coordinating the next day's job, 'The Never-Ending Hustle', just like with the band. And at this point, I'm not as young as I was. To take all this on was going to take some thinking.

Pat didn't like the terms of the contract; it stated that I would be the owner and he would be the silent partner. Which meant he'd be getting half of my profits as long as I owned the company. That way, I wouldn't have to put any money up front to be a partner. Pat and I talked about this in depth and asked ourselves what that meant. The one thing that neither one of us liked was that we were going to be stuck in San Jose, and the price of living was going sky high.

It would be too easy for me to fall back into my hustling mode because of all the people I knew. I tried through my probation not to do any dealing; money dictated my life and pulled me in a couple times, making big deals for the Mexican Mafia. How could I be so naive as to do that again and jeopardize my family?

Living, working, and being poor wasn't for me. I did what I had to do to give my family what they needed. Sometimes the life you know is all you need. Looking back, I should have been a little proud of myself. I have made myself into a carpenter with Randy's help.

I still felt that music was the high in my life, and it had been three or four years since I had done music. I didn't even listen to it that much during those times, except for at home with the kids. It had taken me years to get over not doing music anymore and look at myself again as worthy because I did enjoy making beautiful decks, awnings, and fences; they were beautiful, and there was a certain amount of accomplishment in learning how to create those masterpieces.

I had reinvented myself, and there was a certain amount of pride about that. There was also a sadness that I carried. Me and Pat discussed the offer, and she was worried about how it would take over our lives just like music did. She didn't like carpentry like she loved music, so our decision was to not accept the offer.

## Letter Number Two

I get the mail, and I see that it's from the County of Santa Clara Judicial Department. I'm shaking in my boots because these never come with good news. It informs me that I have a warrant for my arrest and I must turn myself in. Here we go again.

The first thing I did was call my probation officer and ask him how I violated probation. We had discussed the fact that I still smoked weed and that he would ignore it in the urine tests. He had no authority to make such a deal. When my file was pulled as a random check from his superiors it revealed my cannabis usage and that's why I violated my probation requirements.

The warrant had been issued. I had two days with the warning that if I was stopped on the street or in my car, I would go to jail. Now I had to tell my family that, over the last couple years, I have become a carpenter and regained a little bit of my confidence. Receiving this news totally shook me up.

My voice trembled and cracked as I told Pat I had to go to jail. I remember us hugging each other and sobbing. I had prayed and prayed to never go back. I have made promises to my wife and my kids that I wouldn't go back to jail, and here it is in my face again. She tried to reassure me that I had the strength to make it through it again.

I was ready to skip town and go on the run, and she said to me, "How does that turn out? For the rest of our lives, we'd be running from the law in exchange for 90 days, or whatever you might get, you've got to turn yourself in. I want you to get out of this. Turn yourself in so you can get out of this." She told me that she doesn't want me to go back into that 'dark place' that I have been in for so long. I hear what she's saying to me, but I'm still scared. I just remade my life, and now it's being interrupted once again. Would I have to start all over again? It was way too much for me to comprehend. I am the biggest critic of myself, and now I was beating myself up if I had to go to jail. What was going to happen with my family?

Pat was working at the time with her mother and her aunt May; it wasn't enough to maintain the lifestyle without both of our incomes. I get a call back from my probation officer, and he tells me that I shouldn't worry because he's working on something; he couldn't give me the details at this time. He couldn't tell me what he was trying to do for me but bad stuff would happen if I didn't turn myself in. At this point, I don't believe in myself, and I sure don't believe in him. I do believe in my family, and I would have to do what was best for them. Regardless of the amount of time it might serve, I settled myself down and prepared to go to jail, not knowing how long I would have to be there.

## We're Going to Jail

Approaching this chapter is a little difficult because it's talking about one of the lowest times in my life, and to bring it back up again makes me feel 'some kind of way'. It amazes me the strength that I and Pat had to make it through some of these trials of life. We were each other's rock; we always knew we could go to one another.

I was all alone; I could not help myself or my family, and that left me in a hole that I couldn't climb out of. On my way to jail I couldn't see any future for myself anymore. Though I didn't know how long I would be in jail; I had to turn myself in. I wanted this to be the beginning of us getting out of this situation; they have been messing with me my whole life. I couldn't see it ending because though I couldn't change my color. I realized that I could change my attitude.

I was young and had a big ego. I had much to overcome and a lot of hard work to do. Me and Pat were emotionally wrecked, and the kids weren't happy that I was going to have to go to jail. We tried to explain to them the best that we could, but the kids were mad at both of us.

I knew that this was going to scare them in a way that they would probably carry with them for the rest of their lives. I had done it; I had made them feel this way. It tore me in half, along with the fear that I had no idea who I was. It seems like over my life I've always been searching to define who I am, and right when I think I know, something happens. Pat always reminded me of who I was and kept me from going over the deep end.

This time was different; I didn't know how long I was going to be in there.
So that really had me going. I was holding all of it in, hoping that no one could
really see the scared little boy. I felt like it was all out of my control. I was
frightened, feeling like a failure, still putting the front on, 'I can handle it'. That's
what I wanted everyone to think.

I couldn't figure out what was best for me. How can I do that for my family?
All my confidence I had gained was gone. The night before I turned myself in, I
spent time with the kids and the rest of the night with Pat. We cried, made love,
cried again, cuddled, and talked into the early morning.

I don't believe we got any sleep that night. Turning myself in to be locked up
was the hardest thing I ever had to do in my life.

## They Finally Got Me

It's the morning, and I have to turn myself in, and my whole family is
emotional. It's time for me to leave, and all of the crying and emotional pain
that was going on was intense. I had to turn myself in. If I didn't, I would create
another problem.

I'm getting out of the car when she grabs me and tells me that she's there for
me and that she's 'got my back.' I shouldn't worry about our relationship; she
still believed in me; she had made all of that perfectly clear the night before.

She wanted me to get it in my head; she could see the turmoil going on in
my brain and that I'd been taken down a couple notches. I had a lot going on
in those moments; I took about a hundred steps before I walked in the door.
I would have to compose myself. You're going to jail; you've got to be 'hard'.
At least that's what I thought at the time, and I hadn't awakened that tough
guy animal in me since I was a teenager. The way I thought about it was that
a prisoner has to pay two sentences: the time you spend in jail and then how
people treat you on the outside because of the things you've done.

Pat was going to have to tell her family and my family that I was in jail and
that they finally got me. She told me what she thought her parents would say:
"We told you so, he was no good," and for her parents, me going to jail made
them right because that's the way they wanted to look at it; they didn't want to
look at the family. We had created the harmony that my family enjoyed. They
always questioned our ability to raise our kids, and me going to jail made them
righteous, you know.

This wasn't my first time going to jail; the other times I knew exactly how
long I was going to be there. This time was different. I was going to be waiting
to hear from the people in charge, and we all know how long things can take
when you're dealing with the government.

The other times that I have been locked up, I just slept and fasted and didn't
really eat their food; this time I was going to have to eat their nasty ass food.
A week goes by and I still haven't eaten anything, and I'm starting to feel it.

I bought me a jar of Skippy peanut butter, and that's what I ate the rest of the time that I was in there. Two weeks go by, and I finally get a message that I have a meeting with my probation officer coming up. I don't want to get my hopes up too high; I need to know how long I'm going to be here. I talked to Pat and the kids at least once a day.

Now, this is one of the things that was so special about my wife. While I'm locked up, she's called everyone that she can that has anything to do with my case and talked to my probation officer, trying to persuade him to be lenient with me.

She lets me know that she's talked to him, that he's worked something out, and that I will find out when he shows up.

It hit me really hard that someone else had the power to affect my life in any way they felt was right. I did this to myself and to my family, and over the time I was in jail, I admitted that to myself and tried to learn how to live with it and do better. That old saying popped into my brain: "A Hard Head Makes a Soft Behind." I don't know if that truly fits my situation but that's what got me through those days in jail. I wasn't going to be hard-headed anymore; I could only pray.

## Give Us Free

I've been in for about 3 weeks, and finally my probation officer shows up. I am so nervous because this man holds my future in his hands.

As I'm trembling inside my body, I'm trying to be cool on the outside, like everything's all right, even though I'm screaming at the top of my lungs. Silently inside every word he says is like a drum beat in my brain. It only finally gets to the part where he tells me that I will be sentenced in a few weeks and that I will be getting out of the San Jose city jail now. The arrangement that he explains to me is that I would probably get up to 6 months in another location. Although he was trying to soften the blow, it was up to a new judge now how much time I would get but I would be off of probation.

I didn't realize how big of a gesture that was. I was told that I could get two and a half more years of probation. I knew that I couldn't handle that, so his news was big, and I was getting out of this place. All I had to do now was get home and wait for a court date. At least I am a free man for awhile. Eventually they were going to be sending me to Elmwood. I didn't know much about Elmwood then, but I was going to find out.

I go home, and it's a joyful time that I'm back in the house. My sentence date is still hanging over me, and with each passing day, the tension gets a little thicker. I had to work through some serious emotions. I had a lot of anger and no one to blame but myself.

It's important to be good to yourself so that you can be good to someone else. You don't realize that until you are good with yourself.

A month and a half goes by, and I finally get my court date. During this time I have just tried to make as much money as I could. I am hoping and praying that my family can make it through this next phase of my incarceration.

I go to court, and for once, the judge is a little more human than the rest of the judges I've had. He gives me a 120-day sentence, and at the end of my time in jail, I will be off probation for good. He made reference to all of my character witness statements that Pat had provided the court. The judge said that I had more than 10 different character witnesses who spoke very highly of me and had convinced him to give me a lighter sentence.

Pat had gotten statements from Randy, the guy I was working for, my mom, several people that I had worked with over the years, and even the doctor that got our kids here to write one. I mean, she went all out, and her efforts improved my situation. Now that is, 'having my back'.

Well, the day finally approaches, and it's time to say goodbye again. The kids are not happy; they don't understand, and we don't understand. We're not much help to them in processing this whole thing.

Just like the first time I said goodbye to them, we're all emotional wrecks. I kissed them all goodbye, and Pat dropped me off at the intake center. I was not arrested then. Well, that wasn't a good day to be turning myself in. I waited for 4 hours, and then they told me to come back the next day. I would have to go through this whole emotional thing all over again. I didn't want to face my family.

I walked the streets for hours. It bothered me so bad that I finally rode the bus home. We were all emotionally spent. The family tried to comfort me and assure me that they will always be in my corner. None of us could see the future, but I could feel the love and hope they had that everything would be all right.

## Camp Elmwood

The next day comes. It's time to turn myself in; this time they arrest me. One

of the things that I remember was about 15 people waiting like myself, and I realized how much your clothing tells who you are. People from all walks of life—motorcycle riders, businessmen, and street kids—have identifiable personalities until they tell you to take your clothes off. We're all standing there naked; the vulnerability has rolled in now. It's time to be embarrassed. As they ask you to bend over and spread your cheeks, they look up your ass. All designed to keep drugs out of the place and also to get you in line.

Because you're getting ready to be controlled every minute of the day, you have to go do all of the paperwork to find out your medical conditions, things that you are allergic to, and different stuff like that.

From my visits to the jail, I learned a few things, and I promised myself I wasn't going to eat peanut butter ever again after the two weeks that I ate it in jail last time. I told them I was allergic to peanut butter because I heard from someone that it was a big part of the diet.

After your intake, they put you on lock down for 72 hours to determine if you were violent or out of your mind. After 72 hours, it's time to go to 'genpop'. Now you're allowed to go into the 'general population' of the jail.

The clothes that we had to wear were kind of like a surgeon's clothes, highly worn out; they barely stayed up on you. The clothes were a crying shame. I noticed that some people had blue jeans on. I later found out that those people were called trustees, and that's how they were identified in the jail; a trustee was appointed by the officers. They were inmates who were trusted a little bit more than just the regular inmates and had a little more privilege, more visiting time, and better clothes. You had to work for it, and I knew that I wanted that position after the second week I was in there.

Elmwood was kind of what I imagined the army base to be: about 12 to 15  long bungalows where the convicts slept, and then a variety of smaller places. Wood shop, metal shop, classrooms, and the mess hall where you go to eat. Inside the bungalow were bunk beds about 30 inches wide. There were 60 inmates, about 10 toilets, 10 urinals, and about five showers. There was also a little area where you could make hot water for a cup of soup, hot chocolate, coffee, or tea. You have to provide for yourself; the only thing that was free in there was the water.

After 72 hours, I was finally put into my assigned bungalow and was able to call. We're both still shaken up from this experience, and we didn't talk too long because we didn't know what to say to each other. I told her about my living situation and how horribly it smelled in there, sleeping with 60 other men. It was unbearable at this point. I told her I was going to make it through this, and for her not to worry, I was lying to her and myself because I had so much fear wrapped up inside of me that I didn't know what to say.

## We Are Family

The first thing I can say is that sleeping was incredibly hard. The constant noise was driving me crazy. I had a lot of adjusting to do, and not having smoked a cigarette in a week was driving me nuts too.

To my surprise, I got a visit from two family members who were incarcerated as well. *Papoose* and *Little Bubba* were Pat's cousins. They looked up to us like an uncle and aunt. I hear their big voices hollering, "Uncle D!"

I am truly surprised I wouldn't have to take this journey by myself. They knew about the system very well; they had spent most of their teenage years in juvenile detention and progressed to jails after they were 18. They had a reputation on the streets, but I didn't really know much about it until other inmates were telling me about their adventures. They were well known in the world of criminals. I say that lightly because I never looked at myself as a criminal, and three-quarters of the people in there had gotten caught up in a variety of small crimes.

Over the couple days that I was in there, I discovered that there was a 'pod boss' who ran our bungalow. The pod boss controlled the TV. I thought the TV might be an escape, but watching it and all of those people talking just made me have more anxiety.

My nephews walked me over to the pod boss. Let him know that I was their uncle and that, "Nothing better happen to me." If there was any 'funk', he'd better let them know. That's when I realized how much juice they really had. I have watched plenty of movies, and this was a scene right out of one of them.

Over the next week, they schooled me on the things that were going on in Elmwood. I asked them for their advice on some ideas that I had about how to *move right* in this place. They gave me a pack of cigarettes and told me that each cigarette was worth three items: a cup of soup, pastry items, and things like that. If I sold at least 15 of them, I could fill up my drawer with food. I was hesitant to take the cigarettes; I hadn't smoked in a week.

I left all the money with Pat. You have to do what you have to do to survive. Having those cigarettes meant that I had to learn all the ways of smuggling because you were constantly checked, and if they smelled cigarette smoke on you, it would be an immediate shakedown of your possession. Fear comes with the hustle game, and I knew one thing about myself: I was a hustler.

## The Hustler In Me

They explain to me how to cut your coat with the razor blade and hide your cigarettes in your sleeve. Cut the top of your pants so that you could slip money into them and other different ways that you could smuggle stuff.

I didn't want to put my wife in jeopardy. But what I didn't know is that Pat was compiling her own information on all of those different methods of sneaking contraband into jail. The other women who had partners incarcerated informed her of several different ways that she could sneak money into me.

She already knew the penalty for sneaking money into jail, which was that you would not be able to visit anymore. If you sneak drugs into the system, you would get an extended sentence, just like if they caught you on the street.

I held off on having her do anything for a couple weeks. She insisted on keeping it up so that I could eat better. She would roll the money up really tight and, when we held hands, pass it to me. When you go back inside, they don't pat you down; they strip you down, and you have to shake your clothes. If you put anything in them, it will fall out.

Well, I figured out a way to get the money in. I wore two pairs of socks, and I would slide the money in between the socks as far down as I could. When they said, "Shake it", I would hold on to the money so it didn't fall out. I've been holding my breath the whole time this has been going on because if you get caught, you get punished.

Just like in the drug game, you have to make one big purchase so that you can come up. Back then, I believe cigarettes were probably around $3 a pack; in jail, they were $20 a pack. If you sell 10 cigarettes, you get 30 items. Three items per cigarette was one of my first hustles there at Elmwood.

In the first couple weeks of being there, I was highly emotional and felt very lost. Hustling was something familiar. It filled a part of me. I fell right in. It motivated me. I knew I could hustle. Now I had to focus on finding the strong person I knew I was. Facing obstacles and achieving them has always taken me to a higher place. To a better understanding of who I am, my strengths, and my ability to see things through a clearer lens. To me, every experience is a lesson. What was I supposed to learn from this experience?

Through our life experiences, we are asked to deal with how we look at ourselves internally. Internal self-identification and external self-identification sometimes don't match up. From our experience, we hope to come to terms with ourselves and deal with who we really are.

Fear grows in darkness. It's essential that you have light and transparency, and I was trying to get that clarity about what's really going on with me. I tried to live my life the way other people consider right, and failed.

I worked hard in life and could never get ahead without dealing. I didn't let it get to my inner soul while thinking about it. Was life unfair because of the color of my skin? Did I lack the opportunities that most American kids have? It lurked there underneath the surface of my thoughts. I used that pain to justify my actions and knew now wasn't the time for me to turn over a new leaf.

I was going to have to survive in this place for the next three and a half months. I talked to my kids every night and cried after it every time. I missed being a father, and it was starting to occur to me. That's all I needed to be; I just had to get out of this mess. Now that I'm in jail hustling, is that who I really am? Is that all I am?

## Working Her Magic

One day I got a *slip*. A slip is a piece of paper that is considered your past. If you get stopped, you show them your slip. I was asked to go to the administration office. I get to the office, and I'm sitting down. They call me into the room, and the captain and the sergeant are sitting there.

In his first words, he says, "Hall, you've got a hell of a wife," and I'm wondering with a little anger. 'What the hell do you know about my wife?' That's what I said on the inside. I paused my reaction and let him finish talking. He said to me that he had received 27 calls from my wife, and he finally called her back, and she convinced him to just sit down and find out who I really was.

A big sigh of relief came over me, and I'm thinking in the back of my brain, 'What has Pat been up to again, working her magic?

They let me know that I might be in jail and that there were things that I could do without just sitting around. There were classes available, and they gave me a list of jobs that I could go out for. Since I had already worked in the laundry during my work release, I chose that job. I started the next day, and I also signed up for a culinary arts class along the same lines as what I took in high school. They let me know that this wasn't a normal procedure, because my wife was so convincing, they were going to take a chance on me. What they told me was, "Don't let your wife or your family down; here's a chance to make this experience a little different."

## I Got A Job

What I realized was that Pat's ability to find out about things was amazing. She was going to make my life in here better because half the inmates didn't know anything about the stuff that I was told or given the opportunity to learn about.

I had an understanding with the captain and the sergeant. All I had to do was try to strengthen myself for myself and my family. That meeting with them gave me a little hope; it parted the dark clouds just a little bit.

The next day, I went to work. Luckily for me, the guy that I did my work release with was still the supervisor. They used civilians for those types of positions. Fortunately, the last crew was rotating out. He made me the lead man, which made me have to answer a lot of questions from the other inmates. My story was legit, so it didn't get ugly.

It was important for them to understand. I didn't want to be known as a snitch. Bad things could happen. A couple more weeks go by, and I get a job in the kitchen. Now I do not have to eat any of the meals that are made for the inmates. The cooking crew I was on made the food for the Correctional Officers, or 'C.O's. You had to be trusted, and staying busy, having goals, and meeting them in jail lifted me up a little bit.

I couldn't control anything that was going on at home; things were getting very tight. Pat informed me on her first visit that we were losing the house, which took me back into a dark hole.

We hadn't seen each other in a month, and she had to let me know that it took great strength for her to do that. She thought I might have to be restrained or something because I was going to go crazy; she hadn't told me on our phone conversations, she had to see me face-to-face. She had to let me know; she said that she had to work some things out with her mother. Pat had asked her mother to borrow money; her mother said, "No."

This was the beginning of her getting us under her control. Pat was always good at navigating through our situations, and I prayed that she could this time. The hardest thing for me was not being able to solve the problem; we've never been in this bad of shape before.

The only thing I knew was that it was all my fault. Me and Pat got into a couple arguments over the phone, with me trying to tell her how to fix stuff, but I wasn't there. I couldn't tell her how to do anything; through my guilt, I was an asshole. She didn't appreciate it. She didn't come to visit me for a week until after she got everything situated, which was now our new life. She worked at the Cupertino facility for her mother; she had De with her, and Laticia ended up moving in with Norma, her aunt. My family is split up. I don't have a home to go to when I do get out of here, and I'm trying not to feel so guilty, but it was all my fault. I knew that whatever they were going through was because of my actions. All I could do now is keep busy and try to make the days go faster because my wife is mad at me and my family is all split up.

The captain and sergeant gave me another job. Now I have three jobs and a cooking class. My new job is passing out the slips every night for 2 hours. Passing out slips, which were telling people that they were being released. I went to every barracks that they had, which made my hustling a little easier. Now that I have that pass, my mind goes into overdrive, and I figure out ways to make money in jail.

One thing I found out about having that job was that when you get that slip, you don't care about anything else, so you give all of your canteen away. I was on the receiving end of a lot of those. I had a lot of stuff I didn't want much of. I ate every day when I cooked for the Corrections Officer. So all of this stuff was extra. I would have to escort them to the office in order for the inmates to be released. I was like that angel, bringing them a gift or something—I don't really know—and I didn't turn anything down.

These are the things I was up to while I was in jail. I started making a little money behind them. The thing that surprised me was how much cash was in jail. I would sell ham sandwiches, cookies, cigarettes, and food items. I would only sell the ham sandwiches for cash. I made and smuggled a lot of sandwiches.

Here we go again. People would come to me, and I could get them what they needed. I was doing this for my family; at least that's what I told myself. This hustling thing was addictive to me, for sure.

It kept my mind off of all of my other problems and kept me from going crazy. I couldn't do anything in anyone else's life but my own. I had to do this so I could get back to my family. I didn't like the situation. I felt like my whole life had been taken from me.

Some people enjoy the time away from the 'rat race', as they called it. To me, this was a rat race, and I wanted a one-way ticket out of this hellhole. I used to wonder if this is how slaves felt when they wanted to leave the plantation. Their family was there; it was hell; they had to stay or put their family in danger trying to escape.

I'm on a mission to make as much money as I can, and because I have this trustee job, I get more visiting time on Wednesdays and one day on the weekend.

After Pat stopped being mad at me because I was *acting the fool*, she didn't miss a visit, and when she would come, I would sneak her money. She just shook her head at me and said, "Please don't get more time." I promised her I wouldn't; I didn't have too much faith in myself at that time. What I did believe was that I had the power to change this.

Pat believed I could. Her belief in me got me to start making a plan for our future. I was going to change everything up.

I was going to be on the straight and narrow. I'm walking around with two thoughts in my head: on the one hand, I'm hustling and putting myself in danger, and on the other hand, I'm trying to make a plan.

I started going to the library and using the computer for the first time. Back then computers weren't part of our lives like they are now. I had shipped hundreds of personal computers when I was working at Apple and had never used one. I started searching for jobs in other states. I had to get away from the life that I had lived in San Jose. I thought moving somewhere else where I only had to depend on myself and not hustle might be the way to go.

## Pat's New Job

Pat had worked in electronics just like I did in the earlier years and worked for her mother part-time at her care facilities. She didn't find much pleasure in it at first. Then her heart started growing for the individuals that she was taking care of. These care homes are places where parents, who cannot handle the physical or mental handicaps of their children, can have a place stay.

We didn't know this type of place existed, and it was hard for us to accept the fact that parents were giving up their children. For me and Pat, that would never be a possibility.

We had discussions about whether, if our children were born with those issues, we would still keep them and care for them. The care that my wife was giving was excellent. She really put her heart into it, and considering the place that she was in, she was a soldier and carried on.

I'm glad she found that part of her heart because, despite all the stuff we have been through, caring for other people always took her mind off of her immediate problems. Now, when we talk, she tells me about problems with people she worked with. Others would not do the job right, which meant clients wouldn't get good care, and Pat wanted to make sure that everyone was treated with respect. She really took her new job seriously, and I could really see just how much love she was capable of giving.

## Gotta Keep Busy

At this point in my incarceration, I'm working in the laundry, the kitchen, and the front office, and I have a cooking class. I can't control the things that happen to us, only the way we react to them. I'm hustling in every way that I can. I'm selling ham sandwiches and cookies from the kitchen. I'm selling cigarettes, and I make handmade crosses out of pieces of sticks that I find on the ground and carve them down with a smuggled razor blade. In prison, the weekends when you get a visit are most important. People like to give gifts to their family. I sold a lot of crosses. I had several pictures drawn for me that I gave to my wife. I couldn't believe all of the talented people that were locked up—some great artists. I still have some of those artworks to this day.

## Drama In the Bungalow

I kept myself busy as much as I could. I was hustling well enough that I was giving Pat money to put up to save for us when I got out. There was always drama in the bungalows—a lot of temper tantrums. People's girlfriends breaking up with them and a lot of other different reasons for the anger.

One time it was directed my way, so I had to prepare myself for battle. The word had been put out that this guy was looking for me with bad intentions. It kind of knocked me off balance because I hadn't had a fight in years. I referenced some old prison movies, put a lock in the sock and was ready for battle.

Before he got to me, my nephews found out about it and 'jacked him up'. That was the only time I was really scared in there. I really appreciate my nephews for the rest of their lives; unfortunately, neither one of them got to live to be old men; their way of life would eventually take them out.

## Got to Get Fitted

Working in the laundry also gave me the opportunity to make money there. Each week, you were allowed what they called 'your roll.' Which was underwear, socks, new pants, and a top. I passed out the roll, and for a little extra, I can get you a better pair of blue jeans. It was a booming business because everybody who got a visitor wanted to look their best, and I had the best-dressed crew in the jail.

I was kind of allowed to do that because people wanted to work for me. My crew looked so nice, and my boss liked it because he never had to look for workers anymore. We got the new blue jeans straight off the truck, and that's what my crew would be wearing. It wasn't hard for me to get people to work in the laundry. You wouldn't believe how much clothes meant in jail. For them to be in new clothes was *money*.

I was researching jobs with my new skill as a carpenter. I knew that I couldn't live in San Jose anymore. I knew that by living there, I would probably fall back into hustling. It was time for a big change. I thought leaving and moving to another state might be the answer.

Arizona was booming at this time. There were a lot of jobs and affordable housing. I had sent out a bunch of resumes at that time, when faxing was the thing. I got a couple people to respond to me. That was my big plan. Now I had to talk to Pat about this whole thing. I had my mind set. That's what we had to do in order for us to have a life.

## Shining All the Time

I'm about 2 months into my sentence, and I'm doing pretty well. I'm keeping busy so that I don't trip over this stuff that I can't control. Pat's doing well in her new job. She's finding it satisfying now.

I'm going to be graduating from the cooking class, and my family gets to come to the ceremony. I'm doing well at this point. The Correction Officers like me. I'm known by the inmates; if you want something, find Doc; he can get it for you. What amazed me about myself is that I was able to adapt and try to get all I could out of this experience. I was working on myself constantly, reading, and trying to improve my outlook on life. I had to accept things the way they were and deal with reality, not fantasy. For the first time in my life, I cut my mustache off. I had the clean-face look, and my wife was definitely surprised. That was the last time I cut it off because she liked it.

## Laticia Is Not A Baby

Laticia, who was a young teen-ager, did not visit me in the first part of my sentence. She was now living with her aunt and had a hell of a lot more freedom than me and Pat gave her. She was really feeling herself, and I understood why she was basically taking care of herself.

My actions had knocked the childhood out of her; this was her new reality. Laticia was so angry with me, and she informed me in numerous ways that I am no longer your 'baby girl.' She also worked for Dorothy at that time; she paid rent. What I noticed was that she knew a lot of the people who were locked up.

It made me take a step back and ask myself, "What was my daughter really up to?" I did a little investigating and asked those people that she had acknowledged, what the relationship was between them. I found out she wasn't out there sexually; I had raised a little hustler. I'm doing my 'dad thing,' trying to protect her, and I'm locked up.

I had to let that go and promise myself that I would get my family back together. I blamed myself for everything. I fought depression every week and was kind of unsure about myself. I was wondering if I could put my family back together. I doubted who I was and if I had the strength to put that picture of my family back in my mind. I had to keep telling myself, "Pat believes in you, so believe in yourself; you can't let her down."

Her belief in me was my motivation to make it out of this nightmare and to repair what I had broken. I taught my kids to "don't lie to themselves." I had to follow my own advice, forgive myself, and 'own up' to my mistakes.

## Broken Heart

Those last chapters that I wrote really hurt my soul. I thought I had gotten past all of that stuff that went on when I felt like a loser. This world without Pat is really strange, and I have gone through many different phases of grief, feeling sorry for myself and angry at the world.

The loneliness is hard to deal with. For 50 years, I had my best friend with me. These are some of the thoughts I've had over the last 10 months. I'm trying to do better and get on with my life.

## In My Feelings

Let me ask you what it takes. What would it take for me to be free from this

grief? Everyone has forgotten about me, and I feel compelled to speak up. It's like being in the cemetery of the living. Now that she's gone, you get to see everyone just continue to live while they act like you're dead, and it hurts.

I felt like I've been left on the shore of a deserted island. People don't truly break if there's someone there to help them heal. When someone you love becomes a memory, that memory becomes a treasure to hold and never let go of. Everybody's healing looks different. I can't go to somebody and be like, "Help me heal." You've got to go on that journey by yourself. I'm a flower in the middle of a storm. I've had a couple pedals knocked off, and I'm still here. Healing is a journey and a process, and nobody can put a time limit on it. The most help I got was from my children; they are my lifeboat. Focusing on my children helps me. I just try to be a good dad and be there for my children. We all have a big hole in our hearts. We're leaning on each other to get through this grief.

To me, being a father was the most important thing in life. Growing up without a father felt like you were always missing something. On some levels, I'm glad I didn't have him, because if he had been in my life, I wouldn't be the person that I am today. Pat's being a mother was a miracle in her life, and after that, she knew she was God's child.

## A Combination of Thought

Ever since the day that she left, I can't find myself. I get lost inside my body. A part of me has died. Grief doesn't keep a schedule; it shows up when it wants to, and when it does show up, I try not to let it consume me. I really want to believe that there's something greater on the other side and that we will be together again. I'd like to get to the place where I'm excited about life again.

When Pat and I met, we were young and naive; we believed in each other, and we planted a tree. The tree grew, and so did we. Would it bear fruit? We didn't know. We believed in each other and what God told us in our prayers at night. Keep living and loving, and everything will turn out all right. Now, two young trees have grown. Sprinkled with kindness and nourished with care they are the fruits of our labor. My family is not only my greatest weakness but also my greatest strength. A father's job is to protect what gives him meaning.

When someone is grieving, it's like a big sign to stay away. People don't know how to deal with grief; they don't have the right words to say, so they don't say anything. Life doesn't last forever, which is why it's so precious. We recently celebrated our 50th anniversary. It's the what-ifs that always haunt me. What if you were still here?

## The Routine

When we were young, someone said to me, "I don't like the routine of marriage." That's what I loved about it—the routine, the constant knowing that someone loved you. Let me elaborate. You get up every morning and brush your teeth. If you don't, your whole day is messed up. What I had for the past 50 years was waking up in love.

**The Routine:**

To wake up to someone else's concern for you.
Waking up knowing where I'm at is where I want to be.
When I had an itch, she scratched my beard.
Doing the little things to get her to smile.
Grabbing her soft hands and putting them on my cheek.
Me holding her steady as she tiptoed to give me a big hug.
We both loved being in love.
Never forgetting where it started.
The tender kisses on the lips and the cute names that we called each other.
Tell each other we love each other every day.
Find ways to be happy.
Never make excuses not to be happy.
Remember, you can't be in love unless you're vulnerable to each other.
Always have faith in one another.
Always be willing to hear each other.
Pick the other one up when one is down.
Always be willing to let each other grow.
To remember how much I mean to my family and how much they mean to me.
To live in the moment and not in the past.
To see it clearly so that we could get it right.
Marriage's DNA is friendship.
"Love is like two pieces of ice. At first, they're rigid and don't fit together; if you take some time, those pieces of ice melt and you become one," said TD Jakes.
Sleep is the only comfort I get, and when I wake up, I feel like I'm in a *sci-fi* movie—a bad sci-fi movie. Just the thought of never seeing her face again collapses my ego, but there is some relief in writing our story. She would be happy, and I'm pleased with that. To be with someone for such a long time, you take for granted just how well they know you.

When my mom passed, I realized that nobody knew me from birth. Now I have the same feeling because she knew everything about me. Things that I didn't even know about myself.

'God, I understand that this is part of the journey.' But damn, in the last month of her life, we talked about this and tried to get an understanding of what I was going to go through. I never imagined the depths of sorrow and not having the comfort of her smile and the joy that her laugh would bring me. It's a strange new world, and I have to take it day by day. Let's see what tomorrow brings.

## Day Pass

The first step was admitting what I had done. The second step was getting into the right mindset. How do I get the shame off my back? I kept busy and tried to strengthen myself. I lifted weights for the first time in my life every day, surprising myself that it was something that I could never keep up with on the outside.

I was keeping myself busy with all of the jobs and school when it was time for me to graduate from the class. I had never been in the top five of any other class I ever took. I surprised myself by getting the second-highest score in the class. Laticia, Pat, and De were coming to the graduation ceremony, and I was ready to see my kids. De wasn't able to come all the time, and Laticia didn't want to come; her mother was making her come this time. I was excited to finally see my kids.

It was about 20 of us who were going to be able to see our family that was graduating from the cooking class. The last time De visited me, he was really upset. He went to hug me, and the C.O. told him he couldn't do it. He walked in with an attitude and was determined to hug his dad this time; he was allowed to, and everything went fine.

Laticia wasn't as mad at me as she was on her first visit; she still had a little attitude toward me that I was kind of used to. Laticia was always real about her feelings, and when she was upset with you, it was hard for her to hide it. We had a good visit, and she was proud of me that I graduated from the class. About 20 of us got certificates of completion. I did get a diploma in high school, but I didn't walk the stage, so this was my moment. It was great to show the kids that I had finished this class, and I hoped that it would be a motivator for them to succeed.

I have about 30 days left on my sentence. A couple days went by, and the captain called me to his office. I thought, 'The jig was up.' I thought maybe he found out all of the different hustling schemes I was doing, and to my surprise, they praised me for how well I had done in the time I was there. They told me that I had gained a day pass. I didn't know what that was; it gave me the opportunity to leave at 8:00 in the morning and come back at 5:00p.m.

Of course, when you get back, you will be drug tested. I didn't care;
just to get a little break from this madness and be with my wife and kids
meant everything. The day came for my day pass. Pat picked me up, and the
importance of having my freedom came rushing back to me. It was emotional
because we both have been through a lot over these months, and once we got
together, we couldn't hold it in. We cried it out and got back to the time that we
once had. A lot of things have happened in the months I've been gone.

Pat has been working with her mother, and there is always some drama.

Now her grandmother needed her, so she quit working for her
mother and started taking care of her grandmother. At that
point, De is living with Sandra's Pat's aunt, and Laticia is with
her aunt, Norma. I'm trying to figure out how I'm going to get my
family back together. I've got 30 days to figure this out, and with
Granny being sick, I know that Pat's not going to want to move
to Arizona. I had to come up with another plan. I didn't know
what to do at this point, but I had a little confidence in myself.
I've been working hard on my self-esteem. I started sending out
resumes in San Jose. I knew I had to get out of there, so this was
something I could do temporarily. I could have gone back to
work for Randy; he really wanted me to buy the company from
him and was really disappointed. I didn't want to go through that mental battle
again, trying to figure out if I should do it or not. I knew that if I went back, I
might never leave San Jose.

## Short Timer

I have about 2 weeks to go before I get out of this place. Anxiety is starting to
creep back into my life. I have a fear of the future, and I'm not really sure how
I'm going to get my family back. I find out that they towed my Volkswagen away,
so now I don't have a house or a car, I don't have a job, and I cannot stay at
Sandra's house or Pat's aunt's house. I'm going to have to move in with my mom
for the first time since I left her house way back when.

The anticipation of getting out is starting to get to me. The fear of the future
is great. I can't really figure out how I'm going to make things better. I have been
put in my place, I have been humbled, and I was really unsure of myself. They
said that the last few weeks were really emotional, and I was a *short-timer*.

Now I was experiencing the doubt and anger of not having the life that I
had created before. The fear of getting back on track without going back to
hustling made me have all kinds of thoughts, and none of them were good. In
the last couple weeks I was in jail, the anxiety was so great that I started having
flashbacks about my childhood. I fought so many silent battles that I really
didn't share them with anyone, not even my family. I didn't think anyone could
feel my pain, and being in jail that long gave me a lot of time to think.

I was always trying to be the strong person—you know, the big brother, the husband, the uncle, the son. That, 'everything's fine' guy.

## Flashback

I had a lot of internal stuff come bubbling up, so let me tell you about those nightmares. When I was a kid, I used to get splitting headaches that felt like I was in hell. After that, I got nosebleeds that had to be cauterized, and the dreams I had in jail were of me with blood all over the place. In the dream, the bleeding never stopped, so it seemed like something was always going on with me. All I tried to do as a kid was find happiness.

I busted my two front teeth out on the bicycle going down the hills in San Francisco. The point of impact when I knocked them out played over and over in my head. Knocking my teeth out caused me a lot of humiliation because I had two silver caps right in the front. They used to say, "Hi ho silver!"

All I did was fight; that was my mentality, and being sad was my friend. Being in jail had brought back those childhood feelings once again, all alone. What I did realize was how badly I needed Pat.

From our conversations, she realized how much she needed me. We are 20 years into this marriage, and our love just got stronger because sex has jumped to another level. We truly felt like we were making love; it was always good, but now it was great. The absence had made our hearts grow fonder.

As we have seen in this world, not all couples get to that level. We knew that we had something special. I don't know about a lot of things that Pat went through when she was a kid, but from what she did tell me, her mother had her at a very young age. That's why she had such a great relationship with her grandparents; her mom was way too young to be a mother. All through our marriage, Pat and her mother's relationship was a true 'love and hate' situation.

I do know that being in foster care tried to suck the love out of her, and that's why she was such a rebel and would do anything for the people that she felt loved her. Being in foster care is where she got to learn about white people in a more sincere way and not just from television, so being prejudiced against someone for being a color wasn't in our DNA.

## Time To Get Out

It's the day I get to leave this place. I haven't gotten any sleep in the last couple days, waiting for this day to come. I've never been more afraid of my future than I was then. The thought of not having a home to go to or a car to get around just depresses me more and more every time I think about it.

I'm trying to convince myself that I can put my family back together. I'm very unsure of myself, as I have promised. I wouldn't hustle anymore. How was I going to make this happen? I can't work in the job market like I used to.

I'm a felon. "What am I going to do?" I ask myself over and over, trying to hold back the tears of my confusion. I'm excited about leaving this place so I can begin this journey without knowing what's ahead of me.

All I had were the words of my white grandfather to give me strength; he always used to tell me, "If it's meant for you, nobody can take it from you, so go and get it!" I knew that I would need more than some good words to make it through the next chapter of my life. I finally got the slip for my release, and it seems like it took them hours to fill out the couple pieces of paper for my release.

Of course, there were some correctional officers who just thought I was a criminal. Another *Nigga*. They had seen thousands and told me they'd see me back there in six months. They made a bet right in front of my face. The captain and the sergeant walked up and told me that they better not ever see me back there because I had everything a man needs.

A woman who loves me and some great kids. I promised them that they would never see me again. It wasn't often that they would get that personal with an inmate. Thanks to my wife, as I walked out of the big swinging doors, the next thing I knew, I was running towards the parking lot.

I wanted to get as far away from that place as quickly as I could. To see my wife's smile on her face meant everything. To kiss her tender lips and to smell her aroma. I have been around hundreds of men for months. Yeah, the day passed; the time went by so fast that it seemed like we didn't even have that day. I'm free; no more tickets, no more charges, and I'm off probation. Now we have a whole lot of things to work out.

## Brand New World

Coming back to the world was a little difficult. My family had lives on their own at this point. Laticia was living with her aunt Norm and Pat and De were now staying at her aunt Sandra's house and taking care of her grandmother.

I'm staying at my mother's house again, sleeping on her couch and I have no job. That's the first order of business after spending a little time with my family. Then me and Pat went to a hotel for a couple days and discussed our future. At this point, I didn't really know what we were going to do.

I realize now how scared and confused I was and back in those days, you didn't talk about depression, I did. I felt like I have been knocked off my throne. It took me months to get over the depression of leaving the music, I sunk everything into my family. Eventually I was able to come out of it. Now that I don't have a home, I don't have a car. It's kind of like starting all over again from scratch and having to sleep on my mother's couch every day was a reminder of how low I had come. I didn't have that confidence that I once had. They were missing pieces I was determined to find. I searched for jobs and eventually got a job through a temporary agency.

I was finally making a little money, it only lasted a couple weeks or so and
I'm still spiraling down. In my mind, I felt like my daughter had lost respect
for me and that was eating me up inside. De was still taking karate at the time,
so I was able to take him to his lessons even though I had to ride the bus. He
enjoyed that experience a lot more than I did.

## More Changes

I've been out of jail about a month and a half and I get a knock at the door at
my mom's house and it's my connect, the guy affiliated with the Mexican Mafia.

He says to me that enough time had gone by and was I ready to do business
again, I asked him what he meant by enough time had gone by? He told me
that they were waiting to see if I snitched and I didn't, so they were ready to do
business with me again. He gave me $500 and his phone number. Told me to
give him a call, because of his visit, I had more questions than the obvious.

Question 1: How did you know where my mom lived?
Question 2: How do you know if I snitched or not?
Question 3: Have they been watching me?
Question 4: Was I in too deep and didn't even know it?

I hadn't done business with these people in over a year so I was really
confused. A strange paranoia came over me that was filled with fear. I knew
the reputation of those people. Was I that important now? The next thing for
me to do was let Pat know and she calmed my nerves by reminding me she was
friends with his wife and had been talking to her every now and then over the
last couple years. They found out what was happening with me through his wife.
That didn't answer all of my questions and at that point, I knew I had to make a
change. I'm not making enough money to take care of myself, let alone get my
family back and it's making me more and more depressed.

The world keeps changing. My mother informs me that she and my baby
brother Tony are going to be moving to Sacramento in a month. Now what am
I going to do? I'm sleeping on her couch. I can't keep a steady job. All I can get
now are temporary ones.

My relationship with my daughter is all messed up and now I have to worry
about where I'm going to lay my head. Pat's family was convinced I was no good,
so they were no help. Now I really have to come up with the plan, which gives
me a new reason to be scared.

I would be homeless, with no car to sleep in and nowhere to go. I still carry
the fear of being homeless to this day. At this time in my life my mom is moving,
so I've got to do something. I give Randy a call, my old boss and he's happy to
take me back. I'm working and trying to save as much money as I can, it seems
damn near impossible. This wasn't going to work.

I'm in San Jose, I don't have my family and I can't see in the future how I can get them back.

## Where's My Daughter?

At this point, Pat is still taking care of her grandmother and her family has planned a trip out of state. I believe they went to Louisiana because a lot of Pat's cousins, aunts and uncles live there and are going to be gone for a week or so. Her Aunt Sandra was going to Tahoe with her aunt Norma, so they asked me if I would babysit the house. I didn't have anywhere to sleep, so I said yes.

My mom had moved to Sacramento by this time and where I was going to be staying was around the corner from where Laticia lived, so in the evenings I would try to go over and make our relationship a little better, she was already what I called grown. What did I expect? She was working and paying rent; I wasn't in her life. It took me down a couple more notches, I was determined to gain her love and respect back.

One night I walk around the corner hoping to spend some time with Laticia, when I get there, she's sitting in her aunt Norm's Cadillac listening to music with one of her girl friends. I get a strange feeling and see that she doesn't want to spend any time with me.

I say to myself, "This girl is going to take this Cadillac." So I tell her, "Laticia, do not take this car." She gives me that sweet, innocent look implying, 'I wouldn't do anything like that, Daddy.'

I leave so she can visit with their friend. A half hour later, I get a call from Sandra's son, Jason, who tells me Laticia has taken the car. Back then, we only had beepers. I blew that up. I called every 30 seconds, hundreds of times. I'm thinking about her safety, I'm also feeling how she defines me.

I've prayed that nothing happens to that car; I would have to pay for it. When I don't even have a house or car myself, I'm going nuts. I did not want that responsibility to fall on me. About an hour goes by and I get a call from Jason saying that she's back. At that point, I needed some answers because she had never lied to me like that.

I take off walking to go to where she's at. I'm mad as hell and confused, thinking that because of what I had done by going to jail, I had kind of created this situation. I pray and ask God to give me the strength to get through this conversation without totally going crazy and doing or saying the wrong thing. I knew that this was a crossroads in our relationship.

She's 15 years old and I can push her away forever if I don't handle this situation right. What could I do? She didn't live with me anymore, so punishing her didn't make sense. We had a conversation and she promised me that she would never do anything like that again. In her telling me the story about when she was gone, I could sense an attitude that she still had. I asked her what her attitude was about being the one who stole the car.

She told me, "Yeah, Dad, I didn't get in any accidents and nothing happened to the car until I drove into the driveway."

I saw Jason standing there with the shotgun and he almost made me run into the fence. He scared me and almost made me wreck the car. He didn't have to do that. All I could think of in my mind was that, 'You're so much like your mother.' I wish that she was here. She could handle her daughter, because that night I didn't know who she was.

I'm looking at a young woman who's going to do what she wants to do.

I question myself if I could still be a guiding light for her, or is that all gone now? Going too jail stripped almost everything from me. I felt like a hollow shell with no insides. Everything that I believed about myself was gone. I blamed myself more than I blamed Laticia for taking the car. I felt like it was all my fault. All I wanted was for Pat to come back to town and she would know how to handle it.

## The Big Talk

Pat would be home in a couple days and I would have to tell her about Laticia's adventures. She would know what to do. We always raised our kids together and I needed her advice more than ever.

Laticia's attitude hurt my heart and I could feel the emptiness. Rejection hardened you. I didn't want that to happen to me. I was searching for that love that I had before I went to jail. And I'm telling myself that I could have that back no matter what it took.

I realized that I had to live life and quit expecting it to be how I wanted it to be. I had manifested the other things that I had accomplished in my life. Now it was time for me to manifest my future!

Pat tells me she'll talk to Laticia and I'm hoping that she'll get through to her. I'm not sure where this attitude might take me. During our talk, Pat let me know that she was tired of the situation; she wanted her own house again and was counting on me to make that happen and she was disappointed in me because I hadn't made it happen yet.

Now that I'm out of time, I have to do something to get my family all back together. The distance was tearing us apart. To be truthful, I didn't have any faith in myself, so it was time to dig deep and find that man that I used to be, or better yet, find the strength in the man that I am now. Pat also told me that she was starting to get an attitude and act differently since I hadn't been around as much.

I remember being in panic mode. Pat wasn't happy and I'm losing my kids. My nightmares are coming true unless I do something. And I can't do it through hustling, so the decision was made in my mind to get out of San Jose and see what I could create. Where I'm at, sleeping on other people's couches was driving me crazy.

My mom was in Sacramento and D'Lamont lived in Sacramento and by this time, my baby brother Tony had moved there too. All of my support was gone in San Jose and if I kept living like this, it was going to push me back into hustling. And me and Pat had made the decision: no more drugs, no more dealing. Try to make it the straight way.

## The Big Move

I gave D'Lamont a call; the bond that we had created over the music years was still there and he agreed to let me stay at his house until I got back on my feet. I had a little bit of a plan now, I would have to talk to Pat because I was going to take De with me. He had just gotten out of school for the summer, so I wanted him to come with me to start our new life.

I realized how insecure I was. I knew if I wanted my family, I was going to have to show up. Me and D'Lamont talked regularly until I left San Jose. Through our talks, I started to gain some respect for myself again. He would always say, "You forgot who you were, your 'Doctor D' man." I had to step into my fear so I could move forward. I knew that having my son with me would keep me looking forward; letting him down wasn't an option.

Pat wasn't happy about my plans at first, she realized that we had nowhere else to turn. We took the little money that we had and I bought another Volkswagen bug.

It was a car I didn't have to take to the repair shop; I knew how to work on it. Me and my son packed up the bug and headed to *Sac Town* (Sacramento, California). We were greeted by D'Lamont and his family during the time we played music together.

He had gotten married, had two beautiful daughters, purchased a nice home and had a great job at the Rainbow Bakery. He was doing well and that inspired me to get my family back and have something that resembled what he had. We would talk for hours and those talks helped repair my confidence in myself. De was comfortable; he had gained two more cousins and he was able to see his cousins who lived with his grandmother on a regular basis now.

He was doing great and D'Lamont had a swimming pool. That's what De did all summer, three or four times a day. He loved it.

## Happy Anniversary

Writing this book has been my companion through the grief. It has been almost a year, and this is my first birthday without her. These days coming close to her birthday have been really hard because I always try to do something nice for her. She always celebrated her birthday to the fullest. For her, it was the day she turned 17. Her lucky numbers are 7/11. That birthday gave her freedom. So her birthday was important to her, and she always enjoyed July very much.

Her grandson, Darshan Hall's birthday is two days after hers. Two days after that, 7/15, is our anniversary. That would make this year 51 years together. July was always a happy month. But now that she left on the 17th, I have mixed feelings. Almost a year has gone by, and loneliness is the biggest obstacle at this point. My daughter comes and sees me two or three times a month. And what's so amazing to me?

When she comes and cooks, she wakes the house up like a mother would. The house comes alive. I cherish those days. Missing the grandkids is hard. I've tried to figure out little games to play over FaceTime and am enjoying how smart they are. It's going to be our 51st anniversary. Difficult to think about. I wish she was here. I'm starting to understand that I will miss her for the rest of my life. I will long for her understanding. Her patience and her love to see me as the man I am. A flawed man, but she loved me anyways. Not many people get to say that they were married for 50 years, and I'm very proud of that. To think back on all these memories, it went too fast. I miss you. Happy Birthday and Happy Anniversary Pat! I'll love you forever.

## Got To Get A Job

I was so tired of feeling like a man with no future. I had a chance to regain control of my life. De and I were adjusting to the heat. In Sacramento, it's clear that you have to get your work done early. Then you come out in the evening when it's cool.

I started looking for a job after about a week. I applied to all the fencing companies that I could find. I had a tryout lined up through D'Lamont's brother-in-law, John's boss. Things went well, and I was hired. Things went okay for about a month. I get called in the office and find out that he wants to give me a raise and for me to run the crew.

Of course, I accepted it. But getting this position after only working for a month caused jealousy amongst his other employees. The boss had recognized that I had more experience. John, D'Lamont's, brother-in-law, was the most pissed off. We had problems every day. After that, he didn't like me being his boss now.

I don't have time for these games. I only have a couple months before school starts, and I have to get my family a home. I could not help that I had more experience, and I sure wasn't gonna hide it. One of the benefits that I got because of my experience was being dubbed the "Gate Maker."

The gate maker would follow the blueprints on these new homes that were built and lay out they're property lines. And then build fences according to those lines, and then make the gate. Which was always a different measurement. It put pride back in my self. To have this position after only a month. I was feeling better about myself.

A couple months go by, and it's almost time for Pat's birthday. The first couple weeks on the job were really tough to adjust to the heat. But I'm finally getting my legs back. Even though I'm working as much as I can and saving money, every evening, myself and De would go out and work on the Volkswagen. We are sanding it and putting in Porsche parts. I had missed so much time with him. It was important for us to have these moments.

## Time To Move In

It's been about 3 months, and the pressure is building. I have to find something for my family to live in. It seems that the prices in Sacramento are like the ones in San Jose: expensive. It sure is good to know people, so I put the word out. And luckily, my brother Richie's ex-wife, was renting out a place. It's almost time for De to get back to school.

So I have to do something. Even though this house was smaller than we were used to, we decided to take it. What I found out later was that it was in the heart of the ghetto. I'm still working every day, and me and my son have used all of this time to strengthen our relationship. I was determined to get my relationships back on track.

He was so happy to spend the time we had working on the Volkswagen. He loved the job he did putting the dual pipes on. I could see the satisfaction on his face every time we started it up. What I did know is that I was making memories that I never had; these were the memories I only imagined as a kid. To have that father/son time was always what I dreamed abut. But now I had a chance to change the way things had been done and do them differently. He'll have a chance to know what a father's love is.

## Pat's Birthday

Pat's birthday's coming up, and me and De are looking forward to seeing her and Laticia. I'm making arrangements at work to be off until after the anniversary. Which would be after the 15th. Me and De headed to San Jose. We were very excited to see Pat; we hadn't seen her in about 3 weeks. So we make it safely and spend the evening with Pat. Laticia lived somewhere else and was busy, I guess.

I fall asleep, and when I wake up, Pat's not there. De tells me that she received a phone call and ran out of the house. I'm confused; she didn't tell me she had something to do today; it's her birthday. And we had made plans, so what is going on? There were no cell phones back then, so I had to wait about an hour for her to call. She tells me to get dressed. We have to take Laticia to the hospital. I could hear in her voice that this was serious. All I could say was, "What?" She hung up the phone, so I waited for her with all kinds of crazy scenarios going through my brain. We got to the hospital, and she only explained a little bit. But Laticia's health is more important than words.

She was taken to the hospital by ambulance. We did not talk about it until after Laticia was admitted and her condition was stabilized.

## Dangerous Situation

Pat begins to tell me the story. And she is still shaking. She tells me Laticia and a couple of friends went to a party with some guy friends. And those guys talk them into playing a drinking game and smoking a little weed.

What she didn't know that they had laced the weed with something; she did not know what it was. All Laticia remembered was that she got violently sick, and the men were trying to take advantage of her. They were trying to rape me, Daddy, is what she said to me. Even though she was sick, I could see the fear that was growing in my daughter. Pat continues on with the story. And she tells me that her friend rescued her. She locked Laticia in the bathroom and gave up her body for their enjoyment to save Laticia.

I'm listening to this story with a bunch of different emotions: upset with her friends for talking her into it, upset with Laticia for putting herself in that situation, and mad because I wanna' *put my hands on somebody*.

Pat continues on and tells me she told the girls to put Laticia in the car, and she went into the room. And she threw everything she could find at them, trashed the whole room, and slapped them upside the head like she was their mother, telling them that she knew who they were. And that they could be *touched* to.

She found out that they knew one of our friends who was a cocaine dealer and that there would be repercussions for what had taken place. She put all the girls in the car and stated that she would drop them off. One of the girls, Mother's, was a nurse, so she advised Pat that Laticia needed to go to the hospital. After getting that advice, Pat called the ambulance.

She tells me the story, and I am steaming. I want blood. I want revenge. But she would not tell me who they were because of my anger, because she knew what I would do. Pat knew how mad I was at her for not telling me who they were because of my state of mind, and she didn't care; she said "I'm not losing you. Because I know you would kill them for messing with our daughter." She said, "Don't ask me again." And she was firm on that.

I'm devastated inside; I can't protect my family. I've been working so hard to get us all back together. And it shows me that it could all be gone in an instant.

Laticia stayed in the hospital for 3 days, I think. When I was finally able to talk to her, I had got my balls back. I had made up my mind that I was the head of my family. And I was going to fix this. I told her that, "She was only 15. And I was her father, and she was moving to Sacramento, ASAP. No more discussion; you're moving." I was ready for her to argue with me. But all she said was, "Okay Daddy," and I gave her a hug. Laticia has always had me wrapped around her finger. So was it hard for me to demand something like that?

I never pretended to know everything. We always let the kids discuss
the changes that we're going to be making in their lives. But I knew that
individually. We're all lost, and we needed our family structure.

## New Place, New Life

Pat had a little time off, and we moved in. We got all of our furniture and
stuff out of storage and tried to settle into our new environment. Pat got
the kids enrolled in school. Laticia's only got a couple years to go before she
graduates.

At this point in our lives, I'm praying that she will go to college and become a
professional woman. All parents want is to there kids to do better than they did
without the trauma that they had. I am hoping that they will find happiness. As I
live with the fear of knowing how hard it is out here in the world.

## Single Parent

Laticia's out of the hospital, and we celebrate our anniversary. After that, me
and De head back to Sacramento. I made sure before I left that me and Laticia
were on the same page about her moving back with her family. It's going to be
about a month before she comes to Sac. In the meantime, De and I are staying
busy. We built a big island for the barbecue pit. And I also built what we called
"the shack."

Laticia was going to be 16. And I always told my kids that if they had good
grades, once they turned sixteen, they could smoke weed. At home, me and
Pat smoke weed. And we didn't want to be hypocrites. And we also understood
that she wasn't a baby anymore. So I built the shack so that she could have
somewhere to smoke without stinking up our house.

When we weren't home, I was a single parent. Because Pat only comes home
on the weekends. I think everything is going fine. Laticia is showing me her
100% on her test at school. So I'm thinking I'm doing a great job being a single
parent. But I'm missing the hell out of Pat's structure.

Our relationship is a little shaky. But only on Sunday night's before she goes
back to San Jose. The anxiety of us not being together took a toll on both of us.
We knew something had to change.

Unfortunately, things did change, but they changed with a lot of sadness. Pat
lost her grandmother, Granny, one of my favorite people. Pat took it very hard.
That was the woman that she looked up to, admired, and called, "The Queen."

## Got My Family Back

Of course, I do my *daddy thing*, and I put posters all over Laticia's room with
all of her Teddy bears and make it really nice for her. De was finally old enough
to get a TV in his room, and I had all of his karate weapons hung on the wall.
Nunchucks, spears, things like that. I put a TV and stereo in the shack. And all of
my Star Trek stuff was really nice.

The kids seem to be doing well. And Pat is a lot better now. She's got my mom
Back in her life. We're happy Being back together. The Halls, 'Ride or Die.' The
job is going well. I'm keeping busy that way. And we're paying the bills even
though Pat is not working at this time.

Pat started feeling uncomfortable with her body. She said things just didn't
feel right. Come to find out that she has to get a hysterectomy. They found
fibroid tumors as big as a small orange, so a hysterectomy was necessary. But
it put her into full-blown menopause. The operation goes fine, and they put her
on hormone pills. Pat was always hands-on with the kids' school. We got some
bad news about, Laticia. She had been cutting classes, not even going to school.
Except to take the test at the end of the week, pass it, and show it to me.

That's why I thought everything was going all right. I was upset that she
could fool me like that. But Pat did not play when he came to school. Pat didn't
want Laticia to fail because attendance is part of your grade. She took Laticia
out of Sacramento High School and put her in a continuation's school. I guess
that's a school for troubled kids and Laticia did not appreciate it. She was mad
and said that this new school was different from her previous experience.
Sacramento High was 85% black. She said that she wasn't getting an education
there because nobody wanted to learn.

They sat in the back of the class and created havoc. Laticia said she was
used to sitting in front of the class and being one the smartest students in class.
And has worked hard at it ever since she was little. *Sac High* was a different
environment, and if you were smart, they would bully you.

Pat put her in this new school and told her if she was so smart, then she
could *test out*. Laticia took on the challenge and tested out. She graduated a
year early. Her mama was shocked, and let her know how proud of her she was.

After testing out early, Laticia started her college adventure at Sacramento
Community College. She enrolled and got a job, and her first car was a
Volkswagon. I knew how to work on those. But for some reason, we couldn't
figure out why it wouldn't start. Replace the starter and everything. So the only
way that she could drive it was by pushing it, and I believe she had that car for
6 months or so. And got somebody to help her push that car.
Every time she went somewhere, I was impressed.

## Are These My Kids?

A few things I found out about my kids in those first years in Sacramento.
I found out that Laticia, was hanging out with 'Crip' members and 'flew their
colors-blue', but the 'Bloods' were in charge of the area where we lived. I still
don't know how she navigated that whole gang thing. They wouldn't give me
too much information. Pat and I did not grow up in a gang. So we did not
know much about it. From what I understand, the way they saw it, was a way of
making a community a village.

Laticia acquired a new friend, Lucy, whom I now consider to be my second daughter. She wore red and Laticia wore blue. So I don't know how that works. But that's the way that it was in 'Sac.' I never saw guns, and the teenagers that I met always had the highest respect. They called me *O.G.* They called Pat, *Mom's*. Laticia and Lucy are still friends—I should say sisters—to this day. Laticia is the godmother to her child, *Auntie TT*.

Now my son De kind of had me worried. He's a lot different than I am. He has a cool, calm attitude about himself, but don't push his buttons. Something that he had learned from his karate days. When I would get mad, he would tell me his favorite line from his favorite Bruce Lee movie: "Flow like water." He did have a temper, though.

One story I remember is that he'd talk me into getting him a basketball hoop. He came home from school one day and found it broken. He asked who had done this to his hoop. He found out from one of his friends, and as the story goes... He walked around the corner to the kid's house. Asked his mother if he could come outside and talk to him. And when he came outside, De beat him up right in front of his mother. My son was getting his street cred.

I found out shortly after that. He created his own gang, the *O.B.G.* (Original Baby Gangsters), and they are all friends to this day, my adopted nephews. Alex, Danny, Larry, They road bicycles all over Sac, and I'm sure he had as many adventures as I did when I was a kid. Some of the teenagers that were trying to get with my daughter called him "Wild Man," "Baby Pitbull," and "Bruce Leroy" from the *Last Dragon* movie. When those boys came around to see my daughter, he would be right there. Protecting his big sister.

## Is Something Wrong?

We're settling in as a family? It's been a year or so in Sacramento. Pat started losing weight. Which she was happy about at first. I didn't think much about it because through out our marriage. She would gain a little, lose a little, and go back and forth. But she kept losing more and more.

The rest of the family was getting concerned. She wasn't who we'd known her to be. How can I say it? A little irritated all the time, arguing frequently. One night, it all came to a boil. It was quite disturbing; she wasn't patient or courteous at that time, and I asked her to please come out of her *funk* because the kids were worried about her. She told me that the kids didn't care about her. That I didn't care about her. This wasn't the woman I'd known for all those years. Something was terribly wrong. The kids had never seen their mother like this, and neither did I. She broke down and said she didn't know why she was feeling like this. But we agreed to go to the doctor. At this point, she's around 110 pounds. People thought that we were on *crack*.

# *The Halls*

I came to find out that it was a thyroid problem. And she had a form of Graves disease and a hyperactive thyroid. This is serious, and we don't know what to do. Once again, we would have to put our faith in a doctor. After all these years of her taking care of us, we now needed to take care of her. The doctor tells us that she has to have her thyroid removed in another operation.

I had a thing about anesthesia at this time. I didn't trust it, and I was very afraid of it. But she went through it like a champ and slowly recovered. Which we were all happy about.

I know I've talked a lot about the bad times, but as my daughter reminded me, we had some great times as well. The time in Sacramento was educating me on how young people were thinking. Laticia has gathered a group of friends and invited them to what we call movie night. One of the things that I would do is stop the movie and ask them what they thought about the scene. It would stimulate some really great conversations. It gave me a lot of insight into young people.

Laticia is a full-blown teenager. This is the time in life where you wanna know who you are but you haven't grown enough yet. So there's frustration, but she was working it out and keeping her vision of who she wants to be right in front of her. Me and Laticia's relationship was better. She showed me how much she loved me.

On one of my birthdays, she asked me,"Where did you want to go eat?" We went to a steak house. When we got there, I saw a private room and a bunch of seats, and I'm scratching my head. I wonder, "This can't be for me, I don't even know that many people."

A little while later, everyone shows up. My brother and his partner, Ray, teenagers that we had grown to know, and of course, Pat's cousin Rose was there. Laticia and Lucy, my two daughters had planned all of this and surprised me with tickets to go see the Kings of Comedy. Everyone in the room had tickets to go about a dozen people. It was great!

That night, my daughter was making my dreams come true. Now we were back on track, loving each other. I think I might have shed a couple of tears because I realized that I had regained my daughter's love and respect back.

**The Kings Of Comedy Crew**

**Ray, Pat, Dwayne, Tony**

**Laticia, Dwayne & Lucy**

## Remember

Pat became the den mother of the neighborhood. She was taking care of everybody even feeding *cracked out* mother's kids. And then tried to counsel the mother's on being clean and sober so that they could be a better mother. Even though she's going through her own trouble, she never judged anyone. She led with her heart.

I took my daughter's advice and remembered the good times. After me and Pat had known each other for about a month, we started going to concerts. We'd tried to go twice a month. For about 3 and a 1/2 years, we did that. We went horseback riding. She loved to go to Tahoe and Reno. We partied with some rich and famous people. We were invited to cabins and beach-front properties.

We were quite the social butterflies in those early years. One of our favorite things to do was just take a ride to the beach in Santa Cruz, sit in the sand, talk, and then talk the whole ride back. We were friends, and we never lost that. Together, we had this joy of raising our children.

We were proud every time they accomplished something, and we couldn't believe that we helped them achieve that. These two smart kids came from us. And we were determined not to mess it up. And not to let God down for answering our prayers. The most joy I remember experiencing was watching the happiness that was created when the four of us were together. It didn't matter what we were doing as long as we were all together. That was me and Pat's joy; we called ourselves, "The Hall 4."

## The Second Wave Of Grief

I don't know how many different ways you have to grieve, but I thought I was over the worst part of this grieving thing. But I was wrong. I took an emotional hit. All the pain came rushing back in. Just like when she left. The sharp, stabbing pain came back. The crying came back. In my mind, I thought I was putting myself back together emotionally, but the pain of my little dog, Tier, passing brought my reality to the forefront and put it right in my face. Loneliness is the hardest thing. And my two dogs, Shaka and Tier, saved me.

Through this year of grief, I couldn't just lay there and wallow in it. I had to feed them and take care of them. They're the ones who get me out of bed every day. They are what replaced the care I used to give Pat. That part of me taking care of the ones I love is what drives me. I didn't want to be just a me thing. I've lived for it to be a we thing. And now I sit in my loneliness. And so does Shaka, who was his big brother. We had Tier for 19 years. We had Shaka for five of those years. And I watched him go through the dog grieving process. Shaka is not the same dog, just like I'm not the same man I was before she left. I'd like to believe that Tier is in heaven with Pat. It took me three weeks after his passing to start writing again. To go over my life's memories of our love was too much. I had to wait for my grief to calm down.

I have to have something that I'm working towards. To finish this book right now is my motivation. I pray I never have to endure this amount of sadness ever again in my life.

## Life is Gonna Happen

We are all trying to make Sacramento our home. The job was going well, and we were getting things back together. We were all back together, and things were pretty normal. Pat was doing better; she had her new medication. With hormone treatment, she's gaining weight, and things are looking good. Her sickness had scared all of us.

We were enjoying watching our son play basketball. I think they came in second or third place. For the season, he was learning how to be a team player. It was a lot different from his karate. Karate is an individual sport. And now he had to count on other people to be good. Watching them grow into young adults And to see them achieve things was our greatest high.

Pat was finally coming back from that illness. We needed things to go smoothly. But as usual, stuff happens, and I have to deal with someone's jealousy. I had gotten a raise and was running the crew with D'Lamont, brother-in-law. John was jealous because he had worked there longer than I had. I wasn't going to pretend like I didn't know more than him. I did, and that was the reality.

One day, he refused to do what I told him to do. And we got into a big argument. He ended up threatening me. He told me he was going to kick my ass right there. Well, he had 50 pounds on me. He didn't realize who I was. Not easily intimidated. But I took his threat seriously. So as he approached to do harm to me, I drew my hammer out of my work belt like a sixgun. And I told him if you took another step, I was gonna beat his ass with it. I don't fully remember what happened. He either quit or got fired.

Shortly after that, a week or so later, I got a phone call from D'Lamont. Warning me: He was on his way to my house to shoot me. D'Lamont took it seriously, and so did I. I remember the hate in his eyes for me. So what was I going to do? Pat is in San Jose. I have the kids with me. I get them to help me push the old washing machine close to the house so I could get on the roof. I didn't have a gun anymore, but I had a crossbow.

I'm up on the roof, hiding behind the chimney. I was waiting for him to pull up. But he never did, and I was glad. I didn't have to go through that stupid stuff. I did not want to catch a murder case. But I would have shot him with that crossbow. He had me worrying about my life and fearing for my kids. If he decides to shoot my house up, I'm glad he talked himself out of coming over to my house. A couple months later, I lost my job because the owner of the company we worked for got arrested for embezzlement. Luckily, I had only worked a couple days without getting paid.

Now back on the grind, looking for a new job. We were working through a temporary agency. We were able to pay the bills. But that hustling side of me just keeps telling me. You know, it can be easier if you're just selling a little bit. But I had promised myself and Pat that I wouldn't do that anymore. The kids were way too big for us to hide something like that from them. And I was going to keep my word. There's no way I was ever going back to jail; I was scared of that happening again in my life.

## She's In Our Heads

Throughout our marriage, Pat and her mother had a strange relationship. All Pat wanted was to know that she loved her; it bothered her tremendously. Her mother wouldn't express that to her. The relationship I had with Pat's mother was always tense. I knew she didn't like me. And over the years, I had hope that they would see me as a good man. I thought that was happening but while we were living in Sacramento, her attitude changed toward me. At least that's what I thought. Pat's parents had done pretty well for themselves. I'd work for them when they had a janitorial company.

They moved to Fremont, a pretty exclusive neighborhood. They own a couple of care homes and started buying property in Oroville. We had never heard of the place before. We started going up there for Christmas.

Me and De were recruited to cut the grass at these new facilities she was buying. She was filling our heads with what the future would look like if we just listened to them. But I wasn't taking the bait. But the more that we went up there, I could see a possible future. She really was buttering me up.

While we were in Sacramento, she allowed me to go on two trips. One to Kentucky and one to Louisiana. And all the years that she would take my wife and kids I couldn't afford to go to Disneyland, so this was different. She was making me believe that she finally approved of me, and I have been longing for that throughout our marriage. I was so happy, it took me off guard.

## Spirits Of The Past

My daughter and I had a strange experience in New Orleans. Being in the south blows my mind. So many black people own businesses. The fast-food restaurants were better. I love Beignets, they are a cross between a donut and a fritter, made from yeast-risen dough that is rolled out, cut into squares, and deep-fried until golden brown. They are traditionally topped with powdered sugar, Bourbon Street really is a unique experience. At Pat's cousins house they had a crab boiled. I had never had it served this way before.

In a big pot, they poured all of this beautiful food out
on cardboard on a table, and everybody just grabbed it. Pat's cousins and aunts
showed us a very good time. Pat had been there earlier.

In our marriage, I didn't get to go. So she was delighted to take me to all
the spots. And we had a good time. Things got a little strange when the family
booked a tour of a plantation. There's a crowd of people, and we are touring the
mansion. Suddenly, I get nauseous, and I fall to the back of the crowd of people.
I noticed that my daughter had too.

She tells me she's not feeling well. So we exit the house and end up going
and sitting by a tree outside on the property. All I can say is that the feeling
that we had was getting worse. And for some reason, we were emotional. So
we walked up the driveway to the street. And that's what made us feel better
being off the property. It'd triggered something, and then we found out we were
sitting under the hanging tree. All we could think about was how many spirits
there were on the property. And did we tap into something? It didn't affect any
of the other family members. For some reason, we like to think the third eye was
open. It was a very uncomfortable feeling.

## School Days

De is playing football, and Laticia has started at Sacramento City College.
I drive back and forth to San Jose, working for a week or two out of a month.
We're barely keeping our heads above water. But we're all together, and I'm
living this life the best I can. Pat is inspired by her daughter and goes back
to get her high school diploma. Laticia has shown all of us
that she wants to further her education. So she's going to be
moving to Oroville to further her education. We didn't want
to see her go. We felt like we had just gotten her back. But we
knew she had her own life to live. And she would be around
family. She was going to work part-time for Pat's mother.

Laticia started at Sacramento City College and then
completed her prerequisites at Butte Community College
before transferring to Chico State University.

Pat's parents were big football fans. So when De started playing football, they would come down to his games. During those games, Pat's mother would tell us about a possible future in Oroville. But me and Pat were still not convinced. We were trying to make this life in Sacramento work. But it was hard, and we were tired of working harder for half of what we used to make in San Jose. Her proposition was looking better and better, especially now that Laticia is moving there.

## Street-Smart

The part of Sacramento we lived in was considered the ghetto, and I tried to teach my kids everything I knew about the streets. Because the life they lived in San Jose was pretty middle-class.

They had never gone to school with black people, or seen that many black people on the streets? So lessons were learned on how to spot people on dope. How to spot someone looking to take advantage of you and how to spot danger. How to interact with the police. It was a big difference, but they seemed to adapt very well. They used to say that De sounded like a white boy. Well, he learned how to talk, so he didn't stick out so much. And how to handle himself on the streets. Maybe too good.

## We Are Your Parents

I don't remember the time frame, but Laticia had been gone for a while. One night, she shows up at the house. And she has a very serious look on her face. As soon as she walked through the door, De was right by her side. Me and Pat had seen this before. So we knew by waiting for her to talk that she was getting ready to talk him out of some trouble, like she had done their whole lives. She dropped the bomb on us and told us that she wanted De to come and live with her. And we lost our minds. We both took it personally. We weren't good parents? It hit us hard. And at the same time, in the back of our minds. We were feeling guilty about what they had been through over these last years. We couldn't believe what was going on. We said, "No way." Laticia tried to explain that De had gotten himself into trouble, and he needed to come and stay with her. We tried over and over to get them to explain what trouble he had gotten himself into. And to this day, I still don't know what he got himself into. But I could only imagine it was serious for this to be the solution. We talked for a few hours and still never found out what De had done. We were very upset and disappointed. But eventually we gave our permission for him to go live with Laticia.

## Nothing To Lose

Pat's parents had bought more land up on the mountain in Oroville. Which now made what they owned, all together, about 100 acres. She informs us that her plans were to give each one of her kids a couple of acres. And we could live on the property in about 2 years. Me and Pat had a lot to think about. We were both feeling kind of defeated because Dorothy would be my boss *and* landlord.

De moving to Oroville put us in a deep depression. The last thing that Pat wanted was for me to work for her mother. She said that she did not trust her mother, and she prayed that her mother was telling us the truth. I found the courage to talk to my son, even though I didn't know what he had done. I explained that this was an opportunity for him to reinvent himself. He was going to have a new start. People will know you as the person that you portray yourself to be now. I told myself I should listen to my own advice, and get ready for a new beginning. We didn't know much about the city of Oroville, and we really didn't want to move there. But now our kids were there. They're telling us we have a future there.

Life in Sacramento is hell, and at this time, feeling so depressed, we would end up getting high on coke. That was the worst thing that we should have done. The next day, we were so disappointed in ourselves. We felt like we had let the kids down. Now we had let ourselves down. We had broken a promise that we had both made. We didn't enjoy the high, and we're feeling really guilty and sorry for ourselves.

Later that evening, we decided to take a chance. We are moving to Oroville. The whole getting high thing had taken all of our confidence away and had us doubting ourselves once again. All we could do was pray that we would be better. We've made a promise again not to ever touch it. And we kept that promise.

## Believing In The Dream

I believe that this time I was whipped. I didn't have enough of my own dreams to hold on to, so I was going to be part of someone else's dreams. Pat was excited to be moving to Oroville. Because she would be able to be with her children. I was happy about being able to be with the kids. Because we just got them back, that's the way I felt about it but working with Pat's mother and father. Was it going to be a challenge? I hoped that I gained a little bit more ability for them not to control our lives. And gains a little bit more respect from them. All I could pray for was that I would be able to take care of my family.

Pats, parents really had their business going. At this time, they purchased three more houses, which made them own eight or nine different properties.

Five of the homes were transformed into care facilities with multiple exits, water sprinklers, and a variety of other things that a care home requires like, railings and ramps for wheelchairs.

My carpentry skills came in handy the first couple of years I worked on some of those changes. The care facilities are heavily regulated. Everything was done to specs. I also had to do all the maintenance on the properties of all these different properties. Not one property was less than an acre. And some properties had as much as 8 to 10 acres.

Pat and I moved in to what they called mother's-in-law quarters, a small house set aside from the main house. The property we live on contains the office for all the care facilities and an orchard of oranges and mandarin. We love the peace and quiet. And the views that we had from our little place. We would sit in the evenings and watch the sun go down. It was a new lifestyle. We didn't miss all of the traffic and noise that you get in San Jose or Sacramento. Pat And I really love the slow pace.

## Pat Found Her Groove

When we arrived there, Pat's mother offered her a job. Pat said, "No way." She had other plans. With the experience that she had gained from working for her mother in San Jose, she wanted to do something different. She wanted to work with the babies and young toddlers. She had her high school diploma from receiving it in Sacramento, so she applied for the job. She said it felt great not to lie on the application. She has her high school diploma now and was very proud of herself.

The kids were in school, and now it was time for her to spread her wings. She told me, "We're not going to be able to live off of what my mother's going to pay you, so I've got to do something for us. My mother already has you, Laticia, and my son working for her; I'm not gonna be under her grip."

Shortly after we got there, Pat got a few jobs that were temporary. And then she met Mary, Nicholas, and Hailie. Mary is a nurse who works at Oroville Hospital in the infant ward. She had twins. I believe we were premature and needed a lot of care.

Pat was honored that Mary trusted her to take care of her new babies. Taking care of the babies made her heart sing. There were other children that she took care of over the years, but Mary, Nicholas, and Hailie are part of our family.

**Nicholas & Pat**

**Hailie & Pat**

**Pat & Mary**

**Nicholas, Pat & Hailie**

Pat was able to see them graduate from kindergarten, middle school, high school, and then college. She will always be 'Auntie Pat' to them.

## Like Father Like Son

The first couple years had a lot of changes. Laticia is pursuing higher education. De is living with us in our mother-in-law's quarters in a 2-room place. And we were trying to hang on to our sanity. The walls were closing in. When we moved here, De was a sophomore. He had really turned his life around. Me and his mother had a lot of conversations about what made him want to leave Sacramento. He was getting into the streets too deep. The little bit that he tells me now is that he wasn't really liking the person that he was becoming. So when jail or death were the only options, he chose to make another choice, and that was to change his life.

We enrolled him at Los Plumas High School. My son played football; he was a running back, a cornerback, a punter, and a kick returner.

He was a very good player, and the school embraced him. He was very popular and 'Straight A' student. He had reinvented himself. He was back to that happy young man that I knew. Myself and Pat were very proud, De and some friends created what they called conflict management. If the students had issues with one another, they could bring it to the conflict management students. The students were in charge of this program. (No Faculty Allowed) He was a student counselor. He was part of the NAACP and Vice President of Conflict Management.

He was an actor in four plays and the main character in two of them. His

passion for film making came into play when he was given the opportunity to make three films. He loved being the director of his movies, and me and his mother thought that it might be his future Dwayne Hall movie director. That was one of his dreams, and I wanted it to come true. But just like his daddy, that hustle blood started pumping.

He was making money. And I was afraid to ask because I kind of knew how. Pat and I didn't want to be hypocrites. But we wanted to make sure he was doing things safely. I found out he was doing the same thing I used to do. He was bringing back pounds from Humboldt County.

I can't explain how we felt about it. But we were very concerned. He had created a great life for himself. And doing that business put him in danger. We did not know how to tell him not to do it considering our past. Knowing that it could take years for him to come back from it if he got caught. But he was a lot smarter than his father; when things got a little hot, he shut it down.

Oroville (Calif.) Mercury-Register Advertising Supplement, May 4, 2
All For One
Dwayne Hall as Porthos, left, Shane Hemstalk as Athos, Chris Root is Aramis, Luke Ogden as D'Artagnan, Misty Jones plays M'lady de Winter, and Rachel Rash as Constance for the upcoming performance of "The Three Musketeers," directed by June Trask. The performance by the Las Plumas and Oroville high school's theater group,runs May 11-12 at 7:30 p.m. and a 2 p.m. matinee May 13. Tickets are $7.
TONYA PAUL
MERCURY-REGISTER

04/13/2010

He went on to graduate and get his diploma. And he was one of the top students in his class. The class of 2000. De started training as a motivational counselor in high school and attended a seminar at Richardson Spring Camp.

The host Mike Walsh noticed how well he was helping and interacting with his fellow students. He pulled him aside and asked if he would like to shadow him for the rest of the conference. De did, and afterward, he felt he *had what it took*, so Mike began mentoring him. De did the training, passed the test, and eventually became certified. He would work with students, adults,kids, and train corporate employees.

His mother and I were very proud of him, especially when he decided to go to college. He spent two and a half years in college, and then Dwayne III was born. He let us know he was dropping out of college. He said he had to take care of his son like I took care of him. He went on to join the Labor Union. He had done what his father couldn't accomplish. I had tried numerous times to get into the union, but I was denied.

After joining the Labor Union, he joined the Freemasons. Another organization that I was denied membership in, I believe he earned a third degree, then left the organization. He told me that the mentors that I gave him as a young kid were already like minded people who encourage self improvement and helping out the community. D'Lamont, Larry Beck, myself, and of course, Bruce Lee, had taught him well.

I made sure that there were men in his life who would be an example of different approaches to succeed in life. I always taught him that, "Knowledge is power. Get it where you can." I only had my grandfather. I remembered my younger days. I didn't have all the answers. I wanted him to find the answers he needed.

With the birth of Dwayne III, he gave us a new title: grandparents. We really never talk about being grandparents. What we found out was that it was a different level of parenting. Of course, we spoiled him as much as we could. This was the beginning of a whole new existence. As a little kid who felt all alone to have a family and create another generation, we were in heaven. Pat was ready to be a grandmother. She said to me that she had taken care of so many other people's kids that she was ready for this, and she enjoyed it. He became her new obsession. And for me, a new love in my life and an overwhelming sense of pride we had another Dwayne. Look at my family!

# I Want To Meet Mickey Mouse

Pat's mother's business was doing well, and I'm settling into a new life in Oroville. Pat is a little stressed because of the small place we're living in, and it's about time for her mother to keep her word. Pat wanted to move onto the two and a half acres that were promised to her, but her mother is dragging her feet. It's been six months since the agreed-upon date. So Pat and her mother were bumping heads. Their relationship was always strained, and I couldn't figure out what the issue was. Pat really didn't know how to verbalize it, but it was about trust.

She didn't trust her mother. Pat finally exploded when she heard that there was a family trip to Disneyland, and I wasn't invited. Pat was very unhappy about the way that I had been treated as Dorothy's employee. She felt like it was very disrespectful and knew that if it wasn't her mother, I would have never taken the bad treatment that they were giving me. Considering I wasn't invited the other five times, she wasn't having it this time. She wasn't going and her kids were not going either. At this time, I was a necessary tool. Pat threatened to have me quit.

I was cutting the grass and fixing things, the handyman. Buying the food and delivering it to the different facilities. Pat and her mother went round and round for a couple weeks. Eventually, I was granted permission to go to Disneyland . Pat was a little upset with me cause I didn't take it more seriously. But to me, it was different; it's her mother. I guess a little bit of that old saying, "Respect your elders" ran too deep in me to quit. Being upset and mad, I couldn't live in that, so I tried to ignore it even though it hurt deep down inside. To realize that, despite the fact that Pat's parent's still didn't like me after all of these years, we were granted a 'move in' day on Pat's two and a 1/2 acres of property with the mobile home on it. I don't know what was said in the argument, but I was going to meet Mickey.

My kids had been to Disneyland five times, so my daughter promised me that

I was going to get to do it right. Do all the exciting stuff that they told me about over the years. She had a whole schedule figured out. We had breakfast with the whole family. Pat's parents and her sisters. Her brother Ernest and his kids. Tobina, and her boys, which are my nephews.

Laticia informed me that we are not going with the whole group. We had our own plan, she said, "First we're going to meet Mickey Mouse!" And I was giddy, like a little kid. We met Mickey Mouse and went on the rides. I loved everything. The little kid in me came alive.

I had a great time, and my daughter made sure my 2 days were beautiful. But eventually, we drove to Universal Studios. It was marvelous; all of my movie dreams came true, and the ride was amazing! After that, there was the Walk of Fame. I stopped at every souvenir shop. I bought so much stuff. It filled up the whole bed when I laid it out. Such a great time, I have a memory that I'll never forget. What was the best part of the trip? The four of us in the car. Having conversations, laughing and joking like we used to before all of the drama came into our lives. I think we all healed a little bit on that vacation. I didn't know how to love. I didn't know how to interpret it. But I do now.

## You're A Hillbilly Now

Pat is looking forward to moving up on the mountain. It's gonna be a different way of life than what we were used to, but it was going to be our place. A goal we thought we would never achieve. Maybe moving there was a path to our happiness, which I was willing to reach up for and pick the sweet fruit of future.

I'll be able to move in after the orange and mandarin harvest. Pat's brother Ernest and I had been put in charge of the orchards. We work really hard on this new business. We set up distribution for the ripe fruit. We had a couple people in Sacramento who were going to sell them. We also donated fresh fruit to schools. This year we were looking forward to making some money off of the fruit that we'd only given away years before. Then Pat's mother shut it down. We were devastated, and it took a lot of our enthusiasm out of what we were doing. We really felt slapped in the face. It was an opportunity for them to see that we, the youngsters, were capable of handling it. She didn't need the money, she just didn't want us to succeed?

Those are the mysteries of life that you may never get an answer to. I pushed on and waited for the move-in date. It's time to move up on the mountain. Our son is going to stay in the mother-in-law quarters. He was finally going to have his own place. We moved in, and the next morning we woke up. It was snowing. The only way to heat up the house was to burn wood. This was one of the differences from living in the city. But I didn't mind. It was beautiful and very peaceful. It brought some calm to our lives. We met a couple, the wife works for Dorothy. And they had a place about a mile away from us.

Ray and Stephanie introduce us to other people who live on the mountain. Stephanie was a nurse for Pat's mother for a few years. And what we found out was that everyone grows weed. And me and Pat wanted in. We found out that they were making enough money to last them the whole year without having a job.

We learned everything we could about the business. We were invited to trim buds for people, and we made money doing that. I was picking up on all of the different techniques for how to grow it. After a couple years, they started really trusting me and Pat. They asked us to watch their gardens when they went on vacation. Because people would definitely steal it if no one was home. And there had been a couple of home invasions.

For us to be let into the circle that quickly was unusual. I guess they could feel our vibe. After all, we had been in the weed business for years. We got paid in pounds, so that was the beginning for us. We never had to pay for weed anymore. Being *trimmers* on the mountain. It was an exclusive club. They didn't let just anybody in me, and Pat felt privileged to have gained their respect and trust. We now were considered part of the community.

There was a couple who shared the same property line with us. Tina and Jerry taught us everything from seeds to clones, irrigation, and pest control. How do I fertilize the plant? How do you know when the bud's are ready? How do I trim the buds? How do I cure it? What was the right price to sell it for? You could get from $2,500 to $3000 a pound at this time. During this time, weed was starting to become legal, and you could get a license for a medical condition. It was legal to grow six plants per person. So that meant we could grow 12. We got our licenses. About 3 years after being up there, right after our 30th anniversary party in 2002, that's when we started growing.

## Happy 30th

It kind of snuck up on us on our 30th anniversary. We were surprised at the devotion we had given to each other over the years, and our relationship was tighter than it had ever been. I had not taken any hard drugs; cocaine, for 7 years or more. And not having that in our lives was liberating. We celebrated it; we had done it. We had eliminated it from our lives. Because it was a destructive element. There was a time when we thought we would never get off of it.

Being grandparents had changed us; we would just laugh some times at each other while we were making the mobile our home. We really enjoyed that lifestyle. We planted a bunch of flowers. I built a front porch and a back porch. My carpentry skills came in handy. De and I built Pat a pond,and she filled it with Koi fish. She had her little piece of heaven. I got a dirt bike, a 3-Wheeler. And would go on adventures like when I was a kid, me and my dogs exploring the 30 acres. I had always loved the property and couldn't wait to explore it.

We were very proud to be living on the family's property. But it was time for me to become an entrepreneur. Pat's mother was cutting my hours. It eventually turned out that she wasn't giving me a check at all. I worked enough to cover the rent. Oh, yeah, she still charges rent. It's kind of weird. So I created what I called, "Doc's Shop." I had been at Pat's mother's beckoned call for the last couple years. But when I started my own business, I would schedule times to work for her, and she did not appreciate it. So our relationship was rocky. One day, while cutting Pat's mother's lawn, an elderly lady came up to me,

Carmen, and asked me if I had time to cut her lawn. I agreed to, and it turned into me cutting her grass every week. She really appreciated my work ethic and asked me if I would cut one of her friends lawns before I knew it, I created, *Docs Shop and Lawn Service.* The lawn service had about 40 clients. Doc's Shop consisted of woodcraft, including custom cutting boards, shelving and silhouette designs, as well as specialty baskets designed by Laticia. Me and Laticia would make the specialty baskets during Christmas. Valentine's Day was also an appropriate holiday; it was very good money and with all of my new customers, I was finally making a decent living. Pat's working hours were very liberal, and she helped me grow the business. She would get paid for doing different things around these elderly people's homes, and had those special ones that made her feel like she was their granddaughter.

It is time to start planning the anniversary celebration. We decided to renew our marriage vows and celebrate our 30 years together. Somehow, Pat got in touch with my old boss, Randy, and persuaded him into building us a gazebo. That's where we would renew wedding vows. He kept his word, and we had it finished in a day. It was everything that Pat wanted, and my daughter was handling everything else. Food, invitations, wardrobe, and music.

Pat and I had something that we wanted to do to represent the strength of our family. We needed to make a gesture to show our kids how much they played a part in our lives. We felt like we grew up with them. They taught us as we taught them. So I had some rings made. Pat didn't have her wedding ring anymore; it was stolen. So I designed a family ring with each of our birthstones on it and our family name on it. The weekend was approaching, and I was all about my feelings, and what we had been going through over the last 30 years. I was sorry for what I had put my family through and grateful that she could love me for all these years. With all the mistakes that I had made, she still believed in me, still loved me, and still trusted me. And I'm trying to convince myself once again that I am worthy of her love.

Guests started arriving the day before some of my childhood friends. Some of my band members, a big portion of Pat's family, and my family. People came in their campers and camped out. It was one of our best weekends to reconnect with those people that we hadn't seen in a long...long time.

They were here to celebrate us and our relationship. During this weekend, we were told that we had been the inspiration for a lot of couples. They wished that they could have the love that me and Pat displayed. It blew our minds that they were looking at it this way.

I realize that I didn't know how to receive love. I didn't know how to interpret it, and I was my own worst critic. But I knew Pat, and my kids loved me. Thank God for knowing that. Laticia never told us the number of people that were coming. I started questioning her about how much meat she had me barbecuing. Because I'm thinking along the lines of 40 to 50 people. It turned out to be about 125. It blew my mind that so many people came to celebrate me and Pat.

It's time for the wedding. Everybody is getting into their places, and Pat's mother still hasn't shown up. She lives three minutes from us. And we had to wait on her for over half an hour. We were very confused about why she did that. But we did not let her ruin our day. She finally arrived. We settled our nerves and went on with the ceremony. My son was my best man, and my daughter was my wife's maid of honor. During the ring ceremony, I looked up and saw all those people, and the love was so powerful that the whole 30 years came flashing back all in a few seconds.

This was my true love, my family, and the little kid in me said, "You did it, be proud." Then the tears started coming out, and the crowd of people was reactive to my emotions. After we gave each other rings, we stopped the ceremony and announced that the kids would be receiving rings as well. We gave our kids rings to show our appreciation for them being in our lives. And that they were a gift.

I looked up during the ceremony because I heard all the woo and awe. Saw all the people that were there to celebrate me and Pat. Some were crying, wiping tears. I had what I call one of my, "God Moments." It became perfectly clear to me in those moments that I was truly loved. And the emotions rushed over me. My vulnerability was on full display. And in the depths of those moments, I realized that I had created a family. A loving family, and I truly felt blessed.

I don't normally drink, but I had a couple with my buddy Howard. And he said to me, "I didn't wanna make things sad, but I was wondering. Are you on the witness protection program?" I laughed and told him, "No." Howard remarked, "Because you're out here, where nobody could find you. And I remember the trouble that you got yourself into." We laughed about it. And I had another drink.

I'm sitting in the gazebo, I finally have a moment to myself. I'm looking up at the house and enjoying seeing all the people partying and enjoying themselves. It was an emotional day, and I had way too many drinks. It was the first time I had been drunk since my band days.

My daughter was looking for me. She tracked me down at the gazebo. And I shared my appreciation for how she had pulled it off. I was very proud of her; things went great. Another display of how well rounded and intelligent she was. I was overjoyed that Pat and I had raised her! Laticia walked me to the house and to my room and tells me, "I think you're a little drunk." I said, "Yeah, I think so." I wondered if she saw me throw that drink away.

The day was beautiful, except for Pat's mother's attitude. Pat didn't know why her mother was doing these things to make her upset. But life was beginning to go well for us, and we were not going to let the things that she had done to us, knock us off track.

It was an emotional day for many reasons. But it was a loving, enjoyable day—one of the best times of our lives. And she married me again—the first time we got married it wasn't what we had planned for, but this time it was all we had promised ourselves way back when we first got married.

We said we would do it again one day, and we made that dream come true. We did it our way. We didn't have much, but what we did have was pure joy and love. Happy 30th anniversary to the Halls.

## Pat's Garden

After the anniversary party, it was time to get our plants in, and we were very excited to apply all the stuff that we had learned over the last couple of years. If we could make some money, it would be great because we'd be able to do the repairs on the mobile home; it needed a lot of attention. And do some more stuff with the property. Whatever money we were going to make off of the weed, we were gonna put it back into the property and make it everything that Pat wanted it to be. We had a good start on it. We had the pond and the gazebo. And plans to make my grandson's a clubhouse.

It was becoming what Pat dreamed about. I could see the pride and pleasure she was experiencing. She felt it when she was talking about the property; she loved it. The first year of growing, we did not do as well as we expected, but we made about $7000. Getting back in the game wasn't easy. It took us about 6 months to get rid of what we had grown. We spent the money pretty quickly and had to buy a car. I got my teeth fixed, and life ate through the money pretty quickly. We were looking forward to the next planting season and we were determined to do better.

## My Momma In Oroville

Pat was full of joy when she found out my mother was moving to Oroville.

All the kids that my mom raised—my sister's kids—are grown now. And Sacramento was expensive, so she moved to Oroville. Luckily, she found a place two apartment complexes away from Laticia's place. My mom was all alone now. Probably for the first time since I was born. She was happy with me and Pat watching out for her now. Laticia got to know her grandmother on a different level. They spent a lot of time together. They went to the casino two nights a week. Laticia took her grocery shopping; they had dinner date nights; and spent time just hanging out doing homework with my nieces and nephews. They called my mom's *Nana*. My mom didn't have a key to Laticia's house, but she walked in whenever she wanted.

Laticia tells me those years are cherished, and she grew a different kind of love, respect, and admiration for her because those moments allowed her to learn my mother's story. We are firm believers that, in order to understand why people move the way they do, you must know their story. Laticia is the first granddaughter on both sides of the family. And she looked like my mom more than any of her other grandchildren. She was the baby that bonded Pat and my mom. Through Laticia, both of them had their first. First daughter, first granddaughter.

## Fuck Cancer

(For the people who have read this far into my story, I want you to know that this is hard. Bringing up stuff like what's to come. I buried it away and locked it in a box so that I didn't feel the pain or sadness.)

A couple years later, living up on the mountain. Pat discovered a lump in one of her breasts, her right breast. So we took her down, and she got a mammogram. We had to wait for the results. The beginning of agonizing moments. The waiting to find out if it was cancer. It was. Our world was rocked.

Along with the diagnosis of cancer, we also received information about what caused it. It was the hormone pills she had been taking for a few years now to fix her thyroid problem. Her treatment was going to be radiation, I believe, for about 8 weeks. The radiation really zapped her strength and caused slight burns. During her treatment, she stayed home most of the time and spent her time in the garden. One day I came home. She told me to water the plants, and I noticed that the plants had jewelry on them. Come to find out she had named them. Pat could never grow anything before she got cancer. Now she had a green thumb, and everything she touched grew amazingly!

**182**

She said that working in the garden helped her deal with the situation we were in. Through our relationship, Pat went to church, but now she is calling on our Lord. "Father God, help me be here to see our grandson grow up." We prayed every night for healing to come. Pat didn't want me to tell the kids what was going on; she didn't want them to be scared. Which told me how scared she really was. I was scared, but we always put on a brave face for each other.

## Remission

Pat had finished her treatment, and we were waiting for the results. And it's harvest time for the most beautiful plants we've ever grown. Pat had really done her thing. The results are in, and I hear a word for the first time that will be coming into our lives over the next 20 years - remission. Pat was in remission; no more cancer. At least that's what we believed when we later found out that once you get it, you always have it. There's always a chance of it coming back. Now she would have to be checked every 90 days to make sure it wasn't coming back. All we could do was pray it didn't.

## My Baby Brother

Tony

On October 30, 2004, my baby brother, Tony Fetyko, was killed in a car accident, leaving my mom and Laticia's place. He had come up on the mountain to visit me and Pat earlier that day. Kalani Fetyko. My nephew was driving, the son of my other brother. Richard Fetyko, the 'Baby Bull.' Richard is 5 years younger than myself. Kalani had his two children with him, and a drunk driver came over the lines and hit them head-on. The guy who was drunk was never charged. We found out why; he was the brother of one of the Orville police officers. The kids only had a couple cuts and bruises. But my brother wasn't so lucky. He had cut one of his main arteries. My nephew was devastated by his death because he was the one driving. His guilt to consume him for the rest of his life.

## Laticia's Journey

Laticia moved to Chico in December of 2004 to focus on her last semester of college, and since she had worked her whole college career, she experienced what she calls the, "Privileged College Experience."

In May of 2005, Laticia graduated from Chico California State University, earning a Bachelor of Science in Recreation Administration with a concentration in Resort and Lodging Management. She also won an award for, 'Most Outstanding Senior.'
She walked twice that day with a huge class of maybe 1,500+ students and then again with the African American students that were a part of the Black Student Union. Due to her maintaining her 3.8 GPA, she was asked to give a speech at that more intimate graduation ceremony of 25–30 graduates and their families. She moved to San Diego and started her career on July 11, 2005. Of course, her brother and I drove the truck, but Pat didn't let Laticia know that she cried because she moved to San Diego. A lot of things happened in 2005; we were granted our second grandson. DJean was born in December of 2005.

## One Of The Best Decisions Of Ours

Over the last couple of years, we have been talking to people, and they would ask, "How did Pat get cancer?" And when we would tell them how they would say, you guys should sue them. So we sued the health provider because the hormone pills Pat was being prescribed, gave her cancer.

They had come back with a settlement of $75,000. Or a lifetime of medical care. We chose a lifetime of medical care instead of the money. We had a great harvest that year. I had saved about $10,000. We saw her medical bills rise while she had cancer. And we were looking at fighting cancer again. We knew that $75,000 would not go too far for her treatment to save her life, which is expensive. One of the things that we asked for, with the advice of our doctor, was to be eligible for all experimental drugs and new techniques. The research that we did shows that new treatments are coming out every year.

## Who's Gay?

During the time that Laticia was in San Diego, me and Pat did fly down. Her job was going well, and she bought us tickets to come. She said she had something to tell us. And she could only tell us in person, "Oh man." We were a little nervous. What was Laticia up to now?

She picked us up from the airport and gave us a tour of the city, her favorite eating spot, then we spent time on the beach. But throughout the day, we could see Laticia's nervousness increasing. She takes us back to her house. Gives a joint to me and asks me to relax.

She says, "There is something that I have to tell you and mom." Pat is impatient and anticipating what Laticia has to say. Pat says, "Just tell us Ma." Our nickname for Laticia is *Lil Ma*.

She takes a deep breath and says that she is a lesbian. I rock back in my seat and pause for a minute. A little shocked because she had boyfriends. And I asked her, "Are you sure?" She told me, "Yes." And I ask her again? And her answer was the same: "Yes."

And I said, "I just wanted to make sure because, in this world, how I see it? You already have three strikes against you; you're a woman, you're smart, and you're black. And now you're gay? You realize you're going to have a lot of haters in this world."

Luckily, I and Pat had been through a similar experience. When my little brother, Tony, told me and Pat he was gay, he wanted to know. If he was gay, were we going to let him see Laticia? Were we going to let him be an uncle? I told him to just be a good uncle, not the *gay* uncle. If you do that well, when she grows up, you won't even have to tell her you're gay; she'll love you for being Uncle Tony.

He had shared stories of people who were totally rejected by their own family members because they were gay. He shared with us how hard it was for him to make up his mind to live in his truth. He had taught Laticia. It was best for her to live her truth, and don't be afraid to tell your parents. She was a little nervous because she had friends who's parents would never talk to them again. But she didn't have to worry about that. She wasn't getting us out of her life that easily.

Her mama said to her, "Live your truth and don't have us worry about you like that." She promised her mother she would not hold anything back. We let her know that we were her parents, and we were very proud of her. It didn't matter who she slept with or who she loved; she would always be our baby girl.

## Grandparents

Having our two grandsons bring us a little piece of heaven right here on Earth, we were obsessed with them and spent time with them whenever we could. We were granted new names. I was *Poppa*, and Pat was *Gramzie*.

My two kids used to tease me and Pat. They said we had gotten soft. We weren't raising the grandbabies the same way we raised them.

The grandbabies—we're not them. We did not have to practice discipline. Their parents were already doing that. When they came to our house, which was every weekend, if we could get them, it was always about fun and discovering new things. I would put them on my 3-wheeler and get the dogs, and we would have adventures all over the 30 acres.

Pat would always have some new toys or something fun to eat. It was a great time in our lives. Their lives gave Pat the strength to fight for *her* life. She was determined to see them grow up.

## A Mother's S.O.S.

By November of 2006, Laticia was living in San Diego but moved back to  Sacramento when her mother had to announce that she had stage 4 breast cancer in her right breast. It took Laticia less than a month to transfer her job and pack up her apartment, and the three of us drove down to bring her back. She resettled in Sacramento to stand by her mother's side as we prepared for battle! And she got a job at the Hyatt Regency Hotel.

The treatment this time was going to be chemotherapy. It really caused havoc on her body. They had to put a port in to administer the drugs, and this stuff was powerful. She would be nauseous and sick for 3 days after the treatment and with the chemotherapy. Pieces of her hair started coming out. So she had me shave her head. And I shaved mine too. But she used to rock her bald head. She was beautiful.

When Pat got overwhelmed, she would cry and tell me that all she wanted to do was see her baby's boys grow up. DJean who was our youngest grandson at the time. He saw her port for medication and asked, "Who did that to you, Gramzie I'm going to beat them up!" One of the lighter moments during this tough time.

At this time, I was depending on my prayers to God that she would be alright. The fear would come and go, like the grief I'm going through now. All I could do back then was remember that she needed me to be as strong as I had ever been. For me to be her strength when she didn't have any.

My two children were my strength when I didn't have any. Pat was in remission. She had won the battle for the second time. By the time Pat started felling better we have other responsibilities now.

## Barbara June

That's my momma Barbara June, *Nana* to my kids. Laticia is her first  granddaughter. On the night, my baby brother was killed, she had a small stroke. Tony was her favorite, and the rest of us brothers and sisters knew that. Me and him used to joke about who was going to take care of her in her old age. Now that he was gone, it was left up to me. She started having little accidents. When we took her to the doctor we found out she wasn't taking her medicine right. He informed me that they were going to put her in a home. Alzheimer's and dementia were setting in. It's a horrible disease. It's a memory problem. She came to live with us.

Pat was in remission at this time. And she took excellent care of my mother while I was working. My mom loved being on the mountain, and it was a wonderful time for me when we would take walks on the property and talk.

So I would look forward to those times when her memory was still intact. It was hard to watch as her memory became less and less of the person we all knew. But she did let me know in those times that she was proud of me.

I'm very glad that I've overcome the stuff that I've been through. And in her eyes, I have been a great father, husband and son. Some days, she didn't remember who the grandkids were. I'm so lucky that she never forgot who I and Pat were. Before she was bedridden, she would ask Pat to take her to the garden. She loved the smell of the Indica plants.

We did the best we could to make her comfortable, and for her to keep her dignity was important to my wife. It was Barbara's strength that made me who I am today, and she also gave my wife the love that she never got from her own mother. Nana passed in 2006.

## Life Doesn't Stop 4 U 2 Catch Up

The death of my mother Barbra was hard on both of us. Everyone who knew me as a baby is gone now. Edna, Pat's Granny passed away years ago and now Barbra who was like Pat's grandmother, the matriarchs of both our family's, are gone. The women from whom we all came from, have left us and we're on our own now. All the family recipes are gone .

The holidays would never be the same without them. All their love and guidance we will have to share with those who remain. Pat, Laticia, and Francine have some of her recipes, and when you eat those special dishes, the memories of my mother come rushing back.

We're living life in the best way we can because life throws these moments at you and makes you grab on to what you have, love, or live in sadness and grief.

Pat's treatment had gone well, and we were happy with the results, but in the meantime, I built my business up to the point where I didn't have to work for Pat's mother, Dorothy, any more, and she wasn't having it.

She insisted on me working for her like I had before; those days were gone. After months of not getting a paycheck, I would always try to work things out with Dorothy. But Pat was fed up; she said we gave my mother seven years, and all we did was get poorer. One day Pat gets a phone call and tells me she has to go talk with her mother. When she comes back after her conversation, she tells me that we have to move; it rocks my world.

I asked her what happened, and she told me that her father had been
snooping around and found our garden. I asked Pat if I could possibly have a
conversation with her mother, and maybe turn things around.

So I grab my cannabis license or *script*, which stated that we had permission
from California to grow 12 plants. She didn't care; she fell back on being a
godly woman, and growing weed was wrong, so we had to go. I tried my best
to get Pat's parents to change their minds. But their minds were made up, and
I couldn't believe that they would do something like that to their daughter. It
hadn't been too long since she went into remission. They had given Pat two and
a half acres and then took it back. I couldn't believe it. This wasn't what Pat's
mother told me on those long rides up here to Orville, it was all about lifting up
the family. This didn't look like family to me. I even tried to persuade her into
selling us the 2 and a 1/2 acres. We had $20,000 to put on it that we made from
the harvest.

Her answer was still, "No." Pat has come to the end of her rope. The anger
she had for her parents was something I had never seen before. She gave us 30
days. All I could do was bitch about how wrong the whole thing was and how
unfair it was when did everything legal. Pat got mad at me and told me to, "Stop
living in the past." This was her parents' property, and there was something else
for us out there. But I had seen the pride and joy that Pat has living there. But
she was right.

It was their property, and we've gotta move. We're packing up and have
nowhere to go. The 30 days came, and on day 31, she had the police serve us
with an eviction notice. I thought they might calm down but with that move, I
knew there was no hope to stay.

One way that I got my anger out was by tearing down the gazebo, the front
stairs, and the back porch. I paid for all the Lumber, so it was mine. I built them,
so I can demolish them. Now we have 15 days to evacuate the premises. The pot
harvest was just a couple weeks away, and then we'd be out of there.

We ran into the new laws. When you fill out an application for a home, you
have to pay $50. Whether you get it or not, me and Pat couldn't wrap our minds
around that. We're putting in the application, but there are no guarantees.
That's not the way the world used to work in our day.

Pat tells me she has a line on a house, and it isn't in the ghetto. We checked
it out. It's only two bedrooms, a big front yard, and a place to grow in the
backyard. It wasn't in the ghetto, so we checked it out first. And what was cool
about it was, this was one of Pat's aunt's friends who she worked in the Silicon
Valley. So they rented it to us, and we've been here ever since. They gave us
a fair deal to move in, and our rent was lower than what Pat's parents were
charging. Pat didn't speak to her parents for almost a year. And I kinda' just
wrote them off the list as being the parents that I looked up to. I had believed
in them. But their actions showed me that it was all a lie; every man for himself.

I thought they were successful people. I thought if I put in the work, I would be judged fairly and rewarded. It didn't work out that way and now it was up to us.

## Starting Over Again

During the years that Pat had cancer, she joined up with the American Cancer Society. They do an annual Breast Cancer 5K walk in the month of October. Laticia, who was a manger at the Hyatt Regency, Sacramento, made sure they were one of Pat's many sponsors every year Pat participated.

From 1998 to 2016, Pat completed each 5K walk to the finish line. Her other sponsors who walked by her side wore shirts that said, "We Walk In Support of Patricia Hall." During the years Pat was in remission; her shirt said, "Survivor."

Pat started to get involved with all things breast cancer awareness and support-related. Her spirit and heart were so big. While receiving chemotherapy, she would be counseling other patients receiving their types of therapy. Once she started going to chemotherapy in Chico, California, at the Enloe Medical Center, the essence of her care taking for others reappeared with a vigor like when she was young.

Sometimes other patients would need emotional or financial support, and Pat always had knowledge of resources. People don't think about it, but these so-called little things are expensive yet very important for women to keep their dignity. Many lifestyle changes are necessary. Special bras, breast inserts, wigs, bonnets, transportation needs, information on new medications, and the list goes on and on.

Not only did Pat help fellow patients, she was embraced by the nurses because they could feel her generous heart reaching out to those in need. She was always well taken care of. She would go to, 'Survivor Events' in a lot of cities. Her group would paint rocks with inspirational messages then leave them to be found by patients.

She even walked in a fashion show in support of breast cancer. Laticia was right there with her every step of the way. One of the stories Laticia tells is of being there to dress and ensure that her mom's make up was right for the fashion show.

**Cancer Awareness Fashion Show**

Needless to say, Laticia was in a boss/manager mode, so Pat's makeup was done by a professional make up artist. Although other models didn't have a private dressing room, Pat did, and Laticia waited on her all day. Pat's comment was, "Is this how movie stars are treated?"

Pat's friends, who were models, were jealous, so Laticia took care of them as if she were their own personal assistant. Laticia says she did it in gratitude for all the times her mom made her feel like a princess on her school field trips. Yes, Pat was the class mom, recess guard duty, and the favorite parent who chaperoned on all the field trips.

We got news a few months after we moved into the new house. Pat had a lump, and the chemo wasn't working. She was going to have to have her breasts removed in a mastectomy. She led us to believe she didn't mind as long as it got the cancer out and she could live longer.

We shifted our attention to our grandbabies to ease the pain. Pat was a loving grandmother. She wanted them to have memories that would last for the rest of their lives. She was always very keen on knowing the different government funded programs available to low-income people. She had helped a lot of families with her knowledge. Now it was time for her to use it for our benefit. She had arranged to have our windows changed; we got a new refrigerator, a new stove, and a new water heater.

With the addition of that stuff, it was almost a new place, even though it's 90 or something years old. But it was ours now for as long as we could rent it. With the little bit of money we had saved, we made it ours. The second bedroom we set up for the kids. They had a big TV in there for gaming. They were in heaven, and so were we. Over the years, I created different projects to do with my grandsons.

One of the projects that we did was *Homie Park*. It took us about a year to do it. Homie Park came out so well that it's was on display at their school and the African American Family and Culture Center.

Hornte

LURCH

I enjoyed every hour watching them grow and create. It lit something up inside of me. I can look back and know that I made the right choice. My family came before the music.

## Back In Town

We love living on the mountain, but we are moving back to town. We were connected again to the local community. We were closer to the grandbabies. Instead of just seeing them on the weekend, we could pick them up from school. They lived right around the corner, within walking distance.

They would come over during the week. In a lot of ways, we did the same stuff that we did with our kids. Pat took them to the park at least 2 to 3 times a week. I help with homework, trying to get their math, right? Me working on their math was a nightmare. It was a great distraction from the fear I had about breast cancer. I taught them how to ride bikes and took them riding on the weekend as we ran the dogs.

It was time for Pat to have her breasts removed. Things went well, and the operation was a success. Pat began her healing process, and informed the family of her future plans. She was considering reconstructive surgery. During this time, our relationship was good. But it was a little strange, and I was confused. She would not ever let me see her scars from the operation. It was bothering her more than what she told us. It was affecting her self-esteem. She wore a special bra for being out in the world. It didn't affect her social life, but for me, the mastectomy is where the anxiety came from. I tried to convince her I love her just as much as ever, and it doesn't matter to me. But it mattered to her; it was a problem.

With all this going on, we get a summons to court. Pat's parents are suing us for $5,000. They're suing us for not cleaning up the property, which wasn't true. And for it to cost $5000 to clean up the property was ridiculous. When we went to court, they had pictures. What they didn't know is that we had pictures of all the old bikes, moldy beds, and rusty car parts.

Piles of stuff in different locations. Stuff that was acquired through all the years of the family going up there. Those days are over. That's what they showed the judge, but we did not bring that stuff up there, so we didn't take it with us when we moved out.

I guess their motivation was that they knew we had some money cause we offered them a $20,000 down payment to buy the acres they had supposedly *given* Pat. They were trying to cripple us financially in order to put us back in a vulnerable state where we would have to go to them for help.

Well, we go to court, and the judge says that, "Somebody's lying." But he can't tell who. That is because we both had pictures. Who does he believe? The judge says, "This is a petty, family squabble!" He gave us a big speech on how family should be together and help each other. And he thought that this was ridiculous. The case was dismissed.

Pat's father was so mad that he threatened to shoot me right outside the courthouse. He had a hand gun in his truck. I had seen it many times. We did not understand why they were so mad because we were the ones that got kicked off the property. And that was the last time that Pat called him, "Daddy." Pat even tried to file a police report on him for threatening me, but I persuaded her to let that go and for us to steer clear of them until the anger went away. We were free of her parents controlling ways once and for all.

## Living For Ourselves

After that whole episode with her parents, all we could do was work hard for our family. My business was doing well. And Pat was working as a caregiver with Nicholas, Hailie, Chelsea, and Lisa. Pat fills her life with children and babies. They are the ones that received a lot of Pat's time. She had raised Hailie and Nicholas from infants. So they were like our own grandkids. We did a lot of things together. My wife was always doing something to bring joy into people's lives.

Pat calls a family meeting and informs us of the next steps in her treatment. She had made up her mind to have the reconstructive surgery. And we were all a little concerned because this was going to be kind a marathon operation; it could last for 8 hours. But our concerns did not outweigh her discomfort. She had made up her mind, and all we could do was get behind her decision. The operation would be in about 10 months. And the thing that brought a big smile to her face was that she could eat as much as she wanted to. She had to gain weight to have enough strength and fat for the reconstructive surgery. She said, "I'm getting a tummy tuck."

The family was not looking forward to it. But we had to be there for her; it was her life, but I was very concerned about the anesthesia keeping her out for 8 hours. Thinking about that caused me to have nightmares. She finishes the family meeting with, "We all walk on faith lane, right?"

We realized in that moment that she needed our strength, so we gave her a 'Hall Hug' and prayed in the moment. Everything was gonna be alright. Since we moved to Oroville, Pat has been going to church every Sunday. She had finally found a pastor that she believed was speaking God's truth. It gave her strength and the belief that everything would be alright. Her faith in God was her biggest super power.

## The Baby Bull

Richard J. Fetyko, my baby brother, was lost during this time. We didn't get to see each other a whole lot. But every time the Sacramento Kings played the Portland Trail Blazers, we had a phone call to talk shit about each other's teams.

Once Richie came to my house to visit. And we got the chance to watch a basketball game. He gave me shit about my TV. He said, "It's too small." I told him, "It was big enough for me." So he went and bought me a new, bigger one. That was a display of the love he had for me. He said I was, "Big Bro" and I had always taken care of him. He's always loved me for it. He was the band's bodyguard and a roadie for a while. He had dreams of being a professional baseball player when we were kids. He went into the army, later got married, and had two kids. My niece and nephew, Leilani and Kalani. *Big Rich* asked me to be his Godfather, and I said to him, "I'm already his uncle." He said to me, "You can be his godfather too." What was I supposed to say, no? I love that he loved me that much.

The distance between him in Portland and me in Orville, California, was never too far for the love that we had for each other; we have been through a lot as kids and we only had each other to lean on. My sister Francine, Laticia, Pat, and I rented a car and drove to Oregon so that we could spread his ashes at his favorite place on the coast.

Along the way, we stop at all of his favorite eating spots. Unfortunately, he passed away from complications related to being overweight. Tragically, we lost his son, Kalani a few years after that. He never really got over the death of his uncle Tony. Remember, he was driving the car? His death is still a mystery to the family. He was shot under suspicious circumstances. The young man I knew would not have committed suicide. One day, the truth might come out: we lost Kalani in 2012.

## DJ Doc

Pat is waiting for the months to go by so that she can have her operation. I'm trying to have a positive attitude about it. But I'm a little scared. She promised me that she was going to follow the doctor's instructions so that she could be as strong as she could be for the operation. I could see her effort.

A complete lifestyle change. She walked on the river with Lisa and Chelsea at least five days a week. She loved being by the river, and she also made us eat healthier. Pat and Stephanie went to the farmer's market every Wednesday. She also made me go to the doctor; "It was time for me to start being checked on," she said. And I didn't want to go.

However, dealing with her cancer had sharpened her decisions and life choices. So I decided to go see the doctor. I'm at the age where you have to go and get checked out. During that visit, I found out that I had high blood pressure, and they wanted to give me a colonoscopy. My nickname for it is, "Bootyoscopy." Lucky for me, I did it then because I had a couple of polyps that could turn into cancer if they weren't taken care of. I could not tell her anything after that; she would shut down all of my reluctance, quickly. I could see that her being concerned about my health helped her not get depressed about what she was going to go through.

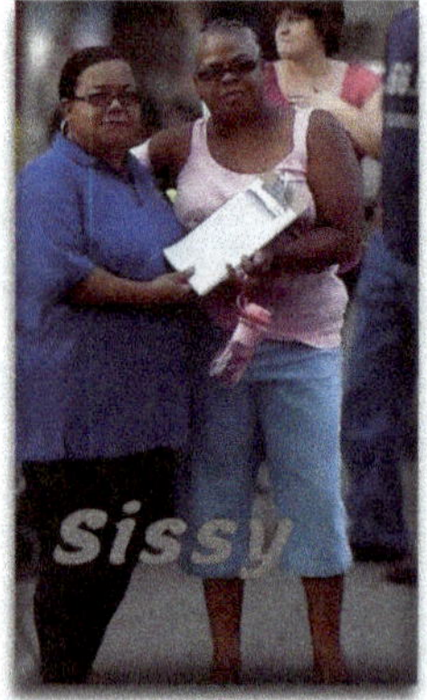


One day I came home from work, and Pat was playing my album, *There Is... Life on Earth*. She started talking to me about music. Asking me if I missed the music. I knew something was up. It was so hard to leave the music industry, and all these years I never even talked about it. So I asked her to get to it, "What's going on?"

She tells me that one of her friends, Sissy, who works at the African American Family and Culture Center, said that they are starting a training class for DJ's and asked if I was interested. I said no in the moment. But it haunted me for the next week. What did I have to lose? Could it fulfill that creative side of me? Did the music still live in me? I told myself, "You had done it before."

When I was a kid, around 17, I worked at the Stanford University AM radio station, and I had a blast. So let's give it a shot. I completed the course. I didn't tell anyone that I was once a band leader. Just some dude off the street. I got my certificate of completion and started the DJ Doc show on KOYO 107.1 FM in Oroville, California. I started out doing to a 2-hour show and eventually went to 3 hours twice

a week. It was a community radio station, so you had to get sponsors for your shows and do P.S.A.'s (Public Service Announcements). I was really enjoying it. I created different segments for the shows, 'Black Hollywood' and 'Gossip.' I wanted to bring in a female to do part of the show with me. First, I had Laticia help me. But then her work got busy, and I recruited 'DJ Coley Cole' about 6 months into it. I got my first award for being the most listened-to show in my time slot in the Northern California region.

You should have seen the smile on Pat's face when I started getting noticed in the grocery store because of my voice. It's a small town, but it was nice to be recognized as a bit of local celebrity. Like being in a band, it gave me a lot of pride and joy. Eventually, about 8 months later, I started teaching the class. I was once again part of the community. Me and Pat both went out and worked on the food give-away. And helped with the music and set up for the reggae shows that the African American Family and Culture Center did every year. Myself and Pat are truly contributing to the community now.

## The Family Is Growing

My son De is working hard on a union job. I am very proud of him - the little boy who turned into a man. He is taking care of his family, and was serious about being a dad. He said to me, "How could you think I would do anything else but take care of these kids?" I took care of him, and was happy to know that he thought I was a good dad.

When we look at De and Maggie we see our younger selves discovering how to be together. They've been married for about 8 years. Maggie tells us that she's pregnant again. We're going to have our third grandchild.

With that news, Pat became more determined to make it through her journey. We pray that it works in our favor so that we can watch these grand babies grow up. It became a running topic in her conversation. It was a little sad because we didn't know if she was going to be able to see them grow up. Or how long she would be with her grandkids. DaVinci was born in 2013. We had our third grandson, and we were so happy. Look at our family, which started out with just the two of us. Thinking about the possibility of leaving her grandkids would always make her cry. And it makes me shiver in my body to even think she wouldn't be here.

The cancer has come back two times now. Would this operation even work? It's getting close and she has to go to San Francisco to see Dr. Vitani, who is the doctor practicing this new technique. She had to agree to go and get checked every two weeks now to make sure that she's got enough fat content and strength. How was I gonna to hold up during this high risk experimental operation? I had my fears. Here we go again. This procedure is brand new. Will the cancer come back again? Nobody knows but God. I just try not to think about it, and I give Pat all the positive energy I could. She does feel pride in being a pioneer and is happy that she's making way for other women with cancer to have this procedure done in the future if it proves to be successful.

## Operation Day

A couple of days before the procedure, we go to San Francisco. We have to check her in the day before to get all her vitals and make sure she's fit for the operation. They said everything was good. Not that we showed it to Pat, but the three of us were very worried, concerned, hopeful, confused, and calling on all our strength and all of God's grace to shine down on us. We would not let Pat feel what we were feeling.

Pat said to us, "We're not going to sit in this hotel room like I'm on a countdown. I want to go out and enjoy myself." We went to Chinatown, and we walked and walked. Pat had us in all of the antique shops. I hadn't seen her have this much energy for years. I guess all the cancer walks and her walking by the river every day really worked. I had to try to put it in my mind that she was strong and believed that. We ate at our favorite place, Hunan Home's Chinese Restaurant. A place that we'd always go to when we were in San Francisco. It had been open since I was a kid. We had many meals there.

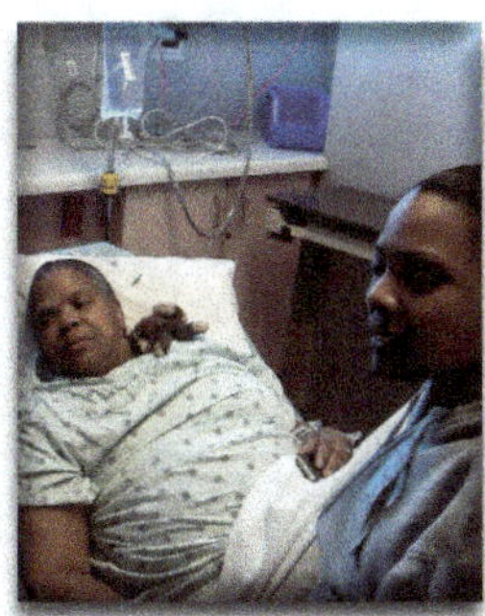

She walked us so much that we were all huffing and puffing, but not Pat; she wanted to keep going. I was feeling bad because I couldn't keep up. She wore the kids out too. Pat was quite aware of the risk involved. But she did not want her fear to take over and make her cancel the operation. She told me later that it was probably the most scared she had ever been in her life. She didn't want us to know because if we started pressing her too hard about our fears, she might not have gone through with it. She did not think she could have handled that. It took everything in us not to tell her our true feelings, which were that we did not care about her breast not being there. We loved her, but this is what she wanted, and we had to respect that.

## The Longest Day Ever

Well, it's the day of the procedure. We get her checked in and try to be as positive as we can. It's time for Pat to go through those doors. The big swinging doors. To the operating room. It's hard to explain the feeling that you have when that door shuts. A feeling of helplessness: You can't do anything. It's in God's hands now, as well as the doctors.

They have her now, and all you can do is pray that everything will be okay. Me, De, and Laticia get in the elevator and collapse into each other's arms. The emotions and the fear just came bubbling out. We regrouped, exited the elevator, and drove around the city for a few hours. We went to the ocean, but the clock was ticking for 4 hours. Now that we understand the phrase a minute feels like an hour, we're trying to feel positive.

We wasted time by going to some of my childhood homes. It was great for my kids to see some of the places where I grew up. Some things are different, but a lot are still the same. Six hours have gone by, and we're all getting extremely anxious. We can't take it anymore. Back to the hospital. The three of us are very impatient. We're bugging the hell out of the nursing staff.

They said it was going to take 8 hours, and we counted every minute and every second. Unfortunately, they said it was going to take another 4 hours or more. We are tripping now. We want some answers. Why has it taken so long? The anxiety is at an all-time high; we have no answers as to why it's taking so long. We walk the hallways and stay in prayer. The funny thing is that we were all silent, but we could feel each other's fear, anxiousness, and this overwhelming feeling of protection.

We are now at hour 9, and Laticia has been pushed past her limit and is now at the nurse's station, demanding information. I'm right behind her, co-signing the urgency of our need to be with her no matter what stage they were at.

Hour 10, and the doctor finally comes out to tell us she is in recovery and

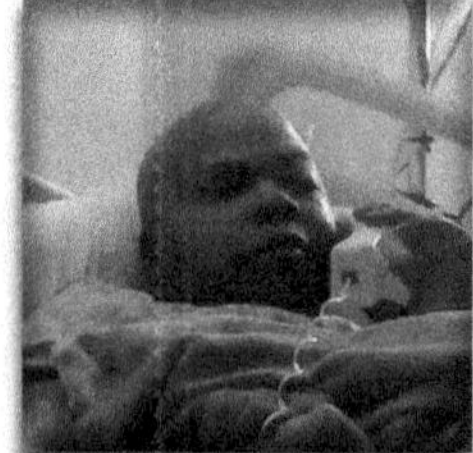

how the surgery went. All I remember is *blah, blah, blah* until Laticia demanded to go see her in recovery. They didn't want to let her, but for whatever reason, they approved. We had been there all day. The night shift was coming back on duty. They knew that we had been there all day into the evening. The operation had taken 11 and a half hours, from what I remember. We finally get into the recovery room to see her. They only wanted one of us in there, but we insisted that all of us go. All of us needed to see her. Luckily, they understood.

The three of us were sitting there for two hours. Waiting for her to start moving, she came back to us and gave us a sign that she was alright. Pat finally opened her eyes, and all of us let out a sigh of relief. She was still heavily drugged at the time, and when the nurses saw her moving again, they wanted to give her more morphine. We protested that. She tried to explain to us that they didn't want her to wake up in pain. But how could she wake up if you wanted to give her more morphine? We said, "No; let her wake up enough to tell you that she's hurting, please." There was a lot of back-and-forth, and finally, we came to an agreement that they would let her at least wake up.

So we agreed and waited longer. Finally, she woke up, still groggy. Pat called out my name. Me and the kids had been so stressed out all day. When we heard her voice, the exhilaration was like I had never felt before. She asked, "Why are you all crying?" That's when we all knew that she was coming back. They had all kinds of tubes coming out of her. She would have to stay in the hospital for three days. That's what they told us. It ended up being five days in the hospital and the kids needed to get back to their jobs. They couldn't hang for a week. Neither could I, because I had clients to attend to. I said, " I Want to stay." She made me go home for one of the longest weeks of my life. It was one of the hardest things I had to do to leave her, but she insisted. We would go and see her every two days. That's all she would allow. She's in the hospital and still trying to watch out for us.

## The Big Comeback

Finally, we got her back home. She still had a couple of tubes that had to be taken care of and kept clean. She wouldn't let me do any of that kind of stuff. She had her cousin Rose, who is a nurse. Other friends of hers, Stephanie, who is also a nurse, Laticia and my daughter-in-law Maggie. Sissy, one of her other good friends, made sure I didn't have to worry about her.

She was going to have to go to San Francisco to see the doctor every week for the next 6 months. She would have to be measured and photographed. I don't know how she went through it.

But that was part of the agreement to get the surgery done. They were amazed at how well she was healing; the operation was a success, and she was in remission! Doc's Shop is doing pretty well, but I'm starting to have back pain. I have to cut down on my days that I work because of the doctor's appointments, and Pat's rules were, "No working on Sunday." That was family time.

Rose & Pat

## New Attitude

After the surgery, you could tell that Pat had a whole new appreciation of life; nothing was impossible. She wanted to have as much fun and adventure as she could. She also made a priority of spending time with the people that she loved. She went to church regularly and gave God all the credit for her success. She told me that she was going to live life differently. She said that, "Something happened during the operation." She didn't know how to explain it. She said that it was like, "My eyes were opened for the first time. I don't know how much time I might have, but I'm going to live it in the best way that I can!" She had never been into politics, but when Barack Obama came along, she was all in.

Being a grandmother was her greatest joy. She started her adventures slowly, taking the kids down to her favorite cousin Rose's house.

They would get into the hot tub. Pat and Rose were cousins by blood and best friends. I think I met her at our wedding. So she's known me our whole relationship and was part of many of our adventures. Pat told me that after that operation, I had been a little bit overprotective. But she knew that I trusted Rose. She was a good nurse. And had always watched out for Pat. So that's why she started going there first. (And to get in the hot tub) If memories were a treasure, we would be rich beyond our belief. Because in those years after the operation, we gave the grandbabies anything we could.

There are a few memories. We had a spa weekend at a resort that Laticia set up for us and our family. Rose was there in order to have the whole family there, and the baby Davinci said, "This is what dreams are made of."

One of my favorite memories was taking my two grandsons to a Sacramento Kings game. They had never been around that many people in their lives. We all got our seats, and the game started, and everyone was hollering, "Go kings, go kings," and making noise with the cow bells. My two grandsons are sitting there, looking a little scared. Like, something is wrong here? I told them that, "Yelling and being loud is what you do. When you come to a game, you let it all out." They were so loud and so exhausted they were asleep before we got out of the arena parking lot.

She also started having family get-together barbecues in the summer. Any holiday was an excuse for her to have everybody come over.

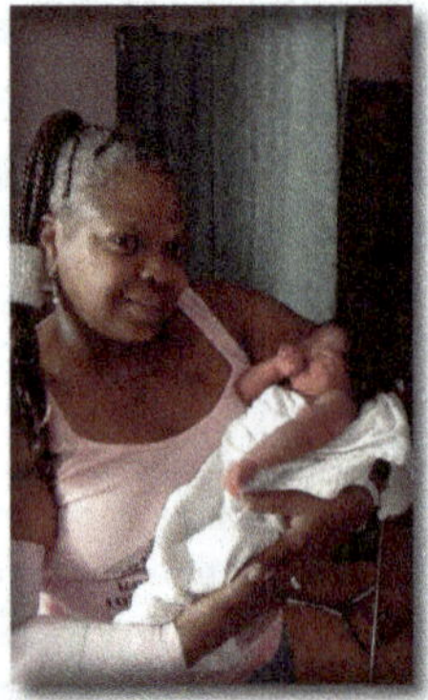
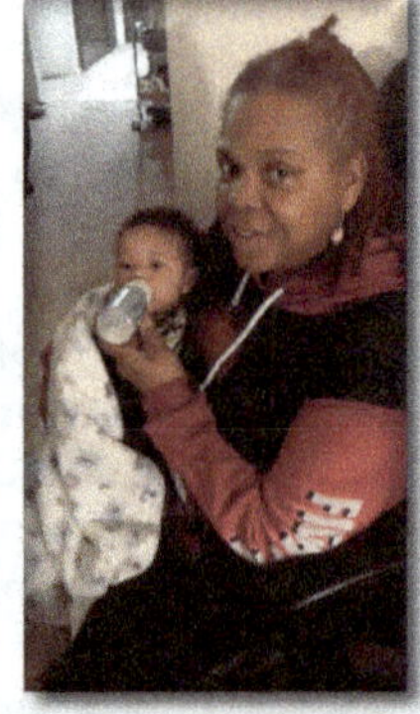

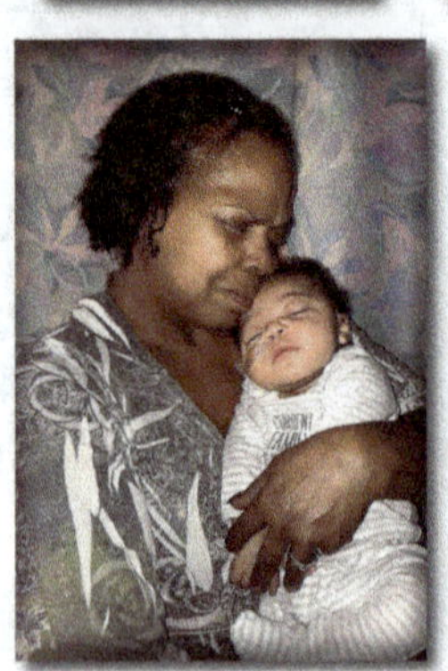

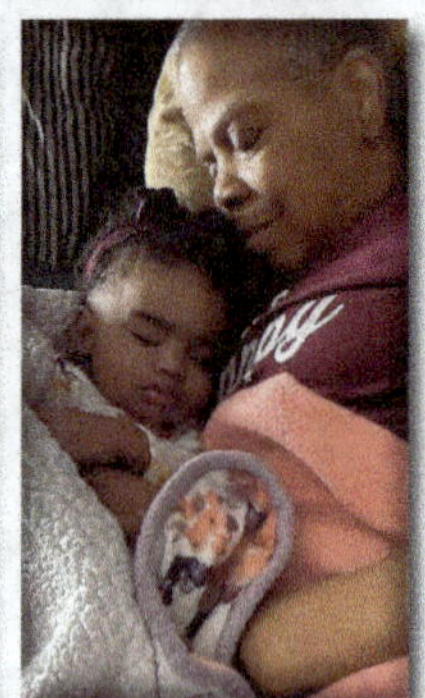

My sister Francine has five kids, my sister Cheryl has six, her brother
Earnest has three kids, her sister Carolyn has three kids, and my brother
Ritchie has two kids. Pat tried to give everyone love. Pat went to all of our
nieces, nephews and their children's  birthday parties. If she was invited
and could spend time with family, she was there. She would drag me along
sometimes.

If a baby was born, she would travel to embrace the new born child. "Nothing
was more important than family," she would say. Pat was happily spreading
all the love she had in her, but she was saddened by the relationship with her
mother.

All she wanted was the love and respect that she deserved. She was a good
daughter. Dorothy never made her feel like that. She never let Pat know that she
was proud of how she turned out. And it bothered my wife a lot.

Pat and her mother hadn't spoken to each other in about a year and a half.
Pat was frustrated, by the way. They could never talk about what the problems
were. Dorothy would act like nothing ever happened. And then gift her with a
trip to Hawaii or Kentucky. All Pat wanted was to be told by her mother that her
mother was proud of her and loved her.

## The Big 60

It kind of snuck up on me. I was going to be 60 years old. I didn't think that I
would make it past 16, and here I am, 60, with a beautiful family, and feeling like
I have my head on straight.

My wife has always let me know that she always appreciates the effort I put
in to provide the lifestyle that we were living. Pat had an idea that she wanted
to run by me; she's got a plan. She decided to tell me after my birthday party.

She and Laticia were planning a big party for me for my birthday. And we
weren't having it at our house. "Rose's house is where your party's going to be,"
She tells me. It's going to be nice. Rose has a beautiful house, so I wasn't mad at
it. We can listen to music and get into the hot tub. Now, when people are trying
to do something for you, let them.

I have been married for a long time. I know
when to roll with the punches.  You should be
happy that they want to express their love for
you. I wasn't a big party guy. That's what Pat
loves doing, but I'm going to be 60. I needed to
loosen up and try to enjoy life. I also needed
to shake off all of the stuff that we had been
through in the last couple of years and just
have a good time. Pat and Laticia went all out. I
don't know where they got it from but they give
me a *Star Trek* cake shape like the *Enterprise* with all the lights.

Pat, Doc, Laticia & Fran

I also received a Sacramento Kings jacket from D'Lamont's family. What I didn't know is that they called James, Ken Mac, and D'Lamont members of my band. We had four members of Manifest Destiny who hadn't been together in 30 years.

James brought some of his equipment and a karaoke screen in case I forgot the lyrics. My cousin Wanda brought her dad, whom I hadn't seen in 50 years. As a kid, I saw how well he took care of her. I only wished that my father was in my life like he was in hers. It was good to see that love that I saw when I was a kid, and he got a chance to see the love and family I had created. They wouldn't let me go into the backyard. They said it was a surprise. I walked into the backyard, and I had my , 'Five Heartbeats' moment. I remember the last scene in the movie by Robert Townsend, *The 5 Heartbeats*, where they let Eddie Kane know he was still part of the group. And as James handed me the microphone, I remembered what Ducks said in the movie, "Man, I ain't sang in years."

I was kind of afraid to let that part of me live again. But I had a great time filling my heart with all the love that they were giving me that night. I could finally let the ghost of my musical past die. I had asked myself for years, "What if I'd kept playing music? ... What if?"

As I look around at my family, and I'm feeling all this love, the question comes to mind, 'What if you didn't stop playing music? Would you have all of this?' And my answer was, "No."

I made my wife cry that night. Seeing me sing again touched her heart in ways that I'll never understand. I saw her and my sister, Francine, hugging like they used to do at my shows. It took me back. I felt that magic again. I felt that I had finally embraced my flaws, and learned from them as well. That question, 'Who am I?' Was answered that night.

## The Plan

A little while after my birthday Pat comes to me with her new idea. She said we've gone long enough without having credit cards. And we don't owe anybody. It's time for us to clean up our taxes.

One of Pat's friends, Mary, the mother of Nicholas and Hailie, helped us design a plan to get our taxes taken care of, and we put those plans into work. Over our long work history, we hadn't filed taxes for about 10 years. We had paid off all of our debt. We hadn't owed anybody anything for a long time, but we didn't have any credit. And the only way we could establish our credit again was to take care of these taxes, so we started down that path. It took us about 2 years but we finally finished up the taxes.

Now the second part of her plan was for us to build our credit back up. So we did that. And then Pat said we were going to class for first-time buyers. We went to the class, and we both passed it, but we couldn't make anything happen that first year. We take the class again and pass it, but still no luck. I'm getting a little frustrated, but I'm still trying to follow her lead. She believed that we could do it, so I put my skepticism to the side.

During this time, my son is trying to find a job that will keep him closer to home. The jobs that he's had are so far away. He would have to drive for two hours just to get to the job. And they only last about 8 months out of the year. He needs something to keep him going all year. He has an opportunity in Sacramento. It would mean that he would have to take the two boys out of school, and they did want to do that. So they left the kids with me and Pat. The kids stayed with us for about 6 months until the job was over.

Pat was in heaven; she had her babies every day. She'd take them to school, to the park, and have birthday parties. She was living the life.

I was doing my *Poppa* thing picking them up from school. I had always used riding bikes for my exercise, and it was great. I loved those days I had with them. At that time, baby Davinci and I

created a special bond. I took them all to the radio station. After a couple years of taking Davinci, he could run the show by himself. They loved being on the airwaves. I created different projects that I felt they could learn from. We were praying that my son would get a job that wasn't so tough, because he had done some crazy things to get a paycheck, just like his father. But he's a little crazier than me. In one of his jobs, he was strapped into a harness and hung over the side of a dam. Hanging 100 feet from the water below, sandblasting it to put a new coat over it.

I was proud that the skills I taught him allowed him to take care of his family. He had expanded on what I encouraged and picked up some new trades that he shared with me; he knew all about concrete now. He was getting ready to learn about solar heating with the company, Urban Design. We only wish that it would all work out at this point. He is a chip off the old block. "Seek what you don't know, keep learning," and, "Keep that food on the table."

My back is really giving me problems now. And Pat's got me going to the doctor every week for blood tests and all kinds of stuff. And we finally get the results back from the X-ray, and the doctor tells us that I need an operation to fix my back. But we only have a 30% chance of it being successful, and I needed to stop working before I ended up in a wheelchair. I had a deteriorating disc.

With that news, we were devastated. I can't work anymore. All I'm thinking is, 'Here we go again.' Right when I get things okay, something goes wrong. What am I going to do about my business, Docs Shop? Over the next 6 months. I hired people to run my business, but it just never worked out. So I had to shut it down because customers were never satisfied with their work.

At this point, I'm around 63–64 years old, and I have to go on disability and social security. Our monthly income took a big hit and made us wonder if we would still be able to qualify for the first-time buyers program. But with Pat's income, she was now working at her mother's restaurant, *Big Momma's Place*. She was the main cook. So we were able to meet the city's requirements to get a loan.

I did a bunch of physical therapy and stuff like that. But with only a 30% chance of success, I wasn't going to get the operation done. Pat agreed that a lot was going on in our lives.

At this time, my son came back in town and got a job in Chico with Urban Design. He was now doing solar installation, and I thought it was a great idea because it's the future, and it kept him working pretty much the whole year.

But with that came the move to Miguelia, right above Paradise, California. After the kids left, the silence was defining.

## The Friendship

Pat and Laticia always had a special relationship as mother and daughter, but we all watched a friendship—a kinder spirit type of relationship—grow when Laticia had her first miscarriage at nineteen.
Although we thought she was too young to have babies at nineteen because she wanted to have a career first, this miscarriage was still very traumatic for her and her mother. Now they were two women who had a shared experience with the pain of loss. They were talking, sharing on a deeper level, and caring for each other. They had walked in each other's shoes with their shared loss. Of which I'm told that unless you're a woman who has been through it, you will never understand it.

Laticia had done great in her career and had saved up money for a house. But decided, at thirty-two, she was ready to be a mother. I don't know all the details, but what I do know is that it wasn't easy for Laticia to conceive. So she and her partner at the time went through IVF (In Vitro Fertilization). Pat was right there too, holding Laticia's hand while the doctors tried to fix her damaged fallopian tubes. The diagnosis was not good and Pat knew what that meant. It would be more difficult for Laticia to conceive than other people.

Pat was upset about the diagnosis, but stayed calm throughout. Being with her during the retrieval of her eggs, holding her hand during the three different times she was implanted, crying and holding her during another two miscarriages, I don't even know how or why Laticia stopped trying, but I could see that emotionally and physically she was exhausted. Laticia and Pat had a lot of private conversations. I was told that Laticia is not going to keep trying to have kids, and we are not going to talk about it.

I didn't have to be told twice. I was feeling sad and disappointed. Not in her but the situation. I know she would have been a great mother because she is a great auntie. This was probably the first goal in her life that she wasn't able to complete. Being a mom was very important to her.

As time passed, Laticia and I spoke about her experience, and did you know that the IVF process cost her over $58,000 and she still doesn't have a child of her own? But I do believe that God has a different plan for her. She's like her mother, and sprinkles love everywhere she goes and has changed many young people's lives, even though she's not a mother. God's got another plan for her; she just has to keep the love in her heart.

## What I Didn't Know

After the kid's move to Magalia, me and Pat put more energy into community service. I work a little harder on my radio show, and at this time I was getting picked on by the general manager, Bobby, of the radio station 107.1 FM at the African American and Family Culture Center.

Let me explain. For the last couple of years, I have been teaching the class for people to get certified, so you'd be able to go on the air. All of Bobby's DJ's were taught by me. And when they had problems, they would bring them to me. Well, he got jealous of that. He wasn't a good person, and I had gained the students trust. And he treated the female DJ's *less than*.

Well, after being held back a couple of times from whipping his ass for disrespecting the ladies right in front of me, I knew it was time for me to go. After leaving, I realized how much being on the radio meant to me. Now, was I good enough to go somewhere else? Did I have that kind of confidence? Did I have enough talent? I was going to find out.

I called all the radio stations in the area and got two interviews. I was hired at both places, and I decided to go with KROV 91.1 FM. It was closer to the house. They had no representation of people of color, hip-hop, soul, or anything ethnic, so now it was my job to bring that to the radio station.

The freedom was wonderful. I did the job of program director for a while, and I introduced them to the Sheryl Underwood show. Another one of hers was *Late-Night Cup-Caking*. They had me for 4 hours a week playing hip-hop. And then I brought another 12 hours of reggae and R&B music.

KROV 91.1
KROV 91.1 FM
CLASSICAL JAZZ OLDIES
DRY BLUES ROCK
R&B GOSPEL
VILLE COMMUNITY RADIO
2360

KROV 91.1 FM
Oroville's #1 Community Radio Station
THE DJ DOC SHOW
The Bird
Rap Hip Hop Fri. - 7:00pm - 10:00pm
(P.O BOX 9) Oroville, Ca. 95965
Phone # 530-534-1200
krov.fm/listen

Now the radio station represented all of the people. My show played all of
the newest music every week. My specialty was playing the rest of the albums
that I called, *The Slice*. So you can really get to know the artist I would play 2 or
3 songs from the album. With my newfound confidence, I added another show.
They gave me a lot of freedom, and I called it, *DJ DOC Keepin' It Real*, where I
talked about politics and the state of the country. We gave a lot of information
about services that people didn't know about and information on breast cancer
awareness. To have freedom was incredible. I was finally allowed to talk and be
me. Within a year, I was recognized for having the most listeners in the region
in my time slot. It was wonderful; I was kind of a ghetto star. People recognized
my voice at the grocery store. Pat loved it.

One day we get an emergency call over our cell phones telling us to evacuate

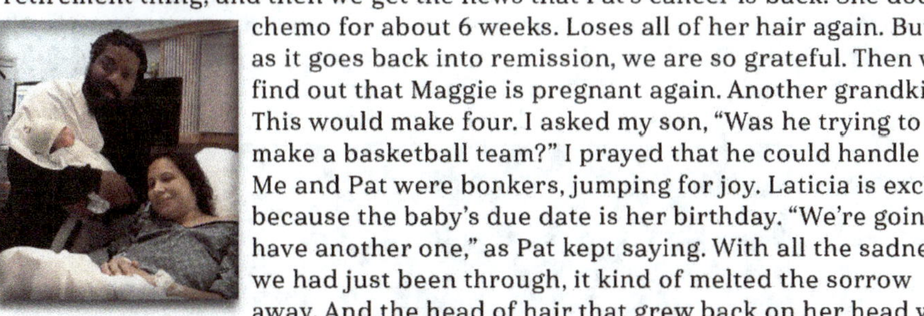

the city. The dam might burst and where we live would
be underwater. We got the dogs, the medicine, and the
paperwork, and we packed up some clothes.

It was the first time we had to make a 'go bag.' Luckily,
Pat's parents had property that was up the mountain, so
we went to their property and stayed for 3 days. The dam
was repaired, but a strange feeling came over us. We never
realized we were in that kind of danger.

I'm starting to get used to not going to work every day. Me
and Pat spend a lot of time together. We have never talked
about this time in our lives. We are starting to like this
retirement thing, and then we get the news that Pat's cancer is back. She does
chemo for about 6 weeks. Loses all of her hair again. But
as it goes back into remission, we are so grateful. Then we
find out that Maggie is pregnant again. Another grandkid?
This would make four. I asked my son, "Was he trying to
make a basketball team?" I prayed that he could handle it.
Me and Pat were bonkers, jumping for joy. Laticia is excited
because the baby's due date is her birthday. "We're going to
have another one," as Pat kept saying. With all the sadness
we had just been through, it kind of melted the sorrow
away. And the head of hair that grew back on her head was
probably the healthiest hair she ever had, and she was very proud of it.

## Now You Really Know

My wife has had me going to the doctor regularly for the last few years.
Ever since we found out about my high blood pressure, it has to be monitored,
checked every 3 months. I go to the appointment, and my regular doctor isn't
there. She was sick or something. She has someone standing in for her who
happens to be a black doctor from Kenya.

The first couple minutes are normally a question-and-answer session, so

he asks me about why I was taking fish oil. I told him that I had been advised by my doctor to take it for high cholesterol, and immediately, in his African accent, he told me, "No, no-no-black men aren't supposed to take that." He told me that I needed to have a prostate test done immediately. He ordered the test for me, and I never saw him again. I go and get the test done. Now we just have to wait for the test results, but he's got me a little nervous. Maggie calls and says that it's that time, the baby is coming, and Pat and Laticia have been there for all the other births. So I knew we were going. Laticia drives from Sacramento, and she picked us up. We head to the hospital in Paradise and the begin the long wait.

I'm at my son's house with the boys, Pat and Laticia are at the hospital. I don't remember how long it was but I got a call about 5 o'clock in the morning saying that my granddaughter is here. Divinity was born one day before Laticia's birthday. So their personalities are similar. We were overjoyed that we got this chance to raise another female. Pat was overwhelmed with happiness and couldn't wait for her to get big enough for Pat to spoil the shit out of her. Pat had another mini-me.

The world doesn't stop, and shortly after her birth, we found out that the owners of the house we rented were going to sell it. We had some decisions to make. The first-time buyer program allowed us to make an offer. We knew how much the city would loan us, so all we had to do was get the seller to agree. Did we want to make an offer on this house, or did we want to try to find something bigger? We decided to put a bid on the house we were in. The relationship we had with the owners was good, so they accepted our offer.

We were now going to be homeowners because of my wife's stubbornness
and persistence. She told me we could do it. It took us four years to put a deal
together, but we finally did it! I didn't always believe we could, but she did.
Pat and I were proud of what we had accomplished. We had done something
in our family that we thought would only be possible to get from her parents:
'generational wealth.' We had done it all by ourselves. We would have a legacy to
leave to our children when we leave this earth.

## I Got It Too

Now we are waiting to get the results from my test. Ever since we found out
about my back, Pat wouldn't let me go to the doctor by myself. She didn't think I
would tell her if I got bad news. So we're sitting in the doctor's office to get the
results of the test. He comes in, and we feel the bad vibes. He says, "I got some
bad news. You have prostate cancer. And the bad part is that it's stage 4." We are
both stunned, and we fall into each other's arms. Pat asked him what could be
done, and he said, "You need to have an operation immediately."

My head is spinning; 'I'm gonna die.' I don't know what to do; I'm freaking
out. All Pat can do is try to calm me down and let me know that there are some
options. But my understanding was that, at stage four, 'You gonna die.'

The way I'm feeling is like I just got a death sentence. I have cancer now, and
the strange thing was, I had no symptoms. I have been feeling pretty good.
I watched Pat go through all of her stuff, and I was just a little scared. I didn't
think I had the strength that she had; they were going to cut me. That's all I
could think about, and they're going to put me under anesthesia. I don't know
if I can handle it. I didn't know how to come to terms with it. Before we left, Pat
made me an appointment to have the operation.

The appointment is a couple of weeks away. I can't remember a time in my
life when I was so unsure about the future. Was I going to have any more life to
live? Thinking about it put me into a deep depression. Now I understand how
Pat truly believed that God had sent the African doctor to me, because he was
heaven sent. If it had been my regular doctor, they would have never found out
about my prostate, and I wouldn't be here right now.

## It's That Time

So I took my wife's advice and got on, *Faith's Lane*. It's time for the operation,
and I'm not really sure about this stuff. I can't put a thought together. I'm so
worried about my mortality.

It's the day of the operation and my family's here. Pat has called Rose; she is
a nurse and could answer a lot of questions. She was always a great strength
for Pat. In my opinion, they were more like sisters than cousins and friends. As
a family in situations like this, we always asked a bunch of questions so that we
knew what to expect, or somewhat knew.

Laticia and De, are here to give me some strength. It's that time, and they roll me in through the big doors into the operating room where there are 5 or 6 people. It's a scene right off the television. They asked me to count backwards from 10, then put the mask over my face. As they put the needle in my arm, I think I counted back to 5.

The next thing I knew, I was waking up in the recovery room with the a ten-inch scar from my groin to my stomach. They had a catheter in my penis and a bag attached to me. It was a strange experience. I had to keep it on for about 2 weeks. The scar tissue from the operation closed my urinary tract. The pain of not being able to piss was the worst pain I ever felt. Once the catheter was removed, I had to go back so that they could laser-open my urinary tract. So I had a second operation within a month. It made me reflect on Pat's first procedure. Mine only took about an hour, and Pat was on the table for 10 hours. I knew I didn't have her strength. I was so grateful I had her to take care of me, because it was a quite an experience. Pat had nursed me through a lot of things through our marriage, but this was big. It shook me to my core to think about having to deal with my diagnosis while she had to endure cancer for all these many years. I could barely handle the paranoia thinking about how many days I may have left. I don't feel I handled it well. Every time I have to take a blood test I wonder, "Is it going to come back positive?" And cross my fingers every time. Now we would both have cancer the rest of our lives.

## The Camp Fire

A couple of months after my operation, the camp fire began. We weren't in danger, but we didn't see the sky for about 2 months because of all the smoke. We got a frantic call from my son one morning, saying that Paradise is being evacuated and Magalia is only a few miles away from Paradise. It's all being evacuated. He informs us that he's going to get his family, and they would be at our house as soon as possible.

His family is in danger, and they just had a new baby. He calls us back once or twice over the next 5 hours. He said that all the roads were closed and he couldn't get to his family. We could hear the panic in his voice, and it had us on edge. Especially when there was no more cell phone service.

After waiting 4 more hours, we finally get a call from Maggie, and she's calling from downtown Chico, somewhere. She and the family were safe. But we had no way to let our son know that Maggie had one of the neighbors take her and the kids down to Chico. Maggie couldn't get in touch with De. We are looking at the news reports on television. We see that Paradise is burning to ashes, and our son is trying to get to his family.

We're desperately trying to call him to let him know his family is safe. We
know he's not going to stop until he gets to his house. And what we see on TV
has us all paranoid and frightened of what could be. What my son tells me is
that he drove every back road he could find as long as it was leading him up to
Magalia.

He did make it home, and the family wasn't there, so now he said he had to
drive back down the hill through all of the fire. It was hard for him to explain in
words that he had witnessed trees exploding, and whole neighborhoods gone.

The places that he used to shop at are all gone, burned to the ground. He
said it was right out of a movie. But it was real life; I could see it would take him
some time to process it all. It was a joy when we saw them pull up and hop out
of the car. It had been a stressful day.

I believe they stayed with us for about a week. And then they were allowed
to go back up to their house. That fire shook up this part of the country. And his
job was going away because of the fire. He had another job offer, but he would
have to move to Las Vegas. That was the last thing we wanted to hear. The kids
were moving to Las Vegas?

But you have to do what you have to do to keep your family strong. And we
always wanted him to do what was best for his family. It's hard to explain the
feelings that my wife and I had about our grandkids moving out of town. Sad
about that, but happy that our son was the man that he is. Our grandkids were
such a big part of our day-to-day lives and we knew it was going to be hard to
adjust, but we promised to come and visit as soon as we could.

## Not the News We Wanted

The kids have been gone for a few months and Pat can't take it anymore. So
we get her a flight to Las Vegas so she can visit her babies. I'm still doing the DJ
Doc show every Friday night from 7 to 10 if nobody else is listening. I know that
my wife is listening and would give me suggestions, and have me shout out too
her friends who were listening. She posted something for me every week.

We are waiting for the results from her last checkup and the news wasn't
good. She now had a growth on her spine close to her brain, and no more
chemotherapy or radiation could fix it. All they could do now was try an
experimental drug that might slow down the growth.

We were all devastated—my family and I. But Pat wouldn't let us live there.
She told us she was going to keep living as long as she could and for us not to
act like she was dying because she was still alive.

This was the beginning of us going to the cancer center every 3 weeks to
get treatment. Over time, I could see the physical change. But everything in me
wanted to ignore it. If you talk to my wife, nothing is wrong, and she continues
to plan trips. She went to Kentucky. She went to the Monterey Aquarium with
Lisa and Chelsea, to Tahoe, and made many trips to Rose's house.

# Lock Down

Here comes COVID, and we are all locked down. And the last thing that we could let happen was for her immune system to become infected. So COVID was a scary time for us. I was healing pretty well from my surgery. We find out that Maggie is pregnant again, and we're going to have grand-baby number 5. And with that news, it gave Pat a new reason for living. She was determined to see this new baby, and she was going to be here when the baby got here.

We cried many nights together, thinking about the possibility of either one of us not being here. "God's got his plans," she would say.

During the lock-down, me and James had been talking and came up with an idea to put our music on video. We didn't have anything else to do, so we figured out how we could work from our computers and link them together, and we started making videos of our music. Over the next couple of years, we will create five videos. Pat helped create her 3D model in one of the videos. She was more hyped than I was.

Since the lock-down, she has become pretty connected with the whole social media thing. She had groups of people that she talked to every week. Cancer support groups, her prayer warrior group, and all of our families. She was really reaching out and touching people.

Every time we put out a video, me and her would celebrate. She told me that years ago she wished that I would have done music again, and for me to be doing it now warmed her heart.

We were going to have our stuff on YouTube. We were finally going to have the world hear our music. I was stoked, and Pat told anyone who would listen to watch my channel. We renamed the band *Funky Rockits!* Making the videos was a nice distraction from this stuff that we both had been going through.

Cancer was zapping her strength at this time. She was still trying to do her walks every day. But the cancer was finally catching up with her, though she continued to travel. She went to Kentucky to attend Carolyn's sister's daughter's wedding. I didn't want her to go, but I couldn't talk her out of it. The thing that made me give in was that she would be flying there with her sister. Tobina. Pat was losing the strength in her legs, but partied like a rock star with her fancy walker that I got for her. She's never let anything slow her down, not even cancer.

We had been locked down for what seemed like a year, we all seemed to lose track of time anyways. The lock-down was hard, and in that time we had only gone to her favorite spot on the river and to the store. I would take her to the river a couple times a week since we couldn't be around people, and being around people was what gave her life. I didn't express it to anyone, but I was getting really scared during this time. I was watching this cancer sucking the life out of my wife. I tried to push my fears to the side and live in the moment.

Our love was deeper than it had ever been. Our shared experience of both having cancer is what brought us closer together. We knew exactly what each other was feeling.

## Big Dog Is Here

We had really gotten in touch with each other. During these lock-down times,  we had so many talks and cleared up so many questions that we might have had over the years. At this time, Pat's mother started reaching out again.        Pat questioned her motives and didn't want to get sucked in to any mind games One day, her mother told her that she loved, respected her and was proud of her. Pat did not really know how to handle it. She waited all her life to hear that, and now that it had happened, she didn't know how to process it. She cried over that, and all I could tell her was what she had told me, "God doesn't always give it to you when you want it. He gives it to you when you need it."

We get a call. Our oldest grandson told us that the baby was coming and that they had called 911. The baby is coming. As the story goes, Maggie didn't realize the baby was coming. It was already too late; the head was coming out. There was no way to get her to a hospital, so my son had to deliver his son, DarShaun Hall, in 2020. They tell us that he came out with the chord wrapped around his neck. But my son's cool and calm demeanor helped him that night. He unwrapped the chord and waited for the paramedics, and everything turned out fine.

## Road Trip

After COVID, we had a couple nice weekends at Laticia's hotel. She always spoiled us and would put us in the best room in the place. The presidential suite or the executive headquarters. Always something grand. Something that we couldn't afford or wouldn't spend the money on. "Only the best for my parents", she would say. She let's us know that she's got a surprise for us. We're going to Las Vegas, and we're going to get to see our baby boy, Darshaun. He's almost a year old now, and we've only talked to him over video chat. But we were going to get to hold him in our arms now. We were both very excited. It seemed like it took forever to get there. We had a great time visiting the kids, gambling, eating, and taking in the sites. We got a chance to catch up with Pat's old friend Mary, and Laticia's childhood friend Raylene. We had not seen them in about 10 years. The two girls are all grown up now.

We knew that the distance between us was going to be hard, but Pat cheered up the minute she heard that they were coming to town and would be staying with us for about 2 weeks.

She was in heaven. I took them to the park by the river. She cooked with DaVinci. She made all the meals that they liked, that only she knew how to make; she was in full *Gramzie* mode. Me and the boys ride road bikes and play basketball. We both got some good sleep the two weeks that they were here; we were worn out every day. It was time for them to go on their way back to Texas. We were both extremely upset. We didn't know if that would be the last time Pat would see them.

A couple months after we get back From Las Vegas, De informs us that he's got an opportunity for a better, higher-paying job, but that would mean that he would have to move to Texas. We were happy for him, but devastated at the same time. It would mean that they would be farther away from us, and that devastated Pat. She was very proud of her son; he was now going to have the title of 'General Foreman,' earning $30K more a year with all the benefits. He had come a long way, and we were very proud of what he had accomplished.

I had seen the anguish in my son over the last 2 weeks. We couldn't even have a conversation about it without breaking down and crying. And never really getting out the fear that we had of losing her. He could see how much weight Pat had lost, and he was worried. His mother had told him to, "Take this job." He worked too long to get where he was, and she would have never forgiven herself if he hadn't taken this job because of her condition.

## A Dark Day

Laticia and I, we're trying to prepare ourselves for what Dr. Robinson was going to tell us. She made sure we were both there before she gave Pat any updates. Through her tears, Dr. Robinson informed us that the drugs were no longer working. If Pat continued taking a cocktail of drugs, she could die

sooner. There was nothing else that they could do but try to keep her vitals right. Pat's visits to the doctor's increased to every week. I don't remember all of the medical terms. Something to do with her white blood cells would get too low. But it got to a place where they basically rejuvenated her blood. We got back in the car from the doctor's visit. We were devastated, and she looked at us two and told us that nothing had changed. She was going to live her life, and for us, please don't mourn for her, at least until she is gone. Every week, the cancer was getting worse. I had to make her stop cleaning the house. Even if it took all day, she still tried to do it. Pat was really starting to need help, but luckily Shaveeta, her pastor's daughter started doing the chores around the house that Pat needed to have done. They talked for hours and became great friends.

What I didn't know was that Pat was telling Laticia what she wanted for her homegoing. She never let me know anything about those conversations. She also started receiving Amazon packages, and some of them she would not let me see. Pat surprised me with an HP computer and bought me a podcast setup so I could do the radio show from home, and a variety of other things.

At the time, I didn't know what she was doing, but I can see it now. What are you supposed to feel when a doctor tells you, "She only has months to live."

But for some reason, I could feel that Pat had already come to terms with her destiny. Pat found peace in it, but I could not make peace with it. I was destroyed inside, thinking that we would not be together. And now it was predicted that I wouldn't have her in my life anymore.

Over the next months, I made sure she had everything that she desired. All the exotic food that she loved to eat, whatever she wanted. The family said, I "Hovered over her like a hawk."

I never understood some of the stories I heard about husbands leaving their wives when they had cancer. I don't know how that's possible to do if you truly love someone.

Pat had something planned before we got this news. She planned to go to a concert at the Gold Country Casino, and she didn't want me to go because it was *Girl's Night*. She informed me that she would be spending the night at the casino.

At this time, I'm watching every move she makes to make sure she doesn't fall and break a bone or something. It was hard for me to see her go to that concert. I was very worried. I was just a little bit overprotective and wanted to spend every minute with her. She wanted to go and spend that time with her friends, and who was I to take those moments from them? And of course, I cringed when they were telling me the story of her dancing with her walker. If I remember correctly, the group was cousin Rose, Stephanie, Pilar, and Lisa. Pat chose to tell everyone in the group about her health condition. I didn't tell anyone anything except my sister Francine and D'Lamont.

Laticia came up every weekend, and people came to our house every day. All of the friends that she had made in town came to visit. People that I didn't even know she knew. She had always told me she wanted to be like Granny. A person who was loved by so many, I could see that she had accomplished that.

## Dog Babies

Teal'c

Worf

Smoke

Worf & Teal'c

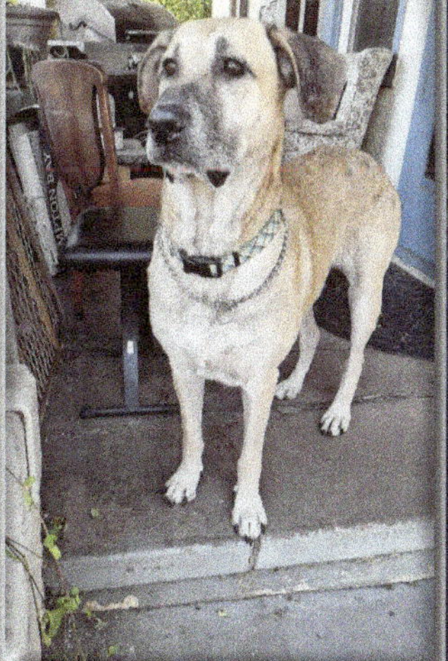

Shaka

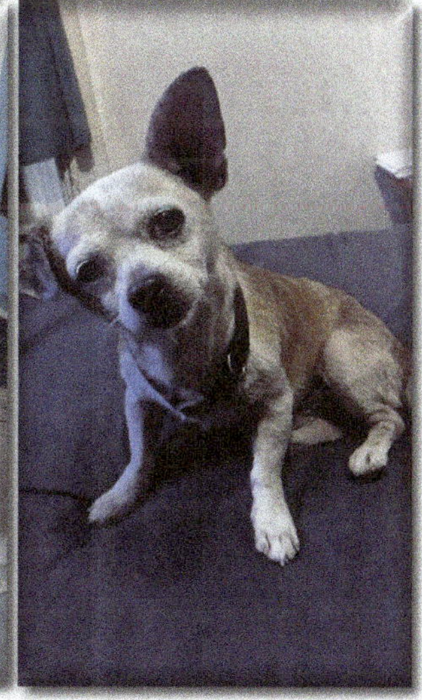

Tear

My wife loved her dogs, and she always had to have a big one. We both
grew up with big dogs, so all through our relationship, we had big dogs. She
loved German Shepherds and Chihuahuas. We even had a wolf hybrid. My
wife spoiled them rotten. She could interpret their bark. They knew who their
master was, and it wasn't me. She had them eating greens and all kinds of
different things; she spoiled them like they were our kids, and they were loyal
to her.

## Hospice

We had one more doctor's visit, and in that meeting, we were told that it was
time for her to go on hospice. With everything in me, I didn't want to hear that.
So my mind shuffled through every story I had heard about hospice, and some
people had lived for a year or more. So those are the stories that I put in my
mind; I didn't want to face the gravity of the situation.

She might only have a couple months. She had fought for almost 20 years,
and somewhere inside of me, I didn't want her to suffer any more. She had
been through some hard times for so many years. I felt it wasn't fair and tried
to believe that God has a plan. As a little kid, I've never understood what His
plan was. I never understood why someone that I love had to be taken from me.
Hopefully, I'll know when, "It's time for me to go."

We don't have the whole picture yet. We're going to have a meeting with the
hospice people. Once we got back to the house, Laticia called her brother and
let him know what we had just found out. De let her know he was on his way.
We had the meeting, and the picture they painted was saddening to us. To think
about a future without her was driving me crazy. All they talked about was pain;
it would become unbearable. She would have to take stronger pain medication
which would basically have her sleeping all day. When Pat heard that, she
politely asked them to leave and told them that, "We'll get back to you." Because
her grandkids were coming, her birthday was coming, and our 50th anniversary
was coming, she wanted to be in her right mind. All me and Laticia could do was
respect her wishes.

We were very concerned about how this whole thing was going to go down;
there was no handbook for this stuff. All we needed to do was give back the
love and attention that she had given us all these years. Hopefully she would
know how much we loved her. Our emotions are on a yo-yo string; you can't let
her see how spun out we were. I'm praying heavily to God that I don't *crack up*
during this time. It's the grief before the grief.

## Pat aka Gramzie

De and his family finally get to town. It was like a shot of adrenaline for my
wife. When she laid eyes on her grandbabies, she was in her happy place. What
we witnessed is what I call a, 'God Moment.'

CALIFORNIA
US
66

CALIFORNIA
US
66

LVV
LAS VEGAS


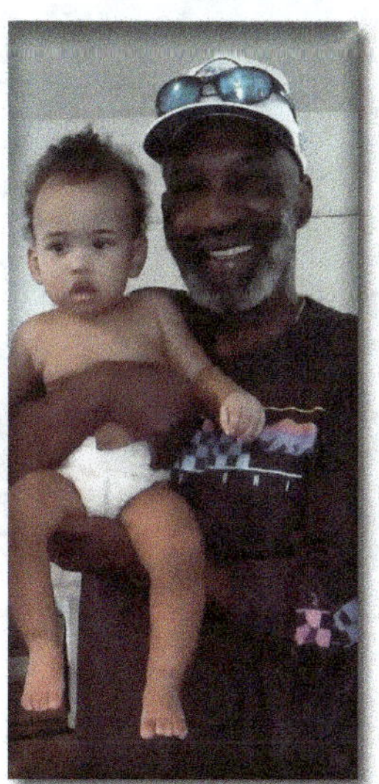

Because her strength came back, me and Laticia are having to tell her to, "Chill out." No trips to the park, but she was in the yard with them every day and watched them from the front porch while they rode bikes and scooters and played basketball in the street. It was the happiest we had seen her in months, and her energy was great.

There was a moment, I remember, that made her cry. The adults were talking and saying: That Divinity looked a lot like Laticia, and Divinity politely stopped everyone and said, "No. I look like my grandmother!"

Pat was so proud in that moment. She said it reminded her of Laticia's enlightened attitude at such a young age. At night, sadness would come when she thought about not being able to see them grow up; that was the one thing that bothered her the most. We would have long talks into the early morning hours during this fleeting precious time.

She had a list of things that she wanted me to do after she was gone. But I avoided the list as long as I could. I didn't want to think about her not being with me. We let each other know how much we appreciated the life that we had given each other. We both didn't want it to end, even though God has plans for everyone.

The grand babies did not appreciate all the people coming by all the time. They said it took their grandmother's time away, and they didn't appreciate it; she had always given them 100% of her attention.

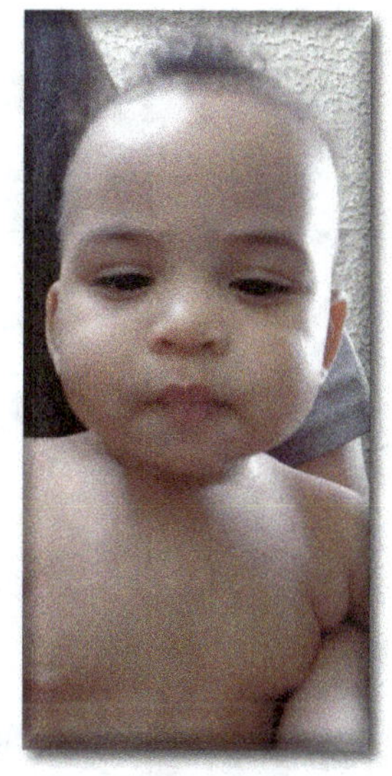

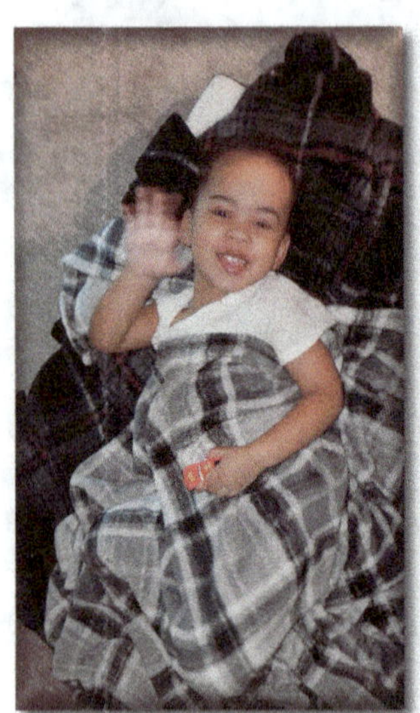  

# Grand Kids

Pat started telling people not to come by while the kids were here. It was strange because people would come up to the door and ask if this was where Pat lived. I had never seen these people before. But when she saw them, she knew their story and everything about them. I was amazed at how many people my wife actually knew. It's that time when De has to get back to work. The family spent about three weeks with us. When it was time for them to go, everybody's emotions were fully on display. The kids were crying, and we were crying. It was a mess.

Pat told me that night that would be the last time she would be able to hold her babies. I didn't want that to be true, and I couldn't find the words to comfort her.

## I Have Things To Do

A few weeks have gone by since the kids left. We had the meeting with hospice, and they instructed me on how to administer her medications. And I didn't want to mess it up; I wrote down every pill. How much water is she drinking? How much was she eating? This was on me. And I was scared. I didn't want myself to be the cause of anything going wrong. They move a hospital bed into the living room to make her more comfortable. She was still resistant to starting the hospice program because her birthday was coming. And she had promised me that she was going to make it to our 50th anniversary, which was 4 days after her birthday. All I could do was believe her. When her birthday comes, we have just a few people come by: her family, my sister, and my niece Brianna. My sister Francine knew her before I did, and their friendship had lasted all these years.

Me and Pat thanked Francine for introducing us to each other way back in 1972. We were supposed to have a big celebration for our 50th anniversary, but Pat was a little too tired. I remember her looking at me with a smile on her face. When she told me, "I made it baby, happy 50th!" It's impossible for me to put into words my emotional state at that time. Knowing that I was going to lose her, not knowing when she would transcend, had really messed me up.

The pain was increasing. Laticia and her partner, Mirage decided to stay over for a couple days after our anniversary. I remember my frustration when Pat stopped eating. Laticia recognized how distraught I was. It took a toll on me watching the cancer sucking the life out of my wife. The day after our anniversary she wouldn't let me give her any medicine.

Before we went to bed, she wanted to talk. We talked until the sun came
up in the morning and probably would have talked longer, but her pain got
too intense. We fell asleep in each other's arms. We hadn't really been able to
cuddle like that because of the pain for a quite a while. But this night, she laid
her head on my chest and cuddled me in her special way.

From what my daughter tells me, she checked in on us three or four times.
For the last month, she was too weak to stand up and shower. We were snuggled
up like young teenagers in love. So I had Stephanie, her friend and her sister,
Cynthia, assist me in giving her a shower, except when Laticia was there.

So this morning, Pat says, "I'm too tired to take a shower." And she just wants
Laticia to wipe her up. A "Monkey bath", as she used to call it. When Laticia was
finished wiping her up, Pat lifted up her shaking hand and touched Laticia's
cheek, and mumbled, "I love you."

Now I have to get her up and put her in the wheelchair. So I ask her to put
her hands on my shoulders. I embrace her to lift her up. As I'm lifting her up,
I pull her closer to me. I feel her breath on my neck. And with that, I knew she
took her last breath. She is gone.

This was different. It was like nothing else that I experienced; the grief
was different. It was so deep. The three of us were standing there in silence.
Suspended in time, the moment seemed to last forever.
She was no longer here. We are standing there, holding back from doing CPR,
to prolong her life. Because that was her strict instruction. She did not want to
be put on life support; that was her biggest nightmare. The hardest thing for me
to do was not attempt to bring her back. She had made me and Laticia promise
her that we wouldn't. Laticia had saved a man with CPR a couple years earlier,
and Pat made her promise not to perform it on her. My memory is like a con
man for me. Because it can lie to me.
I don't remember in detail about the rest of that day. I remember crying
uncontrollably. I do remember playing a video of our lives together that Laticia
made for us over and over again for hours.

## Going Home

I lost my beautiful wife on July 17th, 2022. We arranged her homegoing for
August 4th to give my son time to get here and her sister's family time to fly in
from Kentucky. Over the next month I was lost, confused, scared, saddened, and
full of grief. Laticia was handling all of the arrangements. Surprisingly, Pat's
mother did love her, and she now expresses it with financial help, whatever
Laticia needed to fulfill her mother's wishes.

Over the months, Pat had told Laticia exactly what she wanted. She gave
Laticia the Sausalito dress, the most expensive dress she owned. I bought it for
her 42 years ago, and Pat told her the exact color she wanted. I thank God for
my daughter who had to deal with all of that stuff.

NOT A
THROUGH
STREET

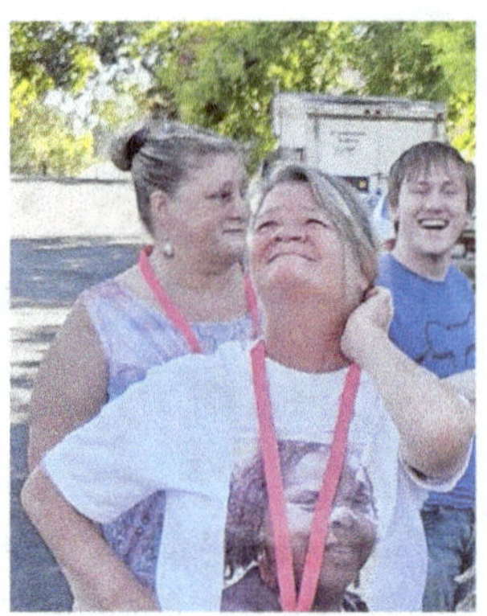

Because I wasn't in any shape to even help, between De and Laticia and Pat's brother Ernest, everything got taken care of.

The day of the homegoing I was like a robot. I don't remember much about that day. But the funeral place was packed. I have been there a couple times for Pats aunties, May, Bert, and Norma. I had never seen it that packed. My wife Pat was really loved. She had truly become a part of the community. Everyone had on purple and white. It was beautiful. Seeing Laticia in the Sausalito dress, she looked just like her mother. It made me drop a tear.

In those long talks, she gave me a list of things that she wanted me to do over the next year. And over the next year, I would find a birthday present and also a Christmas gift for me from her. Even in her passing, she made sure I felt loved. Living without her is like a survival game. She is gone now. All I have left is her memories which give me strength to survive day-by-day. I would complete her list of things.

Finishing this book is finishing the list. She thought our story was unique, and she wanted to share it with our family and the world. For my kids, they should know that their mother was very proud of the people that they've become.

Cancer is a long journey, and you have to just put it in God's hands and keep your mind on being better. And that's what Pat did, and I hope that I can do that too. My wife's only regret is that she wouldn't be able to see her grandchildren grow up to be adults.

She wanted me to live and love again. But I will never find another love like hers; why even try? We never called each other soulmates, but that's what we were.

I pulled my head out of the pages of this book, and two years have gone by. I thank God for my kids taking care of me and showing me that they love me. There is surviving, and then there is living.

I know that God up above
Created her for me to love
He picked her out of all the rest
Because he knew I would love her best
She had a heart that was so fine and true
I give a little piece of it to you
So let's take care for she has done
Cause she was my only one

The question, "Who I am?"
I'd tell you, "I'm Pat's man!"
Heavenly Father up above
Protect all the ones I love
Guide them, keep them, let them know
She will always love them so
The joy that we shared as a family
Was a blessing, precious and holy

## The Gift of Pat Magic

Pat and I felt having our kids was the greatest gift. We got to learn and grow from each other. I mean, the kids taught us great lessons; it is one of God's gifts. I believe in reincarnation, and my mission in this life, was to truly know what love was, to have love, true love. To understand what family was. Love is what saved me time after time. And in my confusing times trying to figure it out.

The love for family is what built the bridge that kept me centered. To truly make your dreams come true, live in the way that people only dream about and to find that special one. When we found each other, we found love, and we held onto it for 50 years.

I knew Pat and my kids loved me. To my kids, "Don't remember how she died. Remember how she lived!" All through our lives, it was important for Pat to have family and friends around her. It took me some getting used to, but I learned to appreciate it. All of the dinners and barbecues were filled with joy and love. It's what she lived for—to be around people, sharing all the love inside of her. She had a lot to give. She was famous throughout the family for her potato salad and 'Monkey Bread.' She called it that because you just tear into it and eat it. Also her, 'Ghetto Chow Mein' and her turkey that she cooked in a brown

paper bag. Pat learned that technique from my mother or one of her aunts', I'm not quite sure. But the Turkey would always be so juicy. She created the family that we dreamed about as kids. I could have never imagined the number of people who truly loved her. My wife was magical. She had that thing that would pull you into your safe place, and you felt like she really cared, because she did. People knew that she cared about what they were saying to her. Marriage may be hard sometimes. But the joy that you receive from it is worth the hard times. To feel like someone truly cares is priceless. To know they have your back all the way, through those ups and downs, is the ultimate expression of devotion. It's a feeling that's hard to explain, but it's there if you can receive it (real love).
My wife taught me that.
That question: : "Who am I?"

"I'm Pat Hall's husband."

## "UWMA"
## Until We Meet Again

# Pat's Family

**Our Nieces**

Cousins

Fran & Maggie

**The Author
Dwayne Erroll Hall**

## Generations

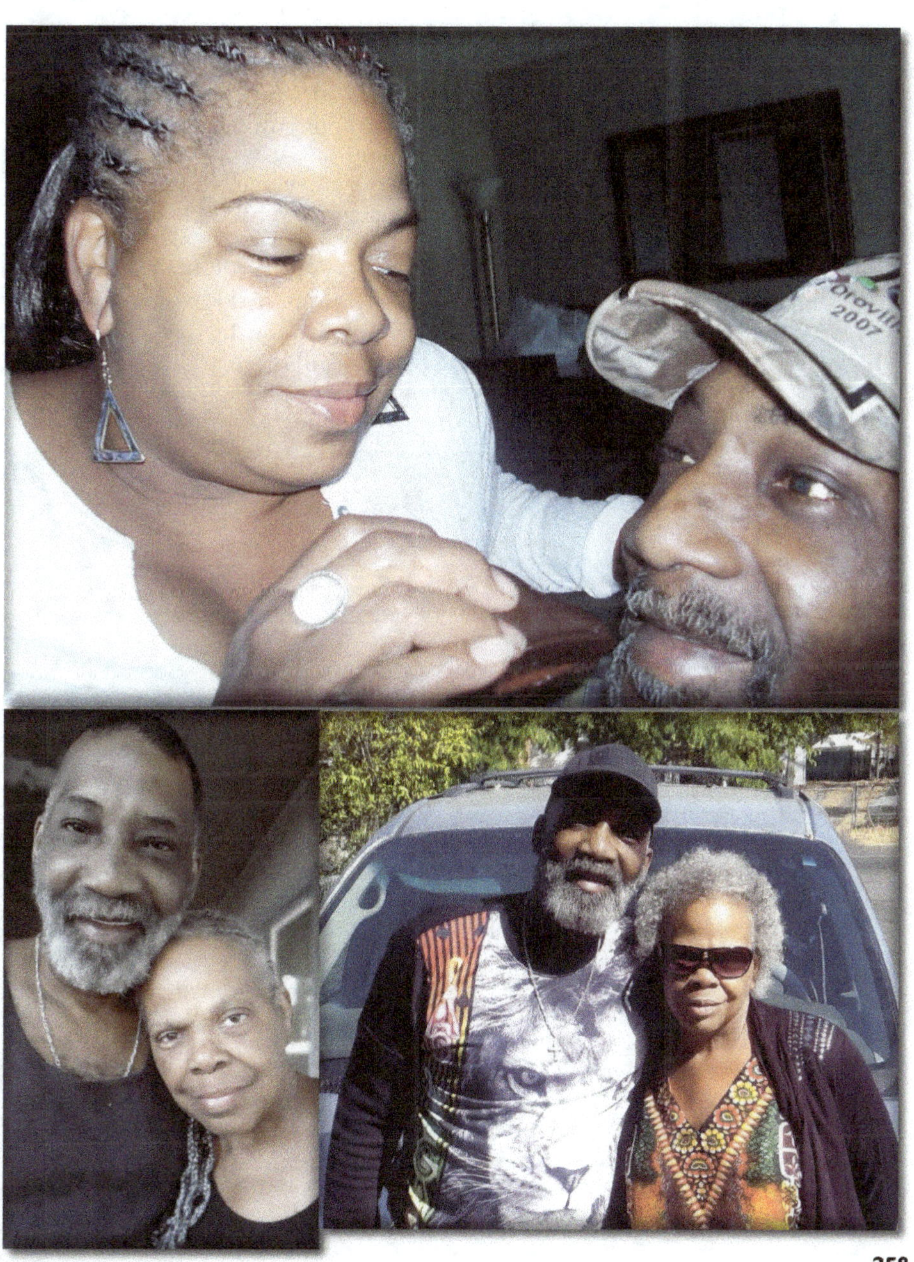

Dwayne Hall, is a poet, author, singer, songwriter, parent and cancer survivor. He says his greatest accomplishment in life was marrying his beloved wife Pat and creating a family together. For without her love, confidence, and supportive partnership there would be no story to tell.

As a final request she asks, "Please write the story of our lives and share it with our future generations to guide and inspire them."
They met as teens, which blossomed into a romance lasting fifty years. Growing up in California during the 60's and 70's Dwayne encountered many social and personal conflicts, which had to be navigated with limited resources.

With so many avenues he could have taken a turn for the worse. To quote Dwayne, "I'm proud of my story, and the legacy I will leave in this world. Though I have no regrets for the choices I have made, I have played many roles! The newest most trans-formative role has been becoming an author."

I would like to thank my two kids who are now amazing adults; I am very proud of you. I would like to thank my grand kids for giving me new life and joy in this world. With each one of your births I know I did something right. Thank you family. I would like to thank all of Pat's friends. You were there when she needed you most. I appreciate you and you know who you are. Thank you Indian princess who always told me I could write this book. Thank you for the motivation. A very special thanks to James Lewis. Without you I couldn't have gotten it done. I also want to show my appreciation for the advancements in technology. This book was written on an Android phone.

- Dwayne E. Hall aka DJ Doc

# INDEX

| | |
|---|---|
| FORWARD | 11 |
| HERE BY MYSELF | 1 |
| OUR STORY AS I REMEMBER IT | 1 |
| A LOT IN COMMON | 2 |
| STEPCHILDREN | 2 |
| NEW DADDY | 2 |
| I'M ALMOST GROWN | 4 |
| A ROCKY START | 4 |
| LOOKING FOR A MIRACLE | 5 |
| TWO MIRACLES | 5 |
| SHE SAW THE MUSIC IN ME | 6 |
| LIFE AND DEATH | 6 |
| THE RULES | 7 |
| WHERE'S GOD? | 7 |
| FINISH WHAT WE STARTED | 7 |
| LITTLE HATERS | 8 |
| SOMEONE ELSE'S SHOES | 8 |
| I CAN LEARN | 8 |
| SECRET | 9 |
| LITTLE BLACK BOY | 9 |
| LEARNING TO HUSTLE | 9 |
| YOUNG ENTREPRENEURS | 10 |
| THE ART OF NEGOTIATION | 10 |
| WILD CHILD | 11 |
| BUSINESS PARTNER | 11 |
| LESSONS IN THE GAME | 11 |
| BUFFALO SOLDIER | 12 |
| WHIPPING HER ASS | 12 |
| RUNAWAY CHILD | 13 |
| YOU GOT A DADDY? | 13 |
| THE LITTLE DARK KID | 14 |
| ARE YOU WORTHY? | 14 |
| MAN MONEY | 14 |
| TWO DIFFERENT WORLDS | 15 |
| MY REAL FAMILY | 15 |
| CHILD RAISING THING | 16 |
| THE DYNAMIC DUO | 17 |
| WANT TO BE A PLAYER | 18 |
| IT'S NOT FREE | 18 |
| MY WHITE GRANDFATHER | 18 |
| MAKING MUSIC | 19 |
| INVESTING IN THE FUTURE | 21 |
| I CAN DO IT! | 25 |
| THE SHOW MUST GO ON | 25 |
| MAN UP | 26 |
| 'RAZOR' JAMES | 26 |
| GO FOR IT | 27 |
| TEAMWORK | 27 |
| CROWD DANGER | 28 |
| THE NO NO'S | 29 |
| COP TROUBLES | 29 |
| BIG BOY MOVES | 30 |
| READY OR NOT! | 30 |
| OUR FIRST MIRACLE | 31 |
| TIME TO GET FITTED | 31 |
| OUR WEDDING | 31 |
| THAT THING CALLED DEATH | 32 |
| TIME TO MEET THE FAMILY | 33 |
| ON THE ROAD | 33 |
| WELCOME TO THE GHETTO | 34 |
| VICIOUS BUSINESS | 34 |
| IN MY FEELINGS | 35 |
| SHE GOT THIS | 35 |
| PROUD MAMA | 35 |
| GROWING UP IN PREJUDICE | 36 |
| BABY BLACK PANTHER | 37 |
| LEARNING THE BUSINESS | 37 |
| THE MIDDLE MAN | 40 |
| CHILDHOOD FRIEND | 40 |
| STOLE MY NAME | 41 |
| BROTHER FROM ANOTHER MOTHER | 42 |
| BILLY THE KID | 42 |
| SHE DON'T PLAY THAT | 44 |
| SHOULD I STAY OR SHOULD I GO? | 44 |
| SWEET POTATO PIE | 45 |
| CAN'T LET IT GO | 46 |
| CALI BOYS | 47 |
| GET TO SEE MY BABY | 47 |
| CAN'T GET AWAY FROM PREJUDICE | 48 |
| WE HAVE A STALKER | 48 |
| WHO MISTRUSTS? | 49 |
| PROVE MY LOVE | 50 |
| IT CHANGED ME | 50 |
| SMOKE IT OR LOSE IT | 51 |
| WHITE WONDERLAND | 52 |
| CAUTION BROTHERS | 52 |
| OUT OF HIS MIND | 60 |
| GOING HOME | 61 |
| SHAKY LOVE | 61 |
| YOU ARE THE FATHER | 62 |
| EITHER / OR | 63 |
| ON THE ROAD AGAIN | 64 |
| BEST FRIENDS | 64 |
| CLUB JEALOUSY | 64 |
| HINDSIGHT 20/20 | 66 |
| THE PLAYER'S MIND | 67 |
| FREE BASE ANYONE? | 67 |
| JUST LIVING LIFE | 68 |
| A LITTLE BIT OF FORGERY | 69 |

| | |
|---|---|
| Best Weed in Town | 70 |
| De Coming | 70 |
| Biracial Blues | 70 |
| Mr. D'Lamont | 71 |
| Look to Your Dreams | 73 |
| Watch and Learn | 74 |
| I'm Black and Proud | 74 |
| Rainbow Hawk | 75 |
| Disbeliever | 75 |
| Ticket Problems | 76 |
| The Simple Things | 76 |
| Stay At Home Dad | 77 |
| Shirley Temple | 79 |
| Good Lie, Bad Lie | 79 |
| Don't Use That Word | 80 |
| Bye Jealousy | 80 |
| Who Are You? | 81 |
| Wrong Move | 81 |
| Meet the Mafia | 81 |
| Time to Record | 86 |
| Cop Hustler | 87 |
| Betrayal | 87 |
| Fool Me Once, Fool Me Twice | 88 |
| Salary Job | 88 |
| Bad Idea | 89 |
| This Is America | 89 |
| Double Duty | 89 |
| We Did It! | 90 |
| In The Grip | 91 |
| The Big Decision | 91 |
| Slipping Into Darkness | 91 |
| A Little Deeper | 92 |
| Close Call | 92 |
| Honest Truth | 93 |
| I Didn't Ask To Join | 93 |
| Missing Her | 94 |
| All About the Kids | 95 |
| The Fight | 96 |
| Little Bruce Lee | 97 |
| Give Them Everything | 98 |
| What You Do For Family | 98 |
| Boss Baby | 99 |
| Crack in the Family | 99 |
| Truth Matters | 99 |
| Warning Before Destruction | 100 |
| Busted | 100 |
| Broken Promises | 103 |
| Little Snitches | 103 |
| Humiliation | 103 |
| She Didn't Do That | 104 |

| | |
|---|---|
| First Impressions | 104 |
| Lying Eyes | 105 |
| One More Deal | 106 |
| Alone | 106 |
| Walk of Shame | 107 |
| Bad Cops | 108 |
| Who Are You Really? | 108 |
| Took My Soul | 109 |
| A Slice Of Hope | 110 |
| Parenting | 111 |
| Pat the Therapist | 112 |
| Believe in Yourself | 112 |
| We're Only Human | 113 |
| Latchkey Kids | 113 |
| The Change | 114 |
| All About the Kids | 114 |
| Pay Attention to Mama | 115 |
| You Must Decide | 116 |
| The Letter | 117 |
| Judgment Day | 117 |
| How Do I Work Now? | 118 |
| The Rules | 118 |
| Probation | 119 |
| It's All My Fault | 119 |
| Bad Reputation | 120 |
| Resistance Is Futile | 121 |
| Follow Orders | 121 |
| She Knows What She Wants | 123 |
| Look to the Future | 124 |
| Mini Me | 124 |
| Pushing The Limits | 125 |
| Never Learn | 125 |
| Keeping It Real | 125 |
| Daddy Don't Play | 126 |
| Phone Magic | 127 |
| Life Lessons | 127 |
| Good or Bad Opportunity? | 127 |
| Letter Number Two | 129 |
| We're Going to Jail | 130 |
| They Finally Got Me | 131 |
| Give Us Free | 132 |
| Camp Elmwood | 133 |
| We Are Family | 134 |
| The Hustler In Me | 135 |
| Working Her Magic | 137 |
| I Got A Job | 137 |
| Pat's New Job | 139 |
| Gotta Keep Busy | 140 |
| Drama In the Bungalow | 141 |
| Got to Get Fitted | 141 |

Shining All the Time ........................... 141
Laticia Is Not A Baby............................ 142
Broken Heart .................................... 142
In My Feelings................................... 143
A Combination of Thought ....................... 143
The Routine ..................................... 144
Day Pass ........................................ 145
Short Timer ..................................... 146
Flashback ....................................... 147
Time To Get Out ................................. 147
Brand New World.................................. 148
More Changes .................................... 149
Where's My Daughter? ............................ 150
The Big Talk..................................... 151
The Big Move .................................... 152
Happy Anniversary ............................... 152
Got To Get A Job ................................ 153
Time To Move In ................................. 154
Pat's Birthday................................... 154
Dangerous Situation ............................. 155
New Place, New Life ............................. 156
Single Parent ................................... 156
Got My Family Back .............................. 156
Are These My Kids? .............................. 157
Is Something Wrong? ............................. 158
Remember ........................................ 162
The Second Wave Of Grief ........................ 162
Life is Gonna Happen ............................ 163
She's In Our Heads .............................. 164
Spirits Of The Past ............................. 164
School Days...................................... 165
Street-Smart .................................... 166
We Are Your Parents ............................. 166
Nothing To Lose.................................. 167
Believing In The Dream .......................... 167
Pat Found Her Groove ............................ 168
Like Father Like Son ............................ 170
I Want To Meet Mickey Mouse ..................... 173
You're A Hillbilly Now .......................... 174
Happy 30th....................................... 175
Pat's Garden .................................... 181
My Momma In Oroville ............................ 182
Fuck Cancer ..................................... 182
Remission ....................................... 183
My Baby Brother ................................. 183
Laticia's Journey................................ 183
One Of The Best Decisions Of Ours............... 184
Who's Gay? ...................................... 184
Grandparents .................................... 185
A Mother's S.O.S................................. 186

Barbara June .................................... 188
Life Doesn't Stop 4 U 2 Catch Up............. 188
Starting Over Again ............................. 190
Back In Town .................................... 193
Living For Ourselves ............................ 197
The Baby Bull ................................... 197
DJ Doc........................................... 198
The Family Is Growing............................ 200
Operation Day ................................... 201
The Longest Day Ever............................. 201
The Big Comeback................................. 203
New Attitude..................................... 203
The Big 60....................................... 206
The Plan ........................................ 208
The Friendship .................................. 210
What I Didn't Know .............................. 211
Now You Really Know.............................. 213
I Got It Too..................................... 215
It's That Time .................................. 215
The Camp Fire ................................... 216
Not the News We Wanted .......................... 218
Lock Down ....................................... 218
Big Dog Is Here ................................. 219
Road Trip ....................................... 220
A Dark Day....................................... 222
Dog Babies....................................... 223
Hospice ......................................... 226
Pat Aka Gramzie ................................. 226
I Have Things To Do ............................. 233
Going Home....................................... 234
The Gift of Pat Magic ........................... 238